Written In Our Hearts

Vegetarian Cookbook

I can't retire
I own *horses*

GONE TO
THE STABLES

Photograph © Courtesy of Annabel Jones

Written In Our Hearts

© 2014 The Davy Jones Equine Memorial Foundation

ALL RIGHTS RESERVED

Cover design by T Lee Harris

Front Cover Photograph © Courtesy of ImageCollect

Photograph on final page © Courtesy of The Palm Beach Post/Jan Tuckwood

Back Cover Photograph (top) © Courtesy of Michael G. Bush

Back Cover Photograph (bottom) © Courtesy of Janice Ausbrooks Jennings

Back Cover Logo © Courtesy of Suzanne Gee

For the love of Davy Jones

This cookbook is lovingly dedicated to honor his memory.

Davy left us too soon on February 29, 2012
while tending to his beloved horses.

We miss you Davy!

Photograph © Courtesy of The Palm Beach Post/Jan Tuckwood

Finally Free

Felt like a daydream, when I heard the news today
Because it's just so hard to believe that you've gone away
Took me back to those younger days, right from the start
All those melodies that you sang were written in your heart
And now you're finally free, like you always wanted to be
Still all those memories where love still abides

Looking back on those HEY-HEY days, it was good clean fun
Forty-five years together, and the journey was a long run
And I'll remember those summer days, when they play your song
I'll close my eyes and see you standing there, and you're still singing along
Singing that you're finally free, like you always wanted to be
Still all those memories where love still abides

And as we look back through the tears and hear all the laughter after all those years
Still all those pictures, they seem so clear, and it just gets me inside
The show is over and the curtain closes, the last train waits to take you home
Still the audience keeps singing your chorus
And if we listen close, we can hear you singing along, singing along
Singing that you're finally free, like you always wanted to be
Still all those memories where love still abides

And as we look back through the tears and hear all the laughter after all those years
Still all those pictures, they seem so clear, and it just gets me inside
Because you're finally free, like you always wanted to be
Still all those memories where love still abides

Felt like a daydream, when I heard the news today...

Chris Pick's "Finally Free"

Written and performed by Chris Pick - Copyright 2013 (BMI)
Arranged and produced by John Roginski of The Monkeephiles
Keyboards, guitars, bass, drums, and backing vocals by John Roginski
Free Download: https://chrispick.bandcamp.com/album/finally-free

Photograph © Courtesy of Michael G. Bush

Contents

Photograph © Courtesy of Michael G. Bush

Foreword

We are elated that the Purple Flower Gang had the wonderful idea to do a vegetarian cookbook and donate the proceeds to the Davy Jones Equine Memorial Foundation. Dad was a vegetarian for most of his life and had favorite recipes he relied on in his busy life as a performer and horseman. Several of those recipes are included in this book.

The continuing support of Dad's fans, friends, family, and colleagues has given us the immeasurable gift of being able to continue his true passion in life, the rescue of retired, abused, and unwanted thoroughbred racehorses. He would be filled with joy to know that the current members of the DJEMF herd — even those with the most severe special needs — are safe, protected, and each thriving in their own way.

We are so grateful to the Purple Flower Gang for their unwavering support and for the very generous contributions they have made to the herd in honor of Dad. We know that he is undoubtedly somewhere smiling broadly!

Much Love from the Jones Girls,

Talia, Sarah, Jessica, and Annabel

Photograph @ Courtesy of John McFadden

Annabel, Jessica, Talia, and Sarah
on the front steps of their dad's home in
Beavertown, Pennsylvania

Acknowledgments

Thank you so much to all of the wonderful fans, friends, and family of David Jones who took the time to submit their favorite vegetarian and vegan recipes for this project. It is because of the combined efforts of many that this cookbook has become a reality and that one more source of revenue has been created to help provide for David's beloved four-legged family members.

Because individual tastes vary greatly, there is no guarantee that every reader will enjoy every recipe contained in this collection, nor were these recipes tested by the team compiling the cookbook. With that in mind, our hope is that you will find many delicious new recipes within these pages printed with love, and that each of us will remember with much fondness the man who inspired this book whenever we prepare these dishes.

We want to send out a very special thank you to Darlene Haines for coming up with the idea for the creation of this book, and to Suzanne Gee for her wonderful expertise and hard work in adapting the photographs used, and to Anita Williams Weinberg for all of her guidance along the way.

Special thanks also to Bobbi Boyce, Tina Howard, David Levin, Sarah Aujero, Jeanette Watkins Jungreis, and Fatima Budica for their valuable assistance, and also to Marian Allen, T Lee Harris, Joanna Foreman, Joy Kirchgessner, and the rest of the Southern Indiana Writers Group for their aid with behind the scenes promotional editing and advice.

THE MONKEES® is a federally registered trademark of Rhino Entertainment Company. There is no affiliation, endorsement, or connection between Rhino Entertainment Company and this book or its editors.

The Cookbook Crew
Cindy Bryant
Jerri Keele
Jody Proetta
Ginny Fleming
Andrea Gilbey
Colleen Gruver

This graphic, scattered throughout the cookbook, was designed to symbolize the forever connection between Davy and his four daughters.

"I have four daughters, all girls."

~ Davy Jones

Photograph © Courtesy of Daryl Goldfarb

Jessica, Sarah, Talia, and Annabel

"Sing like nobody's listening, dance like nobody's watching, and love like you've never been hurt before; and when life gets too hard to stand, kneel."

~ Davy Jones

(derived from a public domain quote by William W. Purkey)

Photograph © Courtesy of Rosinha Viegas

Conversion Charts

Because the recipes in this book have come from around the world, we have provided a conversion chart for temperatures and for dry and fluid measures.

Oven temperature conversions

Gas	Fahrenheit	Celsius	Description
1	275	140	Cool
2	300	150	Cool
3	325	170	Very moderate
4	350	180	Moderate
5	375	190	Moderate
6	400	200	Moderately hot
7	425	220	Hot
8	450	230	Hot
9	475	240	Very hot

Dry measure conversion guide

Imperial	Cups	Tablespoon	Metric
1 oz.	⅛ C	2 T	25g
2 oz.	¼ C	4 T	50g
4 oz.	1 C	8 T	100g

Fluid measure conversion guide

Imperial	Cups	Metric
4 fl. oz.	½ C	125ml
8 fl. oz.	1 C	250ml
16 fl. oz.	2 C	500ml

What's the Difference?

All vegans are automatically vegetarians, but not all vegetarians are vegans. Confused? You're not alone. Many people are unaware of the distinction between these two categories.

Vegetarians eat no meat, but they do eat eggs and dairy products.

Vegans eat no animal products of any kind -- no meat, no eggs, no milk, no cheese, and no animal based gelatin.

Since there are both vegetarian and vegan recipes in this cookbook, we've included icons with each recipe to make it easy for you to quickly identify each type. None of the recipes in this book include meat of any kind. If a recipe does include eggs or dairy products, it will be labeled with the vegetarian icon. If a recipe contains neither meat nor eggs nor dairy products, it will be labeled with the vegan icon.

 Denotes Vegan

Denotes Vegetarian

Appetizers, Snacks, and Sauces

Photograph © Courtesy of Rhino Entertainment Company

Appetizers—The Promise of Good Things To Come!

The appetizer whets your appetite — the promise of good things to come, the beginning of a good meal, or a promise, like a place-holder, of what's to follow, kind of like meeting David Jones for the first time. I was meeting my aunt and uncle at the Imperial Theatre after school. They told me they had someone they wanted me to meet. They were working at the theatre with the cast. I arrived at the theatre that day, but my aunt and uncle were nowhere in sight, so I went in to the stage area and sat down in the first row. The cast had just finished their first dress rehearsal. There were a few members of the cast on the stage. A teenage boy dressed as the Artful Dodger was animatedly speaking with the director. They were obviously sharing a funny story with each other. His beautiful voice was resonating throughout the theatre and I noticed his very heavy English accent. His dark brown hair was coming out from under his Dodger top hat every which way. I was fixated by him and was staring. He must have felt me staring because he suddenly looked down at me and straight into my eyes and winked and smiled. I immediately blushed and he let out this bellowing laugh! Just then, I heard my aunt's voice yell, "David, come on down and meet my niece." The Artful Dodger turns around and runs off the stage and comes to stand directly in front of me. He takes his Artful Dodger top hat off and gives me the most elegant bow. I reach out my hand to shake his, and he ignores my hand and gives me one of the warmest hugs I ever felt and a little kiss on the cheek. The promise of a beautiful friendship to come.

~ Jody Proetta

Photograph © Courtesy of Carol Avins

'Davy's Dangerous Chips'

Contributed by Annabel Jones, Davy's daughter
London, UK

Ingredients:
1 kg Maris Piper potatoes or equivalent, peeled
   and cut into chips (approx. 2 × 2 × 6cm)

groundnut or grapeseed oil/alternatively use
   sunflower oil
salt

Directions:
1. Put the cut chips into a bowl under running water for 5 minutes to wash the starch off.
2. Heat a deep, heavy-bottomed saucepan half-full of the sunflower oil to 130° C. It's important to use a cooking thermometer and check the temperature regularly. Alternatively, use an electric deep-fat fryer heated to 130° C. (CAUTION: hot oil can be dangerous. Do not leave unattended!)
3. Fry for ten minutes, or until cooked through but not browned.
4. Carefully remove the cooked chips and place them on a cooling rack to dry out. If you have time, then place the rack in the freezer for at least 1 hour to remove more moisture.
5. Heat the oil in the deep pan or electric deep-fat fryer to 130° C and fry the chips again until golden.
6. Drain, sprinkle with salt, and if you're feeling really authentic, Sarson's malt vinegar.

To make another Davy fave, the delicious…

'Chip Butty'

Contributed by Annabel Jones, Davy's daughter
London, UK

Ingredients:	Davy's Dangerous Chips (previous recipe)
2 slices of white bread	Ketchup

Directions:
1. Butter generously two thick sliced white pieces of bread.
2. Place your chips on one of the slices of bread.
3. Smother in ketchup and put the remaining slice on top.

Photograph © Courtesy of DJEMF

Annabel with Jess Jones

Vegan Cheese Sauce I

Contributed by Heather Dahman
Fort Wayne, Indiana, USA

Ingredients:
¾ C raw cashews	1 t vegan butter
1 C water	2 T corn starch
4 oz. pimentos or ¼ red bell pepper	salt and pepper to taste
⅛ C nutritional yeast	1 vegan Not-Chick'n bouillon cube (I use
1 t Mrs. Dash Table Blend (seasoning)	Edward and Sons.)
½ t salt	1 C non-dairy milk (I use Rice Dream's rice
½ t onion powder	milk) or an additional C water

Directions:
1. Add cashews and water to blender and blend until smooth and not gritty.
2. Add the remaining ingredients except for the milk (or 2nd cup of water) and continue blending until mixed well.
3. Pour mixture into a large sauce pan. Add the cup of non dairy milk (or additional cup of water) to the blender and swish around to remove remaining sauce. Add to pan. Stir.
4. Heat on medium heat until thickened, about 5-10 minutes, stirring frequently. If you would like a thicker sauce, add an additional tablespoon of cornstarch.
5. Add to your favorite cooked noodles. Enjoy!

Fall Dip

Contributed by Lorrie Malagoli
Forked River, New Jersey, USA

Ingredients:
16 oz. Cool Whip	1 small can of pumpkin
3 boxes of instant vanilla pudding	pumpkin pie spice to taste

Directions:
Combine Cool Whip, dry pudding mix, and pumpkin. Mix well and add pumpkin pie spice.
Serve with graham crackers, fruit, or anything you like ... Soooo soooo good!!!

Vegan "Cheese" Sauce II

Contributed by Karen Baker
Redmond, Washington, USA

This "cheese" sauce is great and delicious on baked potatoes, broccoli, cauliflower, or in place of white sauce for scalloped potatoes, or when used to make macaroni and cheese.

Ingredients:	
½ C of vegan margarine	1 ½ t salt
½ C flour	2 T tamari
3 ½ C boiling water	1 ½ t garlic powder

Directions:
1. In a saucepan melt ½ cup vegan margarine.
2. Use a wire whisk to blend in ½ cup flour.
3. Keep stirring and cook roux until smooth and bubbly, about 2 minutes.
4. Slowly pour in 3 ½ cups boiling water while stirring; do not allow lumps to form while mixture is thickening.
5. Continue to stir while adding 1 ½ teaspoons salt, 2 tablespoons tamari, and 1 ½ teaspoons garlic powder.
6. When sauce has thickened, whisk in ¼ cup oil and 1 cup nutritional yeast.

Leftover sauce will set up very solid in the fridge and you will need to add some water as you warm it up to get the desired consistency.

Pretzel Dip

Contributed by Angi and Braeden Gonzalez
Jackson, Wisconsin, USA

Ingredients:	
1 package of Hidden Valley Dip Mix (original flavor)	6 oz. any type beer
2 (8 oz.) packages of cream cheese	6 oz. shredded Cheddar cheese

Directions:
1. Mix all ingredients together well and chill over night.
2. Serve with pretzels.

Hot Artichoke Squares

Contributed by Jon Provost
Star of Lassie

Ingredients:	
⅓ C finely chopped onion	8 oz. Swiss cheese, cut in small pieces
1 garlic clove, finely minced	2 T minced parsley
2 T cooking oil	½ t salt
4 eggs	½ t oregano
1 (14 oz.) can of artichoke hearts, drained and chopped	⅛ t Tabasco sauce
	⅛ t ground pepper

Directions:
1. Sauté onion and garlic in oil.
2. Beat eggs until frothy.
3. Add onions, garlic, artichoke hearts, cheese, parsley, salt, oregano, Tabasco sauce, and pepper and mix well.
4. Pour into greased 7x11 inch baking dish and bake at 325° F for 25 to 30 minutes.
5. Cut into squares and serve warm.

Serve with thin toast, crackers, melba rounds, or pita bread.

A Conversation Between Jon Provost and Davy Jones

Jon: *If you knew Davy at all, you'd know a "conversation" with him meant he did most of the talking. I mean that in the nicest way. David was so full of energy and ideas, and he always had so much to say.*

I'd seen him at events around town. You'd have had to live in a cave not to know who The Monkees were. He'd heard of me, too, but we'd never met formally. It was Bob Custer who brought us together, one of the photographers for Tiger Beat Magazine. He thought of putting us together for a couple of photo shoots. Bob was a good guy...with really bad teeth. Davy bought him a set of teeth.

Davy: *I can't really remember that, what did I do? Fly him to see his mother or something? Oh yeah, photographer, bald headed guy. (laughs) I did a lot of things. They always say that when you do an act of charity that you shouldn't flourish your trumpets as the heathens do in the streets. I did a lot of shit, flew people here, flew people there. As far as Bob Custer's teeth, Bob Custer took a lot of pictures of us and of me. Tiger Beat flew me to the Bahamas and did all kinds of stuff and he was instrumental in that. He was a nice enough guy.*

I am not quite sure how meeting Jon all came about, to tell you the truth, but Bob came up with the idea and it was just pretty much a free form thing in those days. Everybody that was around, whether it be the Buffalo Springfield or Sajid Khan, we were all these faces that were familiar and all knew each other. Jon was one of the faces that everyone was looking at the time -- same as me and a bunch of other guys; that was basically it. I might have said to Bob that I was a big fan. It was always a very, very strong memory for me – Lassie -- that whole thing is like apple pie and ice cream and cook outs on the weekend, one of those childhood memories... He seemed like the young, fresh kid and he wanted to meet The Monkees and I wanted to meet the kid that was in Lassie and that is how we really got together.

Jon came up to the house a few times...this absolutely lovely Cape Cod style house, trees all around, sitting really pretty on its own acre of land there all the way up at the top of the Hollywood Hills. Phil Ochs was my next door neighbor. Jon and I rode motor bikes and we played pool, I remember that very clearly; he was a lousy pool player! (laughs) No, just kidding!

There was camaraderie in our community. You go to the same parties and, some of the times, you dated some of the same girls. Jon was part of the same little clique because he was known and he had a TV series. It was just our time and that just happened to be the 60s. We were in a happy time; we were working; we had TV series. We were cute little guys and these girls were flashing on us and everything. What I'm saying is that it was a very fun time for us and it was a great time to be in Hollywood.

Jon: *Davy said it beautifully; it was "our time" and not just because we were well-known. It was our generation's time, a thrilling new wave of energy expressed in music, film, fashion, a new consciousness about ecology and the environment.*

In a few years, that wave would carry us in different directions, and, before either of us knew it, decades had passed. When I started to write my autobiography, I reached out to David for a contribution and rekindled our friendship. And when I saw him again, forty years faded away in an instant. His vitality, his joy really blew me away. He was so generous with his time and with his spirit. He loved where he'd been and where he was going. He was more interested in talking about today than reminiscing about "back in the day." David was a man I wanted to spend more time with – but that was not to be.

Photograph © Courtesy of The Jon Provost Collection

Davy and Jon

Grilled Vegetable
and Hummus Wraps

Contributed by Georgeann Maguire
Mechanicsburg, Pennsylvania, USA

Ingredients:
1 C of your favorite hummus
4 wraps (about 9 inches diameter, any flavor)
½ C red onion, sliced thin into half moon shapes
¼ C pine nuts, toasted
2 medium zucchini, cut lengthwise into ¼ inch
   slices

1 large red bell pepper, thinly sliced
2 C lightly packed spinach leaves (or shredded
   lettuce)
1 T olive oil
salt and pepper

Directions:
1. Preheat a grill or grill pan over medium heat.
2. Brush both sides of zucchini with olive oil and sprinkle with salt and pepper.
3. Grill about 5 minutes per side or until tender and slightly browned.
4. Spread each wrap with ¼ cup of hummus and sprinkle with 1 tablespoon of pine nuts.
5. Evenly distribute and layer on top of each wrap: zucchini, red pepper slices, spinach, and red onions.
6. Roll up each wrap. If serving as appetizers, cut each wrap on a diagonal into 4-5 slices. For individual main course servings cut each wrap in half and plate the 2 halves with a salad or other accompaniment. Enjoy!

May be served as appetizers or 4 main course servings.

Zucchini Appetizer

Contributed by Anne Pinna
New Port Richey, Florida, USA

Ingredients:
3 C grated un-pared zucchini
1 C Bisquick*
½ C chopped onion
½ C Parmesan cheese

2 T snipped parsley
½ t oregano
dash of pepper

Directions:
1. Mix all ingredients and spread in oblong pan.
2. Bake at 350° F for 30 minutes until golden brown.
3. Cut into serving pieces and enjoy!

*Bisquick is a premixed baking product sold by General Mills under their Betty Crocker label.

Mini Zucchini Pizza

Contributed by Linda Mach
Kewaunee, Wisconsin, USA

For when you are craving pizza but want to avoid the carbs!

Ingredients:
1 zucchini	dried oregano
shredded mozzarella	fresh basil chopped
spray olive oil	pizza sauce
shredded Parmesan	salt and pepper

Directions:
1. Cut zucchini about ⅛ inch thick.
2. Spray each side with olive oil and season with salt and pepper.
3. Broil or grill each side for about 2 minutes.
4. Top with pizza sauce, mozzarella, oregano, and basil. (Or add more toppings!)
5. Cook for 2 more minutes, or until cheese is lightly browned.
6. Sprinkle with Parmesan before serving. Enjoy!

Southwestern Egg Rolls with Avocado Ranch

Contributed by Dawn Hoffman
Marengo, Illinois, USA

Ingredients:
2 C frozen corn, thawed	½ t chili powder
1 (15 oz.) can black beans, rinsed and drained	1 t salt
1 (9 oz.) package frozen chopped spinach, thawed and squeezed dry with paper towel	½ t cayenne pepper
	4 green onions, finely chopped
2 C shredded Mexican cheese	1 package of egg roll or wonton wrappers
1 (7 oz.) can diced green chilies, drained	1 t ground cumin

Directions:
1. Preheat oven to 425° F. Line two baking sheets with aluminum foil and spray lightly with cooking spray.
2. In a large bowl, mix together corn, beans, spinach, cheese, chilies, onions, cumin, chili powder, salt, and cayenne pepper. Using a small spoon, scoop a small amount of filling onto the wrapper. Starting at a corner, carefully start to roll the wrapper. When it's slightly rolled, tuck in the two sides and continue rolling to the last point. Wet your finger with water and dab a bit on the corner to seal the egg roll. Repeat with remaining wrappers and filling, placing them slightly apart on the baking sheet.
3. Lightly spray the tops of the egg rolls with cooking spray and bake for 15 minutes, flipping them at least once during baking.

Avocado Ranch

Contributed by Dawn Hoffman
Marengo, Illinois, USA

Ingredients:
⅜ C mayonnaise
⅜ C sour cream
3 T buttermilk
½ T olive oil

½ T lemon juice
½ green onion, chopped
¼ t salt
1 avocado, peeled and pitted

Directions:
Place all ingredients in a blender and pulse until smooth. Use immediately.

"I'm such a lucky guy. In a world of noes, I get an awful lot of yeses."

~ Davy Jones

Bleu Cheese Torte

Contributed by Marian Allen
Corydon, Indiana, USA

Ingredients:
½ small package bleu cheese
8 oz. cream cheese, softened
¼ C butter, softened
sliced Pepper Jack cheese

¼ to ½ C pesto
¼ C (more or less) finely chopped sun-dried
  tomatoes

Directions:
1. Line a 9x5x3 inch loaf pan with plastic wrap.
2. Combine bleu cheese, cream cheese, and butter. Mix thoroughly using an electric mixer.
3. Place a layer of thinly sliced Pepper Jack cheese in the bottom of the prepared pan. Top with a layer of cream-cheese mixture, a layer of pesto, another layer of Pepper Jack cheese, a layer of finely chopped sun-dried tomatoes, and a layer of cream-cheese mixture.
4. Refrigerate overnight.
5. Turn out onto a serving plate.
6. Remove plastic wrap.

Stuffed Mushrooms

Contributed by Jody Proetta
Putnam Valley, New York, USA

I serve these for the holidays as appetizers.

Ingredients:

20 very large white stuffing mushrooms with stems removed and stems finely chopped
homemade tomato sauce without meat, about 1 quart
1 bag of shredded mozzarella cheese
¼ C grated Parmesan cheese
1 container of whole wheat flavored bread crumbs

6 large cloves of garlic, minced
1 large sweet white onion, chopped
dried basil leaf flakes
dried parsley flakes
dried oregano flakes
3 T virgin olive oil
3 oz. finely crushed pine nuts

Directions:

1. In a large frying pan, sauté your onion and garlic and mushroom stems in 3 tablespoons of olive oil until soft.
2. Now add ¾ cup of whole wheat bread crumbs to frying pan and mix well. Add crushed pine nuts and mix.
3. Add a full tablespoon of basil, parsley, and oregano each.
4. Transfer mixture to large mixing bowl and add the grated cheese.
5. After you have cleaned your mushroom caps, place them in an aluminum baking pan. Stuff each mushroom with your mushroom mixture.
6. Add your tomato sauce to the baking pan; the tomato sauce should not completely cover your mushrooms.
7. Add your mozzarella cheese so each mushroom cap is covered with the grated mozzarella cheese.
8. Bake in 350° F oven until the mushrooms are good and tender. Should take at least ½ hour to 45 minutes. Check on mushrooms so they don't overcook. I usually take a toothpick and pierce the side of a mushroom. If the toothpick goes through easily, the mushrooms are done. Enjoy.

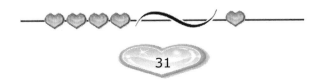

Zucchini Parmesan Crisps

Contributed by Cindy Bryant
Muscatine, Iowa, USA

Ingredients:
1 lb. of zucchini or other squash (about 2 medium-sized)	¼ C shredded Parmesan cheese (heaping)
1 T olive oil (I use garlic infused oil)	¼ C Panko bread crumbs (heaping)

Directions:
1. Pre-heat oven to 400° F. Line two baking sheets with foil and spray lightly with vegetable oil.
2. Slice zucchini or squash into ¼ inch rounds.
3. Toss with oil, coating well.
4. In a bowl or plate, combine bread crumbs, Parmesan cheese, salt, and pepper.
5. Place rounds in Parmesan-bread crumb mixture, coating both sides of each round, pressing to adhere. The mixture will not completely cover each round, but provides a light coating on each side.
6. Place rounds in a single layer on baking sheets. Sprinkle any remaining bread crumb mixture over the rounds.
7. Bake for about 22 to 27 minutes, until golden brown. (There is no need to flip them during baking. They crisp up on both sides as it is.)

Ranch Cheese Ball

Contributed by Sharron Ganjei
Wetumpka, Alabama, USA

Ingredients:
2 (8 oz.) blocks cream cheese, softened	1 (1 oz.) envelope ranch dressing powder
1 ½ C chopped pecans	

Directions:
1. In medium sized mixing bowl mash softened blocks of cream cheese together.
2. Gradually mix in ranch powder making sure there are no dry spots.
3. Once powder is evenly mixed throughout, form cheese into ball shape.
4. Roll ball through pecans until ball is completely covered.
5. Cover ball with plastic wrap. Refrigerate at least 8 hours. Serve with crackers.

Zucchini Appetizer With Sauce

Contributed by Jody Proetta
Putnam Valley, New York, USA

I use this recipe for the holidays as an appetizer when I am having guests or family over.

Ingredients:	
5 large zucchini	homemade sauce for dipping zucchini:
1 container of whole wheat flavored breadcrumbs	1 chopped large white onion
	5 cloves minced garlic
3 eggs beaten well	½ C of chopped fresh basil leaves
1 C of grated Parmesan cheese	1 ½ quarts of crushed tomatoes
sea salt and pepper to taste	1 T oregano
3 T olive oil	3 T olive oil

Directions:
1. Make your dipping sauce first. Sauté the onion and garlic in the olive oil until soft, and do this in a large sauce pot.
2. Add the crushed tomatoes and spices including the fresh basil leaves. Let it all simmer on low/ medium heat so it is bubbling gently---if too hot your sauce may burn on the bottom of the pot.
   ~~ON TO THE ZUCCHINI~~
3. After washing your zucchini, dry well with towel.
4. Cut each zucchini in half. Then cut zucchini so you have 2 to 3 inch strips, each about ½ inch wide.
5. Now place your olive oil in a large frying skillet on medium heat. You should have a bowl with bread crumbs and a bowl with the beaten egg.
6. Add the grated cheese to your bread crumbs and mix well.
7. Once your frying pan is hot enough, dip your zucchini strips in the egg and then roll in the bread crumb mixture and place into the frying pan.
8. You will fry each strip until tender/crisp.
9. Place each cooked zucchini strip on a plate lined with paper towel to drain the oil and allow it to cool.
10. When your zucchini strips are all cooked, place them onto a baking pan and sprinkle with salt and pepper to taste and place into a warm oven until ready to serve.
11. Your sauce, once cooked (about 25 minutes), can be left on low until ready to transfer to a dipping bowl.
12. Place a large serving fork onto the plate with your zucchini strips and a large spoon in the sauce so your guests can place the zucchini on their appetizer plates with some sauce.
Enjoy

"How 'bout the flip side?"

~ Davy Jones

Garden Fresh Spaghetti Sauce

Contributed by Georgi and Cassidy Umbdenstock
Coin, Iowa, USA

This is a tried and true recipe that my daughter Cassidy and I created.

Ingredients:	
4 lbs. fresh tomatoes; peeled, chopped, and puréed in food processor	¼ C fresh basil, chopped
2 small onions, chopped	¼ C olive oil
4 cloves fresh garlic, minced	1 t salt
	1 T sugar

Directions:
1. Heat olive oil over medium heat in a large saucepan.
2. Add onion, basil, garlic, and salt.
3. Sauté until onions are tender, around 5 minutes.
4. Add tomato and sugar. Heat to boil; reduce and simmer about 2 hours, stirring often.
5. Serve over pasta or freeze.

"We are only here a short time - Whatcha say - go for gold."

~ Davy Jones

(Daydream Believin' © David Jones 2000)

Jalapeno Pimento Cheese

Contributed by Celine Allan
Dallas, Texas, USA

Ingredients:	
3 C finely shredded cheese (Colby, Monterey Jack, sharp Cheddar)	5 fresh jalapenos, seeded and diced
1 large pepper, roasted and diced (or a big jar of pimentos, drained)	mayo, as much or as little as you like

Directions:
Combine ingredients and enjoy!

Tomato Bruschetta

Contributed by Jody Proetta
Putnam Valley, New York, USA

The appetizer is the promise of good things to come. I don't know anyone who doesn't like bruschetta. If you are having many more guests, you will need to increase the quantity of this recipe. This recipe is one that you will make just before serving.

Ingredients:
10 slices of a rustic bread
5 garlic cloves, halved
10 plum tomatoes, peeled and diced
½ white onion, finely chopped

sea salt and pepper for taste
extra virgin olive oil for drizzling
a bunch of fresh basil leaves chopped to
   sprinkle on top

Directions:
1. Mix the basil leaves and onions with your diced tomatoes in a bowl.
2. Lightly toast your rustic bread on both sides and take your bread out of the oven. Take your halved garlic cloves and rub each piece and side of bread with the garlic cloves.
3. Return to the oven broiler for a few seconds more until done to your liking. Watch closely that they don't burn. Take out when done.
4. Divide your diced tomato mixture among your bread slices and drizzle some of your olive oil on top of each slice and sprinkle each piece with salt and pepper.
5. Serve immediately. Enjoy.

Garlic Lovers' Hummus

Contributed by T Lee Harris
New Albany, Indiana, USA

Ingredients:
2 C (one 15 oz. can) chick peas, drained
3 cloves garlic, crushed (less or more to taste)
approx. 3 T tahini (sesame paste)
juice of 1 lemon

½ t oregano
1 ½ T olive oil
salt and pepper to taste

Directions:
1. Put chick peas, garlic, herbs, and olive oil in food processor and pulse to make a paste.
2. Add lemon juice and process thoroughly until smooth. Add more lemon juice a little at a time if the mixture is too dry.
3. When it's well mixed and smooth, add a little of the tahini at a time until the hummus thickens to the desired texture. Add salt and pepper to taste.
4. Place in a bowl, garnish with chopped onion, chive, cilantro or the like, and you're ready to go.

Cranberry Relish

Contributed by Whitney Plummer
Richmond, Virginia, USA

Ingredients:
1 bag cranberries	2 C granulated sugar
2 oranges	1 box red raspberry vegetarian gelatin*
1 (20 oz.) can crushed pineapple (drained)	

Directions:
1. Wash berries and grind them in a blender or food processor.
2. Peel oranges and also grind them.
3. Add pineapple and sugar to fruit mixture.
4. Let it stand while gelatin is being prepared.
5. Mix gelatin with one cup of hot water.
6. Stir and let stand until it starts to gel. Do not wait for it to totally gel.
7. Pour over berry mixture.
8. Stir and chill. Best when chilled overnight before serving.
9. You can also add ½ cup of pecans if you'd like.

Easy Zucchini Rounds

Contributed by Beth Pinterich
Berwick, Pennsylvania, USA

Ingredients:
zucchini	garlic salt
shredded cheese	Italian seasoning
olive oil or non-stick cooking spray	

Directions:
1. Preheat oven to 350° F.
2. Oil or spray baking pan.
3. Slice zucchini in thin rounds.
4. Sprinkle with garlic salt and Italian seasoning.
5. Top with whatever shredded cheese you like.
6. Place in oven and bake until cheese is melted and zucchini is as tender as you desire.

*Unknown to many, gelatin is a protein that is derived from animal bone, cartilage, tendon, skin. Gelatin is usually found in yogurt, marshmallows, cereals that are frosted, gelatin desserts, and Beano. Animal products are not always explicitly stated on some package labels, and therefore the consumer is unaware they are present in the foods. The good news is that there are vegetarian sources of gelatin readily available in your health food store so you are able to enjoy the delicious recipes here in this book that contain gelatin as one of the ingredients. Vegetarian gelatin is sold as plain or fruit flavored and is used the same way as conventional gelatin. You may be familiar with agar, one form of vegetarian gelatin. Just follow the directions on the manufacturer's label to adapt the ingredient to the recipe, and enjoy.

Texas Caviar

Contributed by Nan Burkhart
Crestline, Ohio, USA

Ingredients:
2 cans white corn
1 can black beans, rinsed
2 tomatoes, diced
1 green pepper, chopped
1 onion, chopped

1 can diced tomatoes with jalapeno
1 C Italian dressing
½ C parsley
hot pepper flakes, to taste

Directions:
1. Mix ingredients well.
2. Shake hot pepper flakes over the top.
3. Serve with corn chips.

No Meat Pasta Sauce Sicilian Style

Contributed by Liliana Radwanski
Belleville, New Jersey, USA

Ingredients:
1 large white sweet onion chopped
1 can Tutto Rosso, Rienzi, or Cento puree
1 can tomato paste
extra virgin olive oil
1 can pitted olives
1 jar capers

1 package mushrooms, preferably portobello
Italian seasoning
salt optional
grated Parmesan, Locatelli, or Romano cheese
great loaf Italian bread or garlic bread

Directions:
1. In a large sauce pot or deep pan, sauté onion in extra virgin olive oil until onions are translucent or golden.
2. Wash mushrooms and slice them unless you bought pre-sliced.
3. Add them to pot or pan. Sauté with slotted spoon.
4. Wash jar of capers. Add them in, stirring.
5. Add tomato puree; stir.
6. Add tomato paste and a pinch of Italian herb seasoning like McCormick's.
7. Slow simmer turning occasionally until thick, 20-25 minutes.

When almost done, boil salted water in pasta pot and throw in your favorite pasta.
I'd say fusilli, ziti, penne, or rigatoni for this dish. Good grated cheese,
fab Italian bread, and good wine and you're in business.

"It may choke Artie but it ain't gonna choke me!"

(quote from The Little Rascals)

Contributed by Donna Loren

I'll make this as easy as can be.

Ingredients:	Dip:
2 large artichokes	½ C Veganaise
cold water	1 or 2 t balsamic vinegar
lemon wedges	salt and black pepper
olive oil	1 t chopped thyme and rosemary
	very finely chopped garlic

Directions:
1. With a scissors, trim off the thorny tip from all the leaves. Cut lengthwise into quarters.
2. Trim the end of the stems. I like to peel the outer skin so the stem will be more tender.
3. Take a tablespoon and scoop out the fuzzy heart and rinse.
4. Fill a bowl with cold water and lemon wedges. Add artichoke asap to retain the fresh color.
5. Pour the contents into a large pot, add salt, and boil.
6. Turn heat to simmer until tender. Drain in a colander.
7. Next, heat a grill pan, coat the artichokes with olive oil, and place in the pan. Check for grill marks - gives it a smokey-chokey flavor. Let cool.

Dip:
1. Mix ingredients to taste and stir until nice and creamy. Makes 4 servings.
   Option: grate a hard boiled egg over dip when served and sprinkle paprika.

Bon Appetit

©2011 Swinging Sixties Productions

Photographs © Courtesy of Donna Loren
and Swinging Sixties Productions

**Donna Loren and Davy
on *The Monkees***

Seattle Peace-Meal Diet
Instant (Almost) Bean Dip

Contributed by Karen Baker and the Seattle Peace-Meal Cookbook
Redmond, WA, USA

Ingredients:

1 (16 oz.) can vegetarian baked beans,
    undrained
1 (16 oz.) can garbanzo beans, drained
1 (16 oz.) can kidney beans, drained
¼ C barbeque sauce
1 T dried onion flakes

½ t garlic powder
3 T Italian salad dressing
1 tomato, chopped
1 avocado, chopped
2 green onions, chopped

Directions:

1. Place all ingredients except the avocado, tomato, and onion into a food processor and blend.
2. Just before serving, stir in the tomato, avocado and green onion.

Makes about 1½ quarts

Mango Salsa

Contributed by Jerri Keele
Salem, Oregon, USA

Ingredients:

2 mangoes, peeled, pitted, and cubed
¼ red onion, finely diced
1 plum or Roma tomato, seeded and finely diced
1 jalapeno, seeded and finely diced
½ red bell pepper, seeded and finely diced

1-2 cloves of garlic, minced
a small handful of cilantro leaves
juice of 1 lime
juice of 1 lemon
juice of 1 orange

Directions:

1. Mix first seven ingredients in a large bowl.
2. Mix three fruit juices in a small bowl and whisk together.
3. Add just enough of the juice mixture to the fruit/veg mixture.
4. Serve with chips, or over greens, or as a condiment.

Breakfast

Photograph © Courtesy of Noel Cutler

**"David used to make the best omelets ever! In fact, his were the only omelets
that I have ever eaten and enjoyed. He made me what he called his Anita special.
I have no idea of the amounts, but lots of everything — Cheddar cheese,
cream cheese, sweet corn, tomatoes, salt, and pepper."**
~ Anita Pollinger–Jones

Dad's Famous Fried Egg Sandwich

Contributed by Talia Jones Roston, Davy's daughter
Santa Barbara, California, USA

Ingredients:
1 t butter (or more)	salt and pepper to taste
1 egg	2 T ketchup
2 slices of white bread	English sweet pickle relish (optional)

Directions:
1. In a small skillet, melt butter over medium heat.
2. Crack egg in pan and cook to desired firmness; flip egg over to get some of the crispy bits on both sides.
3. Place bread on plate; spread ketchup on both slices.
4. Place egg on one slice, season with salt and pepper, and place remaining slice over top of egg.

As Dad would say,

"Bob's your uncle!"

Serve warm and enjoy!

Photograph © Courtesy of DJEMF

Talia Jones Roston with Smither Jones

Micky's Vegetable Frittata

Contributed by Micky Dolenz

*If this isn't vegetarian enough, you can always
go to the garden and chew the bark off a tree!*

Ingredients:	
2 T vegetable oil	6 eggs
2 small potatoes, diced	2 T milk
¼ C chopped onion	½ C shredded mozzarella cheese
½ C red pepper, chopped	½ C shredded white Cheddar cheese
½ lb. asparagus, trimmed and cut in 2-inch pieces	1 T chopped fresh basil
½ t salt	sprinkle of red chili flakes and pepper to taste

Directions:
1. Preheat oven to 350° F.
2. Heat olive oil in skillet over medium heat; stir in potato, onion, and red pepper.
3. Season with salt and pepper.
4. Add asparagus and continue cooking till tender (about 5-7 minutes).
5. Transfer to prepared baking dish.
6. Whisk eggs and milk together in small bowl; pour evenly over dish.
7. Scatter cheeses over top then bake about 20-25 minutes till set in the middle. Garnish with basil and serve.

Photograph © Courtesy of Michael G. Bush

Micky, Davy, and Peter

Florentine Scramble

Contributed by Cindy Bryant
Muscatine, Iowa, USA

Ingredients:
1 lb. spinach, rinsed, chopped, and drained
8 oz. fresh mushrooms, chopped
1 onion, chopped
4 eggs, lightly beaten

4 T Parmesan cheese, grated
3 T olive oil
Tabasco sauce to taste

Directions:
1. Heat oil in a large non-stick skillet.
2. Add mushrooms and onions and sauté lightly.
3. Add spinach and mix well.
4. Stir Tabasco sauce into eggs and pour over spinach mixture.
5. Cook, stirring constantly, until eggs are set.
6. Transfer to serving platter.
7. Sprinkle with Parmesan cheese and serve immediately.

Serves 6

Strawberry Oatmeal Breakfast Smoothie

Contributed by Cheryl Belle
New York, New York, USA

Ingredients:
1 C soy milk
½ C rolled oats
1 banana, broken into chunks

14 frozen strawberries
½ t of vanilla extract
1 ½ t white sugar

Directions:
In a blender, combine soy milk, oats, banana, and strawberries. Add
vanilla and sugar if desired. Blend until smooth. Pour into glasses and serve.

Ready in 5 minutes

Pancakes

Several times Davy and I made pancakes when he used to live near Portsmouth. We would use 4 eggs, a pint of milk, 6 heaped tablespoons of regular flour, and whisk this lot up. Then we would put butter in a pan, lots, pour on the mixture, and then have fun flipping the pancakes. Jess used to love pancakes; she was 5 or 6 years old then.

Plate pancakes up and then cover them in your favourite things. Davy on his would sometimes include sugar, freshly squeezed orange, and good quality runny honey. We could eat loads of these. Jessica liked chocolate Nutella or whatever it was called back then, which melted nicely into the pancake, which had potentially sticky consequences.

~ Lawrie Haley

Photograph © Courtesy of Lawrie Haley

Davy and Lawrie piling into the nuts

Cinnamon Roll Pancakes

Contributed by Linda Mach
Kewaunee, Wisconsin, USA

Ingredients for pancakes:	Ingredients for cinnamon filling:
4 C all-purpose flour	1 C butter, melted
8 t baking powder	1 ½ C brown sugar, packed
2 t salt	2 T ground cinnamon
4 C milk	
4 T vegetable oil	Ingredients for cream cheese glaze:
4 large eggs, lightly beaten	½ C butter
	4 oz. cream cheese
	1 ½ C powdered sugar
	1 t vanilla

Directions:
To make the cinnamon filling:
1. Mix the three ingredients together.
2. Place in a disposable piping bag and snip the end off, or put in a Ziploc bag and snip the corner off.

To make the pancakes:
1. Mix the dry ingredients in one bowl and the wet ingredients in another bowl.
2. Stir them together until everything is moistened leaving a few lumps.
3. Heat your griddle to exactly 325 °F. You don't want these to cook too quickly, and you won't want your cinnamon to burn.
4. Make desired size pancake on greased griddle and then, using the piping bag and starting at the center of the pancake, create a cinnamon swirl. Wait until the pancake has lots of bubbles before you try to turn it. You will find that when you turn it the cinnamon swirl will melt. The cinnamon will melt out and create the craters which the cream cheese glaze will fill.

To make the cream cheese glaze:
1. In a microwave safe bowl, melt the butter and cream cheese and then stir together.
2. Whisk in the powdered sugar and vanilla.
3. Add a little milk if needed to make it a glaze consistency.
4. Place pancake on plate, then cover with cream cheese glaze.

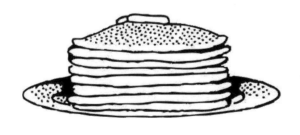

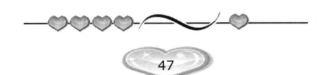

Vegan Scrambled Tofu

Contributed by Heather Dahman
Fort Wayne, Indiana, USA

Ingredients:
1 pkg. firm tofu, drained and squeezed well	¼ t garlic powder
½ vegan Not-Chick'n bouillon cube (Edward and Sons)	⅛ t turmeric
	½ T soy sauce
½ T nutritional yeast	¼ t black salt (optional, but recommended for the sulfur/eggy flavor)
½ t salt-free Mrs. Dash Table Blend	
1 T dried parsley flakes	pepper to taste
½ t onion powder	

Directions:
1. Drain tofu well and squeeze out as much water as possible.
2. Spray pan with cooking spray or melt butter to coat.
3. In large bowl, crumble tofu and add seasoning; mix well.
4. Cook on medium heat until done. I like mine slightly brown on one side.

Optional Add-ins: Vegan sausage crumbles (I like Lightlife's Gimme Lean), broccoli, spinach, kale.

Tofu Pancakes

Contributed by Jody Proetta
Putnam Valley, New York, USA

Delicious way to get protein and have your pancakes too!!!

Ingredients:
3 eggs	2 T honey
1 ½ C milk (use whole milk for this recipe)	1 T baking powder
1 lb. tofu	1¼ t vanilla
1 t to 1 T of canola oil	¼ t salt
	1 C whole wheat flour

Directions:
1. Mix all of the above ingredients, except the flour, in a blender until smooth.
2. Add 1 cup of whole wheat flour and blend once again.
3. Bake on a lightly oiled, medium-hot griddle until done.

This recipe make about 18 pancakes. Enjoy!!!

Breakfast Casserole I

Contributed by Georgeann Maguire
Mechanicsburg, Pennsylvania, USA

This is a make-ahead recipe, perfect to prepare in advance
for a special morning, birthday, or holiday (or serve it at lunch or dinner with
a nice salad). When ready to bake, preheat the oven to 350° F.

Ingredients:
6 slices of bread (crusts removed)	about 2 ½ C of diced vegetables, lightly sautéed
8 oz. shredded cheese (Swiss recommended)	(Use different color peppers or broccoli,
6 eggs, beaten	whatever you like. You can steam the
2 C half-and-half	broccoli just until tender.)
butter for the bread	1 t salt
	½ t pepper

Directions:
To prepare the casserole (make the night before):
1. Spray 9x13 inch pan with non-stick spray.
2. After removing the crusts, butter the slices of bread. Place the bread slices butter-side down in the pan.
3. Evenly spread the vegetables on top of the bread. Sprinkle the shredded cheese on top of the vegetables.
4. In a bowl, combine the eggs, half-and-half, and salt and pepper. Mix well and pour over the cheese layer in the casserole.
5. Cover the casserole and chill overnight.
6. Next morning, take the casserole out of the fridge for 15 minutes before baking.
7. Bake the casserole, uncovered, for 45 minutes or until set.

Hash Brown Casserole

Contributed by Rose Ann Gillett
Beech Grove, Indiana, USA

Ingredients:
2 sticks butter	2 C shredded Cheddar cheese
2 lbs. Ore-Ida brand frozen potatoes O'Brien	3 C corn flakes
1 can cream of mushroom soup	milk
1 medium onion	

Directions:
1. Melt one stick of butter and pour into 9x12 inch casserole dish. Add potatoes.
2. In separate bowl, mix soup, onion, and cheese. Add a little milk until consistency is pasty. Spread mixture over potatoes.
3. Melt second stick of butter and stir in cereal. Top casserole with the buttered cereal.
4. Bake uncovered at 325° F for one hour.

Breakfast Casserole II

Contributed By Darlene Haines
Crestline, Ohio, USA

Ingredients:
8 eggs beaten
6 slices bread cubed
2 ¼ C milk
1 C grated cheese
1 t salt

1 t dry mustard
8 oz. fresh sliced mushrooms
½ C onion chopped (I sometimes use a bunch
    of green onion)

Directions:
1. Combine all ingredients.
2. Pour into a 9x13 inch baking dish.
3. Cover and refrigerate for at least 12 hours or overnight.
4. Bake uncovered at 350° F for 50 minutes. Use clean knife test for doneness.

Anna's Old-time Apple Fritters

Contributed by Roxanne Salch Kaplan
Lake Grove, Long Island, New York, USA

This is my maternal grandmother's recipe from the 1930's (her name was Anna Bauer Ziehl), and my Mom (Eleanor Ziehl Salch) used to make them when I was growing up. Anna passed away when my Mom was only 14 years old so I never met her, but I feel like I did.

Ingredients for plain batter:
1 C flour
1 ½ t baking powder
¼ t of salt
2 eggs
⅔ C milk

Ingredients for apple mixture:
4 large apples, sliced.
2 T powdered sugar
1 T lemon juice

Directions:
1. Sift dry ingredients together. Beat the eggs, and add eggs and milk to the dry ingredients. Beat until smooth.
2. Mix apple slices with the powdered sugar and lemon juice. Add to the plain fritter batter. Heat shortening or vegetable oil in a frying pan. Add spoonfuls of batter and heat until golden brown, turning to cook each side.

You can also add other ingredients to the plain batter to make corn fritters, blueberry fritters, etc.

Enjoy!!

Open-Faced Waldorf Sandwich

Contributed by Tommy James
of Tommy James and the Shondells

Ingredients:

bread	pure maple syrup
Swiss or Cheddar cheese slices	strawberries

Directions:
1. Slice your favorite bread.
2. Cover with the Swiss or Cheddar cheese slices.
3. Place in greased skillet to melt.
4. Add warmed maple syrup and strawberries. That's it!

Photograph © Courtesy of Tommy James

Breakfast Bowl

Contributed by Kim Briggs
Atlanta, Georgia, USA

Ingredients:

3 C cooked brown rice	1 C salsa of choice
1 medium zucchini, cut into ¼ inch slices	fresh cilantro
8 oz. broccoli florets, each halved lengthwise	salt, pepper, olive oil
12 egg whites	

Directions:
1. Steam or sauté the broccoli and zucchini until tender. Meanwhile, cook the egg whites in a large sauté pan and season with salt and pepper. Stir with a wooden spoon until the eggs are white and fully cooked.
2. Fill 4 bowls with the brown rice. Top with the egg whites, vegetables, and salsa. Garnish with cilantro leaves.

Mini Frittata

Contributed by Madelyn Warkentin
Fullerton, California, USA

Vegetarian and Gluten Free

Ingredients:	
10 large eggs	1 C shredded mozzarella
½ C cooked soy-riso (vegetarian chorizo)	1 pinch coarse salt and freshly ground pepper
1 C spinach, finely chopped	1 T. fresh oregano
1 leek, sliced lengthwise (green parts discarded) and thinly sliced into half moons	olive oil

Prep Time: 10 minutes   Total Time: 40 minutes   Serving Size: 12 mini frittatas

Directions:
1. In a large bowl, whisk the eggs and season with a pinch of salt and pepper.
2. Heat a tablespoon of extra-virgin olive oil in a medium skillet and add the leeks. Season lightly with salt and pepper and sauté until slightly browned, 3 minutes.
3. Remove from pan and set aside.
4. To the pan, add the soy-chorizo and cook until it's softened, 5 minutes.
5. Pour the eggs into a non-stick muffin tin (I found that these will really stick to your pan if it's not non-stick.)
6. Sprinkle the leeks evenly into each eggy mixture followed by a good dollop of the soy-chorizo. Go ahead and throw that spinach in there too. Sprinkle some cheese and oregano on top of each frittata.
7. Throw the whole thing into an oven, preheated to 375° F. Bake for about 10 minutes, checking at the 8-minute mark. They should be puffed up and set in the middle.
8. Let cool a few minutes and serve at your next brunch!

Vita-Granola

Contributed by Colleen Gruver
Lynnwood, Washington, USA

Ingredients:	
¼ C oil	1 C of sunflower seeds, pumpkin seeds, and walnuts (or any other seeds or nuts as desired)
1 C brown sugar	
½ C water	
6 C rolled oats (not quick oats)	1 C toasted wheat germ
	1 C raisins or other dried fruit

Directions:
1. Combine oil with sugar and water.
2. Pour over oats and nuts and spread in shallow baking pans.
3. Toss gently to blend . Spread about ¼ inch thick.
4. Bake at 350° F for 10 minutes and then stir and bake for another 10 minutes.
5. Mix in wheat germ and raisins.
6. Cool and store in a sealed container in the refrigerator.

Gluten Free Frittata
with Brown Rice Pasta

Contributed by Madelyn Warkentin
Fullerton, California, USA

Ingredients:	
6 large organic free-range eggs	2 t chopped fresh mint
½ C non-dairy cream, sour cream, or plain yogurt	olive oil
sea salt and ground pepper, to taste	⅓ C diced red bell pepper
1 T chopped fresh parsley	⅓ C diced yellow bell pepper
2 t snipped fresh chives	2 C brown rice penne, cooked to al dente

Directions:
1. Preheat the oven to 375° F. Whisk the eggs with the non-dairy cream till frothy. Season to taste with sea salt, parsley, chives, and mint. Set aside.
2. Lightly oil a 10-inch cast iron skillet. Place it on medium heat and cook the red and yellow pepper for 4-5 minutes until slightly browned and softened.
3. Add the cooked brown rice penne to the skillet and stir gently to combine it with the peppers, arranging the penne evenly in the pan.
4. Quickly pour the egg mixture all over the penne pasta and peppers. Using a small spatula or spoon, shimmy the pasta a bit to allow the egg mixture to seep in and around each piece.
5. After a minute or so on medium heat, remove the skillet from the stove and place it in the center of a preheated oven. Bake the frittata for about 20 minutes until the frittata is set in the center and golden brown around the edges. Use a thin knife to check the center for doneness if you like.
6. Allow the frittata to cool for a few minutes before serving. This makes it much easier to slice.

Dairy Options: Replace non-dairy cream with organic sour cream or Greek yogurt. Add 4 oz. organic goat cheese, feta, or shredded cheese on the top.

Cook time: 20 minutes Yield: Makes 4 hearty servings. Serves 6 as a side dish.

"It doesn't matter if it's 10 people

or 10,000 people; my performance is

the same. I put it right out there."

~ Davy Jones

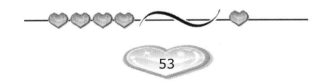

Breads

Photograph © Courtesy of Rhino Entertainment Company

Morning "Gloria" Muffins

Contributed by Karen Steele
Marstons Mills, Massachusetts, USA
http://www.gloriastavers.com

Ingredients	
½ C golden seedless raisins	¾ C chopped pineapple (fresh or canned)
⅓ C walnut halves	3 eggs
2 C unbleached all-purpose flour	¼ C canola oil
½ C granulated sugar	6 T unsalted butter, melted
2-¼ t cinnamon	1 T freshly squeezed lemon juice
1-½ t baking soda	1 t pure vanilla extract
¼ t salt	½ C shredded, unsweetened coconut
1 medium carrot, grated	⅓ C coarse raw sugar
1 Granny Smith apple, peeled and grated	

Directions:

1. Place raisins in a small bowl and cover with hot tap water. Let sit for 10 minutes while raisins plump, then drain and squeeze out excess liquid with your hands. Set aside. Place walnuts on a rimmed baking sheet and toast until golden brown, about 15 minutes. Let cool, then chop coarsely and set aside.
2. Sift flour, granulated sugar, cinnamon, baking soda, and salt into a medium bowl. Mix gently with a wooden spoon and set aside. In a separate medium bowl, combine raisins, walnuts, carrot, apple, pineapple, eggs, canola oil, melted butter, lemon juice, vanilla extract, and coconut, and mix with a wooden spoon until combined. Add dry ingredients and continue stirring just until all the dry ingredients are moistened. It's important not to over-mix.
3. Scoop batter into oiled muffin tin, filling the cups to the top. Sprinkle coarse raw sugar on the tops.
4. Bake on the center rack of the oven at 350° F for 40 to 45 minutes. The finished muffins will be deep brown.
5. Let cool for 20 minutes, then slide a fork down the side of each muffin and gently lift it from the pan. Makes 12 muffins.

From the moment Gloria Stavers saw David, she knew he was someone her readers would love. In the December 1963 issue, she called him "a real show stopper" in his role as the Artful Dodger. "Let's hope he decides to stay in America!" And from that moment on he had a home at 16 Magazine with Gloria as his trusted friend. David visited her offices whenever he came to NYC, and Gloria visited the set of The Monkees. She was there to support him at the opening of his Greenwich Village boutique Zilch and made it possible for 16-ers to send off for the Zilch catalogue. And later, as David started a family, we got to see photos of them in 16. Thanks Gloria, for all the years of loyalty to David and his fans!
~ Karen Steele
www.gloriastavers.com

Photograph of Gloria Stavers © Courtesy of Karen Steele

Pumpkin Bread
with Pumpkin Butter Cream

Contributed by Linda Mach
Kewaunee, Wisconsin, USA

Ingredients:

1 ¾ C all-purpose flour
1 ½ t ground cinnamon
1 t baking powder
1 t baking soda
½ t salt
½ t ground nutmeg
½ t ground allspice
2 large eggs
¾ C packed dark brown sugar (You can
   substitute light brown sugar.)

⅓ C granulated sugar
2 t freshly grated orange zest (optional)
1 t freshly grated lemon zest (optional)
½ C canola oil
1 ¼ C canned pure pumpkin puree
½ C chopped, toasted pecans or walnuts,
   optional (I don't add the nuts to the batter,
   but sprinkle them on top of the frosted loaf
   instead.)

Directions:

1. Position your oven rack in the middle of the oven and preheat oven to 325° F. Grease and flour a 9x5 inch loaf pan; set aside.
2. Combine flour, cinnamon, baking powder, baking soda, salt, nutmeg, and allspice in a medium bowl and whisk until thoroughly combined; set aside.
3. In another bowl, or the bowl of an electric mixer, beat eggs on medium-high speed for two minutes or until lightened in color. Add the brown sugar, mixing for about 2 minutes, then the granulated sugar, mixing for about 1 minute. Add the orange and lemon zests, if using, and beat for another minute. Scrape down the bowl as needed.
4. Drizzle in the canola oil with beater on medium-low. Reduce speed to low and add the pumpkin puree. Mix until thoroughly combined. Add the dry ingredients in two additions and blend for 10-15 seconds just until incorporated. Fold in the pecans using a rubber spatula.
5. Spoon the batter into your prepared loaf pan and bake for 60-65 minutes or until a toothpick inserted in center comes out clean. Cool loaf in pan for 10 to 15 minutes, then remove and cool completely on a wire rack.

If you're going to frost the loaf, you can make the frosting while it is cooling.
See recipe for Pumpkin Butter Cream Frosting on next page.

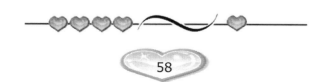

Pumpkin Butter Cream Frosting

Contributed by Linda Mach
Kewanee, Wisconsin, USA

Ingredients:
¼ C (½ stick) unsalted butter, softened	3 C powdered sugar
2 T canned pure pumpkin puree	2 t half and half or milk
½ t ground cinnamon	¼ to ⅓ C chopped pecans or walnuts, optional,
½ t vanilla	for sprinkling on top

Directions:
1. Cream the butter, pumpkin puree, cinnamon, and vanilla, blending well.
2. Add powdered sugar a cup at a time, blending well after each addition.
3. Add half and half or milk and blend well. NOTE: This makes a very thick butter cream frosting. If you want a thinner, creamier frosting, add more half and half or milk until you get the desired consistency.
4. After frosting the cooled pumpkin loaf, sprinkle with chopped pecans or walnuts if desired.

Tofu Raisin Bread

Contributed by Jody Proetta
Putnam Valley, New York, USA

*This bread is delicious with apricot preserves and with a
large salad for lunch or with scrambled eggs for breakfast!*

Ingredients:
2 C whole wheat flour	¼ C margarine
¾ C raisins	4 t baking powder
2 eggs	¼ t baking soda
1 lb. tofu	¼ t salt
¼ C honey	

Directions:
1. Mix whole wheat flour and raisins well in a large bowl.
2. Mix eggs, tofu, honey, margarine, baking powder, baking soda, and salt in a blender until smooth.
3. Pour the blended ingredients into the flour mixture. Stir well.
4. Turn into a buttered and floured 8-inch spring form pan.
5. Bake at 350° F for 45 minutes or until a toothpick inserted into the center comes out clean.
6. Cool 10 minutes in the pan and remove to a rack.

Enjoy this delicious bread!!

No-Fail French Bread

Contributed by Jerri Keele
Salem, Oregon, USA

Ingredients:	
1 (2.5 oz.) pkg. dry yeast	2 ½ T olive oil (I use extra virgin)
1 C very warm water	1 ½ t salt
2 scant T sugar	3 C bread flour, divided

Directions:

1. In a large mixing bowl, dissolve yeast in warm water and let sit until it's nice and bubbly. Then add the sugar, oil, salt, and 2 cups of the flour. Beat until blended. (I use a stand mixer with a dough hook.) Stir in enough remaining flour to form a stiff dough.
2. On low speed, if using stand mixer and dough hook, beat for 5 minutes, or turn onto a floured surface and knead until smooth and elastic, about 8 minutes. Place in an oiled bowl, turning once to oil the top. Cover and let rise in a warm place until doubled, about 1-2 hours. Punch dough down and return to bowl. Let rise another 30 minutes to an hour.
3. Punch dough down. Turn onto a lightly floured surface. Shape into a loaf approximately 16 inches long with tapered ends. Spray or lightly oil a baking sheet (some people prefer to sprinkle corn meal instead.) Place loaf on baking sheet. Cover and let rise until doubled, about 30 minutes to an hour.
4. Preheat oven to 375° F. With a sharp knife, make diagonal slashes 2-3 inches apart across the top of the loaf. Bake for 25-30 minutes or until golden brown and bottom sounds hollow when you tap on it. Cool on a wire rack.

Davy during the filming of a television pilot

Photograph © Courtesy of Michael G. Bush

Orange Date Bread

Contributed by Cindy Bryant
Muscatine, Iowa, USA

Ingredients:
2 T frozen orange juice concentrate	1 ¼ C all-purpose flour
1 egg	¾ C whole-wheat flour
2 T orange zest	1 t baking soda
¾ C pitted, chopped dates	1 t baking powder
½ C brown sugar	½ t salt
¼ C granulated sugar	1 T vegetable oil
1 C plain nonfat yogurt	1 t vanilla extract

Directions:
1. Preheat oven to 350 °F.
2. Spray 4 mini–loaf pans with nonfat cooking spray.
3. In a food processor, process the orange juice concentrate, orange zest, dates, sugars, yogurt, and egg until mixed. (This will cut the dates into smaller pieces too.)
4. Add the remaining ingredients and pulse until mixed, scraping down the side of the bowl if necessary.
5. Divide the mixture between the 4 pans. Spread the mixture so each pan has an even layer.
6. Bake until a toothpick inserted into the center of a loaf comes out clean, about 15 to 20 minutes.
7. Cool the bread in the pans on a wire rack for 10 minutes.
8. Remove the bread to the rack and cool to room temperature.

Pulp Bread/Crackers

Contributed by Tina Howard
Longview, Texas, USA

Ingredients:
2 ⅔ C pulp from juice	additions: spices or nutritional yeast (I like
½ C flax meal (or chia seeds)	garlic salt and cracked pepper)
1 C water	

Prep time: 5-10 minutes (depending if you have juice pulp on hand)
Bake time: oven 350° F for about 30-45 minutes
Dehydrator time: 115° F about 6 hours, or if you want really crispy crackers dehydrate overnight

Directions:
1. Add your pulp, water, and flax into a bowl or mix in a food processor.
2. Add in your favorite spices or additions. Once blended, spread onto a dehydrator teflex sheet or cookie sheet if doing in oven.
3. Dehydrate or bake in oven till desired texture and crispness is achieved.

Quick Focaccia Bread

Contributed by T Lee Harris
New Albany, Indiana, USA

Ingredients:
1 ½ C whole wheat flour	2 ½ - 3 T olive oil
1 ½ C all-purpose flour	grated Parmesan cheese
1 T sugar	1 t salt (I use coarse kosher salt when I can)
1 oz. yeast or 1 ½ T dry instant yeast	
1 ⅓ C warm water	

Directions:
1. Place all dry ingredients in a bowl and blend together.
2. Add half of the water and stir it into the dry ingredients to moisten.
3. Add olive oil and mix well.
4. Add the remaining water and mix together until you can't use the spoon any more.
5. Knead in the bowl, adding more flour or water as needed to achieve a smooth, fairly elastic dough.
6. Grease a round baking sheet. I use a 14" aluminum tray.
7. Pat the dough onto the tray in a round that is about an inch to a half-inch thick (depends on how thick you want the bread).
8. Make dimples in the surface of the bread with your knuckle.
9. Drizzle more olive oil on top and spread with fingers.
10. Sprinkle Parmesan cheese over top to taste.
11. Let rise approximately 10 minutes.
12. Bake at 375 °F until golden brown (usually 20-25 minutes).

Banana Bread
(Aunt Jan's Recipe)

Contributed by Lyn Tomkinson
Finksburg, Maryland, USA

Ingredients:
½ C shortening	½ t salt
1 ½ C sugar	½ t baking soda
3 beaten eggs	¼ C sour cream or buttermilk
1 t vanilla	1 C mashed banana
2 C cake flour	

Directions:
1. Mix ingredients together.
2. Bake at 350° F for about 50-60 minutes in loaf pan.

Thirty Minute White Bread

Contributed by Marian Allen
Corydon, Indiana, USA

Ingredients:	
1 C milk	approximately 6 to 7 C bread flour or
2 T vegetable shortening or butter	all-purpose flour
3 t salt	1 T butter, melted
1 C water	2 medium (8 ½ x4 ½ inch) loaf pans, greased
2 packages dry yeast	or non-stick
2 T sugar	

Directions:
1. Combine milk, water, 2 T butter, and sugar. Heat to lukewarm (105° F - 115° F). Add yeast and stir gently to dissolve.
2. Stir in salt and 2 cups of flour. Stir 3 minutes at medium speed in an electric mixer or 150 strong strokes with a wooden spoon. Add 2 more cups of flour and continue beating for 3 minutes or 150 strokes. Add 2 more cups of flour. Work in with spoon. When it becomes too stiff, work it with your hands. When the dough has a rough form and is cleaning the sides of the mixing bowl, turn it out on a floured work surface.
3. Knead for about 8 minutes with a strong push-turn-fold motion. Occasionally throw the dough hard against the work surface, saying, "Take THAT, [name of anybody you're mad at]! Hah!"
4. Divide the dough in half and shape the balls. Let rest under a cloth for 5 minutes.
5. Form the loaves by pressing each with your palm or rolling pin into an oval, roughly the length of the baking pan. Fold the oval in half, pinch the seam tightly to seal, tuck under the ends, and place seam down in pan. Brush loaves with melted butter.
6. Place the pans in a cold oven and turn heat to 400° F for 60 seconds – 1 minute, no more. Turn it off!
7. About 30 minutes later, turn the oven to 400° F and bake for 25 minutes or until the loaves are brown. When done, they will sound hollow when tapped on the bottom crust with the forefinger. If the crust is soft, return to the oven without the pans for 10 minutes.
8. Place the loaves on a metal rack to cool.

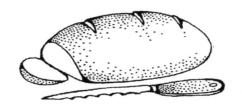

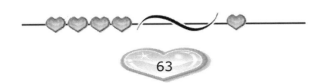

Irish Soda Bread I

Contributed by Jerri Keele
Salem, Oregon, USA

Ingredients:
2 ½ C flour
2 T sugar
1 t baking soda
1 t baking powder
½ t salt
3 T butter or margarine, softened

⅓ – ⅔ C raisins or dried cranberries or currants
   or golden raisins
about 1 C buttermilk
additional softened butter or margarine, if
   desired

Directions:
1. Heat oven to 375° F.
2. Grease baking sheet with shortening or spray.
3. Mix flour, sugar, baking soda, baking powder, and salt in a large bowl.
4. Cut in 3 tablespoons of butter using pastry blender or hands (but act quickly if using your hands so that the butter doesn't melt), until mixture looks like fine crumbs.
5. Stir in raisins/crans/golden raisins (I use a mixture of dried cranberries and golden raisins) and just enough buttermilk so dough leaves the side of the bowl.
6. Dust with flour (or turn out onto floured board and dust) and knead either in the bowl or on the board 1 to 2 minutes, or until smooth.
7. Shape into a round loaf, about 6-7 inches in diameter.
8. Place on baking sheet.
9. Cut an X shape about ½ inch deep on top of loaf with a floured knife.
10. Bake 35-45 minutes or until golden brown.
11. Remove from baking sheet to wire rack.
12. Brush with additional softened butter or margarine, if desired.
13. Cool completely before slicing.

Harvest Pumpkin Apple Bread

Contributed by Cindy Griffin
Wallingford, Connecticut, USA

Ingredients:

3 C all purpose flour	4 large eggs
2 t ground cinnamon	1 C vegetable oil
2 t baking soda	½ C apple juice or water
1 ½ t salt	1 large baking apple, peeled, cored, and diced
3 C granulated sugar	
1 can (15 oz.) LIBBY'S® 100% Pure Pumpkin	

Prep: 15 minutes   Cooking: 65 minutes   Cooling: 10 minutes
Yields: 24 slices (12 slices per loaf)

Directions:
1. Preheat oven to 350° F. Grease and flour two 9x5 loaf pans.
2. Combine flour, cinnamon, baking soda, and salt in large bowl. Combine sugar, pumpkin, eggs, vegetable oil, and apple juice in large mixer bowl; beat until just blended.
3. Add pumpkin mixture to flour mixture; stir just until moistened.
4. Fold in apples. Spoon batter into prepared loaf pans.
5. Bake for 65 to 70 minutes or until wooden pick inserted in center comes out clean.
6. Cool in pans on wire racks for 10 minutes; remove to wire racks to cool completely.

For three 8x4 inch loaf pans:
Prepare as above. Bake for 60 to 65 minutes.

For five or six 5x3 inch mini loaf pans:
Prepare as above. Bake for 55 to 60 minutes.

Buckskin Bread

Contributed by Marian Allen
Corydon, Indiana, USA

Ingredients:

2 C self-rising flour	1 C water

Directions:
1. Mix well. Put into greased cake pan or pie pan.
2. Bake at 400°F for about 30 minutes. Best served hot with soup, butter, or margarine.

Grandma Mollie's Mexican Cornbread

Contributed by Colleen Gruver
Lynnwood, Washington, USA

Ingredients:
1 C yellow corn meal
1 C flour
1 T baking powder
1 t salt
1 egg
1 C milk

¼ C chopped onion
2 T chopped green chili peppers
¼ C margarine or butter
½ C shredded Cheddar cheese or cottage
   cheese

Directions:
1. Combine dry ingredients in a bowl and mix well.
2. Beat egg and milk together. Add corn and mix well.
3. Sauté onion and chilies in margarine or butter in skillet until onion is tender.
4. Add milk mixture, onion mixture, and cheese into dry ingredients. Stir until just mixed and pour into well greased 8x8 pan.
5. Bake at 400° F for 40 minutes or until toothpick comes out clean. It will be moist!

Monkey (Monkee) Bread

Contributed by Kim Pedley
Lindenhurst, Illinois, USA

Ingredients:
½ C of granulated sugar
1 t of cinnamon
2 cans of Pillsbury Grands Homestyle
   refrigerated buttermilk biscuits

1 C of brown sugar
¾ C butter or margarine melted

Directions:
1. Heat oven to 350° F. Lightly grease Bundt pan with shortening or cooking spray. In large storage plastic food bag, mix the sugar and cinnamon.
2. Separate dough into 16 biscuits; cut each into quarters. Shake in bag to coat. Arrange in pan.
3. In small bowl mix brown sugar and butter and pour over biscuit pieces.
4. Bake 28 to 32 minutes or until golden brown and no longer doughy in center. Cool in pan for 10 minutes. Turn upside down onto serving plate; pull apart to serve.

Serve warm

Irish Soda Bread II

Contributed by Connie Gee
Las Vegas, Nevada, USA

Ingredients:
4 C sifted self-rising flour
2 T baking soda
1 ½ t salt
¼ t chilled butter

1 C dried currants
1 C milk
½ C white vinegar

Directions:
1. Plump currants by covering them with boiled water and then allowing them to sit for about 15 minutes.
2. While waiting, mix together all dry ingredients.
3. Cut butter into small chunks and hand knead into dry ingredients until just incorporated. Don't over-knead.
4. Remove currants from water and pat dry.
5. Distribute currants evenly into mixture.
6. Add vinegar to milk and add half of the soured milk to the dry mixture, blending quickly by hand.
7. Add remaining soured milk gradually. Add only what is needed to moisten mixture enough to transfer onto a floured cutting board.
8. Hand knead as little as possible to form a round dome shape and transfer mixture onto a cooking sheet that's been buttered only on the area where the dough will be placed.
9. Re-form mixture to make sure dough has remained in a round shape that is about 2 inches thick.
10. Flour a knife and score dough in a crisscross shape about halfway through. This will help it to rise evenly.
11. Bake for 30-40 minutes in a 375° F degree oven.
12. Remove when top is lightly golden. Don't let the currants burn! The bread is done when you can thump your finger on the top and hear a hollow sound.
13. Can be enjoyed almost immediately. Serve with butter, jam, or just by itself with a cup of tea.

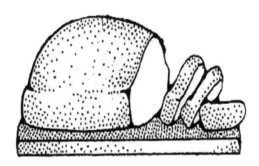

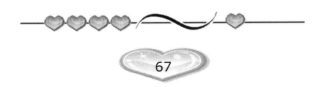

Soups, Stews, and Chilis

Photograph © Courtesy of Rhino Entertainment Company

Lentil Soup

Contributed by Sarah Jones McFadden, Davy's daughter
Santa Barbara, California, USA

I made this for Dad every time he came to visit. He loved soup! This recipe is healthy and filling and super easy to make. This recipe was inspired by one of my favorite chefs, but I made it my own with a few tweaks.

Ingredients:
2 T olive oil (plus a bit more to drizzle on soup before serving)
1 medium onion, chopped
2 celery stalks, chopped
2 carrots, peeled (if you want) and chopped
2 garlic cloves, chopped
1 can diced tomatoes (14 oz. can)

1 pound lentils (approx. 1 ¼ c.)
11 C low-salt veggie broth
4 to 6 fresh thyme sprigs
salt and ground black pepper (I always try to use fresh ground pepper)
1 C shredded Parmesan cheese

Directions:
1. Heat the oil in a large pot over medium heat.
2. Add the onion, carrots, and celery.
3. Add the garlic, salt, and pepper and sauté until all the vegetables are tender (not too soft!), about 5 to 8 minutes.
4. Add the tomatoes with their juices.
5. Add the lentils and mix all together to coat the lentils.
6. Add the broth and stir.
7. Add the thyme sprigs.
8. Bring to a boil over high heat.
9. Cover and simmer over low heat until the lentils are almost tender, about 30 minutes.
10. Season with salt and pepper, to taste.
11. Ladle the soup into bowls.
12. Sprinkle with the Parmesan, drizzle with olive oil, and serve.

Sometimes, I add a dollop of sour cream to the top for a decadent treat.

Sarah Jones McFadden with Whiskey Bee Jones

Photograph © Courtesy of DJEMF

Photograph © Courtesy of Linda Haines Jones

**Linda Haines Jones with grandchildren
Harrison and Lauren McFadden**

Chilled Melon Soup with Basil

*Contributed by Linda Haines Jones, Talia and Sarah's mother
Santa Barbara, California, USA*

Ingredients:	
6 C roughly chopped honeydew ¼ C lime juice, plus more to taste	½ C roughly chopped basil plus more for garnish

Directions:
1. Put all ingredients into a blender and puree, stirring often, until very smooth.
2. Transfer to a container, cover and chill. Serve in bowls garnished with basil leaves.

Serves 4

Vegetarian Chili

Contributed by Theresa Archey
Oklahoma City, Oklahoma, USA

Ingredients:
1 T olive oil
½ medium onion, chopped
2 bay leaves
1 t ground cumin
2 T dried oregano
1 T salt
2 stalks celery, chopped
2 green bell peppers, chopped
2 jalapeno peppers, chopped
3 cloves garlic, chopped
2 (12 oz.) packages vegetarian burger
   crumbles

2 (4 oz.) cans chopped green chili peppers,
   drained
3(28 oz.) cans whole peeled tomatoes, crushed
¼ C chili powder
1 T ground black pepper
1 (15 oz.) can kidney beans, drained
1 (15 oz.) can garbanzo beans, drained
1 (15 oz.) can black beans
1 (15 oz.) can whole kernel corn

Directions:
1. Heat the olive oil in a large pot over medium heat. Stir in the onion and season with bay leaves, cumin, oregano, and salt.
2. Cook and stir until onion is tender, then mix in the celery, green bell peppers, jalapeno peppers, garlic and green chili peppers.
3. When vegetables are heated through, mix in the vegetarian burger crumbles.
4. Reduce heat to low, cover pot, and simmer 5 minutes.
5. Mix the tomatoes into the pot. Season chili with chili powder and pepper.
6. Stir in the kidney beans, garbanzo beans, and black beans.
7. Bring to a boil, reduce heat to low, and simmer 45 minutes.
8. Stir in the corn and continue cooking 5 minutes before serving.

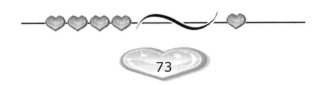

The Working Man/Woman's Express Chili

Contributed by Jody Proetta
Putnam Valley, New York, USA

I make this a lot if I am super busy and don't have time to make a
dinner or lunch from scratch, and I serve it with multi-grain vegan crackers.
My husband is not a vegetarian, but he happens to love this very quick and healthy recipe.

Ingredients:
1 (14 oz.) can of diced tomatoes
1 ½ C of frozen vegetables
1 ½ t of chili powder
½ C water
2 (14 oz.) cans of kidney beans or black
    beans--it's your choice
1 (12 oz.) jar of salsa
1 t of cumin

5 veggie burgers -- I use black bean veggie
    burgers for this recipe, or portobello veggie
    burgers, crumbled up
Optional: Buy a small container of vegan sour
    cream or vegan cream cheese and place a
    dollop on top with some shredded fresh
    parsley to garnish and add a little extra
    Flavor.

Directions:
Combine all of your ingredients in a large pot and simmer for about 15 minutes stirring frequently so they don't stick to the bottom. You can add more salsa if you like it looser. My husband happens to like a lot of salsa.

Kale Stew

Contributed by Marian Allen
Corydon, Indiana, USA

Ingredients:
3 T garlic-flavored olive oil
4 large potatoes, diced
1 large bunch of kale, de-stalked and torn up
8 C water
enough vegetarian bouillon to flavor that much
    water

dried tomatoes
pepper
onion powder
½ bay leaf
1 (16 oz.) can of beans

Directions:
1. Put everything but the beans in a large pot. Bring to a boil, then reduce to simmer and cook about 20-25 minutes until the potatoes are soft.
2. Mash slightly so the potatoes thicken the stew.
3. Add beans and heat through. Remove bay leaf before serving.

Note:
My husband, Charlie, can't eat onions—but if he could I would modify this recipe by cooking real onions and garlic in the olive oil until tender, then proceed with step 1 listed above, omitting the onion powder.

Grandma Angela's Pasta Fagioli

Contributed by Deana Martin

Ingredients:
2 T extra virgin olive oil
1 onion, finely chopped
2 (15-ounce) cans cannelloni beans
6 C of water
salt and pepper to taste

¼ t ground cinnamon (HER SECRET
    INGREDIENT)
8 ounces tubetini pasta
¼ C grated Parmesan or Romano cheese

Directions:
1. Heat the oil in a large pan and sauté the onion for a minute.
2. Add the two cans of beans with the six cups of water.
3. Season with salt and pepper to taste.
4. Add the cinnamon, cover and bring to a boil.
5. Boil for 15 minutes, then reduce heat and simmer for one and a half hours.
6. Simmer very slowly. Check occasionally and add boiling water as necessary.
7. Add the pasta and continue simmering until the pasta is al dente.
8. Remove from heat and serve with grated cheese sprinkled on top.

Serves 4

Source: "Memories Are Made Of This: Dean Martin Through His Daughter's Eyes" - 2004

Photograph © Courtesy of Deana Martin

Davy and Deana Martin

Photograph © Courtesy of Kim Mauger

**Deana with Davy's daughters
Jessica, Annabel, Talia, and Sarah**

Green Soup

Contributed by Tina Howard
Longview, Texas, USA

Ingredients:
6 to 8 big chunks shallots
8 leeks
⅓ C organic olive oil
2 big bunches of asparagus
3 big bunches broccoli (Cut the stems off
    halfway up the shafts.)

2 big bunches of spinach
6 containers (32 oz. each) vegetable broth
sea salt (at least 3 T of coarse grain)
pepper to taste

Directions:
1. Cut leeks just above their white part, about 2 inches. Peel the outer layer off and then slit them open lengthwise, but not completely severed clear through. Rinse them out well.
2. Cut the hard ends of the asparagus off , about 3 inches.
3. Cut the stems of the broccoli off halfway up the shafts.
4. Cut off the tiny part of the dirty ends of the spinach.
5. Peel and slice shallots thinly.
6. Put all the olive oil in a very large, deep pot. Turn the heat to medium-high. Put the shallots into the oil and sweat the shallots. "Sweating" means to cook the vegetables to tenderize them without browning them. Adjust heat as necessary to ensure they do not brown.
7. Add 1 tablespoon of coarse, ground, good quality sea salt to shallots to absorb while they are sweating.
8. Cut the leeks into thin slices and toss them into the oil with the shallots. Sweat the leeks along with the shallots.
9. Chop the asparagus into small bits and then add them to the mixture and sweat them along with the shallots and leeks.
10. When the shallots, asparagus, and leeks are fully sweated and tender, break the broccoli into small chunks and throw them into the soup pot. (If the shallots, leeks and asparagus combo gets too dry before they are tender, just add small amounts of vegetable broth to the mix and keep on sweating.)
11. Let the broccoli sweat a little while (about 2 minutes) and then add half of your vegetable broth. Cook this for about 10 minutes.
12. Add remaining vegetable stock and continue cooking for another 5-10 minutes. (You want the broccoli to be tender, but not overcooked, and you want the color of soup to always remain a nice, bright green.)
13. Add all the spinach and cook for an additional 3 to 5 minutes.
14. Turn the flame off the mixture and season to taste with sea salt and pepper.
15. Transfer the soup into a blender by increments and puree the mixture.
16. Put the pureed soup mixture into one big pot, and then taste and season it to your liking. Only season with salt and pepper. If you desire any other seasoning, create an individual serving, not in the whole pot.
17. Cool the soup before refrigerating and/or freezing.

You are basically adding the vegetables in order of their hardness. The spinach is so soft, you would never want to add it too early. If you do, it can make the soup turn brown. Green Soup is 62 calories per cup. This recipe yields about 23 cups of soup. Make sure your cooking pot is big, or you can halve the recipe.

New Year's Good Luck Stew

Contributed by Colleen Johnson
St. Louis, Missouri, USA

This is one I have been tweaking over the years, and on New Year's Eve 2009,
I believe I got all the ingredients just right. It is filled with all sorts of special ingredients
which I have heard will bring you lots of good luck and fortune in the new year ahead.
I always make this on New Year's Eve. ENJOY!!

Ingredients:
1 pkg. red beans and rice (Mahatma or Zatarain's brands)
1 C frozen black eyed peas
1 can diced tomatoes (14.5 oz.) *not drained*
1 C dried black eyed peas
1 can garbanzo beans (15 oz.) *not drained*

1 box penne pasta (12 oz.)
1 can black-eyed peas with jalapenos (15.5 oz. Trappey's brand) *not drained*
1 pkg. broccoli slaw (Mann's brand 12 oz.)
1 jar Prego Traditional Italian Sauce (14 oz.)

Directions:
1. In the morning, add 1 cup of dried black-eyed peas in medium bowl and cover with water.
2. Later in the day, in a big kettle, bring 4 cups of water to a boil and add package of red beans and rice.
3. Reduce heat to low; cover and simmer 30 minutes or until rice is tender; stir occasionally.
4. Stir in all remaining ingredients except penne pasta; increase heat a little and cover and simmer 30 minutes or until slaw is tender.
5. Prepare penne pasta per instructions on the box. Once pasta is done, drain and add to the other ingredients and cover and simmer on low for 30 minutes.

Note: I like my stew thick and a bit on the sweeter side which is why I add Prego Traditional Italian Sauce. Depending on the consistency, you may need to add water to thin.

Roasted Sweet Potato
and Squash Soup

Contributed by Georgeann Maguire
Mechanicsburg, Pennsylvania, USA

Ingredients:
2 sweet potatoes (med-large size)
1 acorn squash
1 small onion
4-5 garlic cloves, unpeeled
3 ½ - 4 C of vegetable stock
2 T olive oil

For extra loveliness:
½ C light cream
salt and pepper to taste

Directions:
1. Preheat the oven to 375° F.
2. Cut the sweet potatoes, squash, and onion in half lengthwise. Scoop out the squash seeds. Brush all the cut sides with olive oil.
3. In a shallow roasting pan, arrange all the vegetables and garlic cloves. Roast for about 45 minutes, or until tender and light brown.
4. When slightly cooled, scoop out all the flesh from the sweet potatoes and squash and put in a medium-sized pot with the onions. Peel the garlic and add the soft insides to the pot.
5. Add the vegetable stock and bit of salt. When it just barely reaches the boiling point, reduce the heat and simmer partially covered for about 30 minutes. Stir occasionally until the vegetables are very tender.
6. Cool the soup slightly and then, in batches, transfer to a blender or food processor and process until smooth. *see options below
7. Ladle into bowls and enjoy!

*Optional:
1. If adding the cream (and it is equally good with or without), return the soup to a pot and stir in the cream.
2. Add salt and pepper to taste.
3. Simmer for 10 minutes allowing the flavors to blend.
      I have made this without the cream and it freezes well.

Davy said of his performance as Jesus in "Godspell":

"I enjoyed playing Jesus. The only thought
I had once in a while as I was singing
'Oh God I'm Dying' was that someone from
the audience would shout out 'Could you give
us "Daydream Believer" before you go?' "

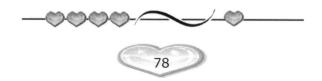

Rootin' Tootin'
Vegetable Bean Soup

Contributed by Beverlie Tyler and Michael G. Bush
(Monkees photographer)

Ingredients:
32 oz. vegetable bean stock
1 cup each :
    chopped carrots
    green beans
    garbanzo beans
    black eyed peas
    black beans
    pinto beans
    light kidney beans
    red kidney beans
½ cup chopped celery
1 small onion, diced

1 bay leaf
2 minced garlic cloves
1 T tomato paste
2 t salt
1 t black pepper
½ t turmeric powder
1 t Italian seasoning
21 oz. can of crushed tomatoes
2 large whole potatoes, diced
1 t dried oregano
2 T coconut oil

Directions:
1. Sauté onions, oil, celery, garlic, salt, and pepper 5-10 minutes.
2. Add carrots and potatoes. Sauté 5-19 minutes.
3. Add everything else and cook 25-30 minutes until carrots and potatoes are done.
4. Serve with crackers. Enjoy!

Photograph © Courtesy of Janet Litterio

Beverlie, Davy, and Michael

Mushroom Bisque

Contributed by Suzanne Gee
Las Vegas, Nevada, USA

Ingredients:
2 C brown button mushrooms, sliced
½ onion, chopped
1 C vegetable stock
3 ½ T butter
3 T flour

1 C milk
½ C heavy cream
¼ t celery seed
2 T sherry
salt and pepper to taste

Directions:
1. In a large pot add stock, mushrooms and onion. Cover and bring to a simmer and cook for 30 min.
2. Melt butter and add to a bowl. Slowly whisk flour into melted butter, making sure there are no lumps.
3. Heat milk in a saucepan; don't boil, just heat through and whisk this into the butter and flour mixture.
4. Pour all this back into the saucepan and bring to a boil, stirring constantly. Once at a boil, lower heat and simmer for 2-3 min, continuing to stir mixture.
5. Add cream very slowly while whisking.
6. Add this mixture into the pot with the cooked down stock, mushrooms, and onion. Stir well and season with celery seed and sherry. Add salt and pepper to taste.
7. Serve with crusty bread.

Serves 4

Myo's Magnificent Chili

Contributed by Reneé "Myo" Baer
Bellmawr, New Jersey, USA

Ingredients:
2 (14 oz.) cans dark red kidney beans
1 packet chili powder (whatever level heat you prefer)

1 (28 oz.) can diced tomatoes
1 large onion, diced
1 large pepper, diced (color of your choice)

Directions:
1. Mix all ingredients together in a large pot.
2. Bring to a boil then simmer for at least 30 minutes (or longer for more intense flavor).

This recipe also works great in a slow cooker!
You can top this with vegan shredded cheese, non-dairy sour cream, crushed corn chips, or tortilla chips — the possibilities are endless! Super easy, extremely filling, and absolutely delicious!

White Bean Soup

Contributed by Jody Proetta
Putnam Valley, New York, USA

If you live in a region where the winters are
chilly and snowy, this soup will warm your soul!!

Ingredients:

6 oz. of dried cannellini beans soaked in cold
    water overnight (the cold water should
    cover them completely)
6 C of vegetable stock (I use all natural low
    sodium)
4 oz. of soup pasta (I like to use small shells for
    this recipe)
6 T of olive oil

2 garlic cloves minced
1 white onion chopped small
5 T of fresh flat leaf parsley
salt and pepper to taste
12 oz. can of diced tomatoes
grated vegan cheese
Italian or French hard crusty bread

Directions:
1. Drain your soaked beans and place them in a large heavy bottom soup pot.
2. Add your vegetable stock and simmer the beans for two hours or until the beans are tender.
3. Now take half of your beans and some of the soup stock out of your soup pot and place in a food processor and puree.
4. Add back to your soup pot and add the parsley and the can of diced tomatoes, salt, and pepper, and simmer.
5. Add your shell pasta to the soup pot to cook with the beans and soup stock.
6. Now place your olive oil in a skillet and sauté the garlic and onion.
7. When finished, take the garlic and onion out of the skillet with a slotted spoon and add to the soup.
8. Continue to simmer soup. Now take your Italian or French bread and pour the remaining oil from the skillet on it; sprinkle garlic powder on the top and add vegan grated cheese and broil until the cheese is melted on top.

Serve your bread with the soup. Enjoy this lovely soup.

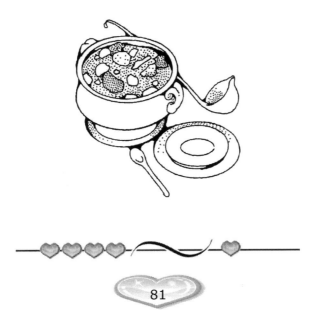

Kelly's Fresh Vegetable Soup

Contributed by Kelly Canney
Henderson, Nevada, USA

Ingredients:
2 medium garlic cloves, minced	1 medium sweet red pepper, diced
2 medium carrots, diced	1 celery rib, diced
2 small zucchini, diced	2 t fresh thyme, chopped
2 C shredded savoy cabbage (or other variety)	6 C vegetable broth
2 C Swiss chard, chopped	2 T fresh parsley or chives, chopped
2 C cauliflower, small florets	½ t table salt, or to taste
2 C broccoli, small florets	2 T fresh lemon juice (optional)
1 medium onion, diced	¼ t black pepper, or to taste

Prep time: 35 Minutes   Cook time: 13 minutes   Serves: 12

Directions:
1. Put garlic, vegetables, thyme, and broth into a large soup pot. Cover and bring to a boil over high heat; reduce heat to low and simmer, partly covered, about 10 minutes.
2. Stir in parsley or chives; season to taste with salt, pepper, and lemon juice. Yields about 1 cup per serving.

Artichoke and Chickpea Stew

Contributed by Connie Gee
Las Vegas, Nevada, USA

Ingredients:
2 T olive oil	1 (15.5) oz. can garbanzo beans (chick peas), drained
1 medium yellow onion, chopped	
6 cloves garlic, minced	1 quart low-sodium vegetable broth
⅛ t red pepper flakes	1 T chopped fresh sage
2 medium carrots, chopped	1 t lemon juice
4 medium Roma (plum) tomatoes, chopped	salt and pepper to taste
2 (15 oz.) cans artichoke hearts, drained and halved	

Directions:
1. Heat oil in a large pan over medium heat and cook onion until translucent.
2. Stir in the garlic and chili flakes; cook until the garlic has begun to soften, about 1 minute.
3. Add the carrots, tomatoes, artichokes, garbanzo beans, and broth.
4. Bring to a boil over medium-high heat, then reduce to low and simmer until carrots are tender.
5. Season with sage, lemon juice, salt, and pepper.
6. Taste and add more salt and pepper if desired. Cook an additional 5-10 minutes.
7. Serve with white rice and saltines.

Serves 4

Vegetarian Lentil Soup

Contributed by David Alexander
Member of The Davy Jones Band
Lynn, Massachusetts, USA

Ingredients:
½ lb. dry green lentils
4 C chopped yellow onions
4 cups chopped leeks
1 T minced garlic (3-4 cloves)
¼ C cold pressed virgin olive oil
1 T sea salt
1½ t fresh ground black pepper
1 T minced fresh thyme

1 t ground cumin
3 C diced celery (8 stalks)
3 C diced carrots (4-6 carrots)
3 quarts organic vegetable stock
¼ C tomato paste
optional: balsamic vinegar, Parmesan cheese, kale

Directions:
1. Get 1/2 pound dry lentils and sprout them by covering them with warm water in a bowl or a Mason jar for 24 hours.
2. Drain lentils and rinse.
3. Leave them covered (not in water) with a damp towel in your bowl or jar and rinse them every 12 hours. Your lentils should sprout in 48 hours. You will yield three times the volume! Google "how to sprout lentils."
4. When your lentils are sprouted, get a large stock pot and sauté the onions, leeks, and garlic with the olive oil, salt, pepper, thyme, and cumin on medium heat for 15-20 minutes until the veggies are translucent and tender.
5. Add celery and carrots and sauté 5-10 more minutes.
6. Add the veggie stock and whisk in the tomato paste.
7. Add lentils, cover and bring to a boil.
8. Reduce heat and simmer uncovered for 30-40 minutes. Check seasoning.
9. Optional: Add some chopped kale at the end for extra protein.
10. For added flavor, drizzle with balsamic vinegar, olive oil, and grated Parmesan cheese.

Knowing David Jones was truly a highlight of my life. We shared so much together from tears of laughter and joy to tears of sadness and sorrow. He was such a huge inspiration to me professionally and spiritually. I will always carry his wisdom and his memory in my heart. Love Still Abides...

~ David Alexander

Photograph © Courtesy of David Alexander

Davy and David

Photograph © Courtesy of Michael G. Bush

Black Bean and Squash Chili

Contributed by Jody Richardson
Montrose, California, USA

Ingredients:

1 medium butternut squash (peeled, seeded, and cut into 1 inch chunks)	2 (14.5 oz.) cans fire-roasted tomatoes, low sodium
1 T vegetable oil	2 (15 oz.) cans black beans, rinsed and drained
½ T vegetable oil	2-4 t chili powder
1 medium yellow onion, chopped	½ t dried oregano
1 green bell pepper, seeded and chopped	½ t powdered cumin
1 stalk celery, chopped	¼ t cinnamon
3 cloves garlic, minced	salt and pepper (optional)
1 C corn kernels (frozen or fresh)	freshly chopped cilantro (optional, for garnish)
1 C water	

Directions:
1. Preheat oven to 400 °F. Line baking sheet with parchment paper or coat with cooking spray. In large bowl, toss butternut squash chunks with 1 tablespoon of oil. Spread squash on baking sheet in single layer. Roast in oven until tender and starting to brown, about 30 minutes.
2. Heat ½ tablespoon oil in large stock pot over medium heat. Add onions and bell pepper stirring frequently until soft, about 5 minutes. Add celery and garlic, stirring about 1 minute.
3. Stir in corn, water, tomatoes, beans, chili powder, oregano, cumin, and cinnamon. Simmer, covered, for 15 minutes. Add in squash and cook for an additional 10 minutes, until mixture is soft. Add salt and/or pepper to taste.
    Serve over brown rice or alone with freshly chopped cilantro if desired.

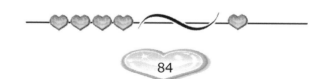

Baked Potato Soup

Contributed by Megan Bartlett
Keene, New Hampshire, USA

Ingredients:
3 T butter
1-2 vegetable bouillon cubes (to taste)
4-5 potatoes (I use red skinned*), chopped
3 T flour
1 (12 oz.) can evaporated milk

2 C extra sharp Cheddar cheese, grated
½-¾ C light sour cream
1 C sautéed mushrooms (optional)
finely chopped chives for garnish

Directions:
1. Melt the butter with the bouillon cube(s) to form a smooth paste.
2. Add the chopped potatoes and sauté them lightly.
3. Sprinkle the potatoes with the flour and stir to coat.
4. Add just enough water to cover the potatoes and simmer until potatoes are soft.
5. Add milk and gently cook until slightly thickened.
6. Add cheese and cook (stirring continuously) until melted and soup is (other than the hunks of potato) smooth.
7. Gently stir in mushrooms and sour cream.
8. Serve with a sprinkle of chives.

* 2-3 sweet potatoes can be used in place of regular ones.

Photograph © Courtesy of Michael G. Bush

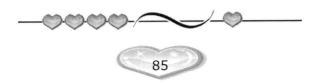

85

Monday's Vegan Cream
of Cauliflower Soup

Contributed by Freddy Monday
Singer/Songwriter
http://freddymonday.com/

Ingredients:

2 heads of cauliflower
1 carrot
1 onion
1 stalk celery
unsalted vegetable soup stock – two (32 fl oz.)
    containers of Pacific Organic Simply Stock
    Vegetable unsalted (water, carrots, celery,
    onions, leeks, mushrooms)

flour
salt
fresh parsley
1 bay leaf – remove after cooking
olive oil
fresh ground black pepper
plain unsweetened fortified rice milk or almond
    milk

Directions:

1. Wash 2 heads of cauliflower. Whack the head in half and get rid of the hard inner core and green parts. Use 1⅓ heads and cut into little florets or finely dice.
2. Finely dice one carrot, one stalk of celery, and one onion. Place pot over medium heat, add 3 tablespoons of olive oil, and then throw in the onions. Stir for 2 minutes or until onions get a little color. Throw in the carrots and celery and stir for a minute. Throw in the cauliflower and stir around to combine.

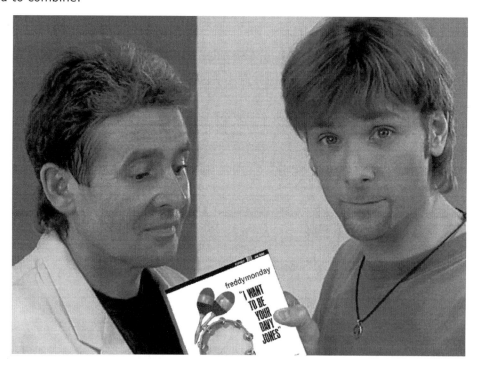

Photograph© Courtesy of Freddy Monday

Freddy and Davy

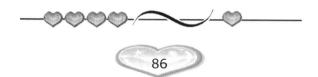

3. Next, add 2 tablespoons fresh parsley finely cut. Cover pot and simmer on low heat for 15 minutes, stirring twice during process.
4. Pour in 2 quarts (64 fl. oz.) of unsalted vegetable soup stock. Bring to a boil over medium heat and then reduce heat and let simmer.
5. White sauce: While soup is simmering, put 3 tablespoons of olive oil in a medium saucepan over medium-low heat.
6. In a separate bowl, pour 2 cups of almond milk and add 6 tablespoons of flour to the almond milk.
7. Mix together with a whisk. Pour almond milk/flour into the saucepan and stir to combine. It will thicken into white sauce. If too thick add additional almond milk. Keep whisking!
8. Pour white sauce into the simmering soup mixture. Throw in a bay leaf. Add salt to taste. I only add a pinch. Let soup simmer for 15 to 20 minutes. Remove bay leaf.

I add a healthy amount of black pepper at serving.

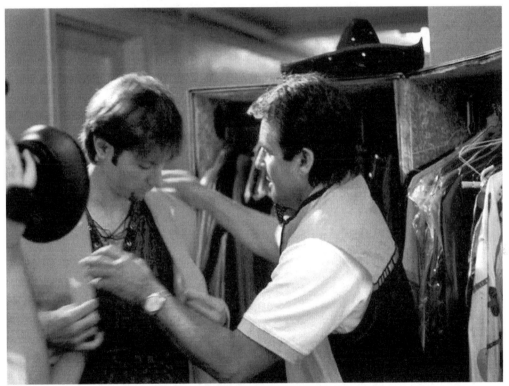

Photograph © Courtesy of Freddy Monday

My fondest memory of David is when he literally gave me the shirt off his back by lending me his yellow suit to use during the filming of my music video "I Want To Be Your Davy Jones." A very cool guy who was selfless, generous, and quite funny… I will never forget our time together.

~ *Freddy Monday*

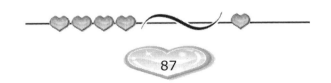

Fave Rave "16" Bean Soup

Contributed by Karen Steele
Marstons Mills, Massachusetts, USA

Ingredients:

1 (16 oz.) package of 16 bean soup mix (throw away the flavor packet)
2 T of chili powder
1 T of cumin
1 onion, chopped
2 cloves chopped garlic
1 t salt

½ t pepper
1 (6 oz.) can of tomato paste
3 pieces of veggie bacon strips (I prefer Morning Star)
2 quarts vegetable broth

Directions:
1. Pour the beans into a pot and fill with water until it covers the beans by an inch. Let them soak overnight.
2. Strain and rinse the beans.
3. Cook "bacon" according to package directions, then break into pieces.
4. In a Dutch oven or soup pot, put 1 tablespoon olive oil in the bottom and sauté chopped onion and garlic until translucent over medium high heat.
5. Add the "bacon" pieces and beans along with the veggie broth and spices.
6. Bring to a boil and the add the tomato paste.
7. Lower the heat to medium and cook for 2-3 hours on medium heat until the beans soften and the soup thickens.

Tenderfoot Chili

Contributed by Karen Jorgenson
Stationed in Misawa, Japan

Ingredients:

1 lb. vegetarian minced "ground beef"
1 can stewed tomatoes (do not drain)
1 can kidney beans (do not drain)

1 package dry onion soup mix
cooked pasta (at least 2 c. cooked elbow pasta, drained)

Directions:
1. Brown vegetarian minced "ground beef" in large fry pan.
2. Add stewed tomatoes, kidney beans, and dry soup mix and heat until boiling. Stir in cooked pasta and mix well.

Serves 4 to 6

Butternut Squash Soup

Contributed by Megan Bartlett
Keene, New Hampshire, USA

Ingredients:
1 butternut squash, peeled, with ends removed
1 onion, peeled and chopped into wedges
4 T butter, chopped into dabs
2-3 C vegetable broth
2-3 T pure maple syrup

salt to taste (no more than 1 t)
cayenne pepper to taste (optional, but divine)
½-⅓ C cream (any kind works, from fat-free half
   and half to heavy)

Directions:
1. Slice the squash lengthways and remove (and discard) the seeds.
2. Chop the squash into 1 inch cubes and arrange the cubes and the onion pieces in a sprayed 9x13 inch pan.
3. Gently pour the broth into the pan.
4. Sprinkle the salt, dab the butter, and drizzle the syrup over the vegetables and broth.
5. Bake at 325° F until squash is soft (about an hour).
6. Allow to cool slightly, set broth aside, and, in batches, purée vegetables in a blender or processor until smooth. (This is easiest if you only use a cup of vegetables at a time and add some water to help it liquefy.)
7. When smooth, pour into a large saucepan.
8. Repeat until all of the vegetables are puréed and in the saucepan.
9. Add all the broth and heat through.
10. Season to taste with a touch of cayenne pepper.
11. To serve, pour into bowls and add 1 tablespoon of cream to each serving (to be stirred in then OR add ½ cup or so to the entire batch before pouring into bowls).

Easy Pumpkin Soup

Contributed by Jody Proetta
Putnam Valley, New York, USA

Ingredients:
1 (15 oz.) can of pumpkin puree
1 C of vegetable broth
1 T of olive oil
1 C of plain soy milk

sea salt and pepper to taste
1 T of honey
butter at room temperature

Directions:
1. Combine all of your ingredients in a pot and mix well.
2. Cook on low/medium heat until well heated. Combine honey with ¼ bar of butter that's at room temperature.
3. Serve your soup with a salad and some warm rustic bread with honey butter.

Enjoy!

Cream-less Cream of Mushroom Soup

Contributed by Lisa Duclo
Vista, California, USA

Ingredients:
3 C chopped fresh mushrooms. You can use any variety of mushrooms you like, but my favorite combination is hiratake mushrooms, king oyster trumpet mushrooms, and white button mushrooms.
1 C chopped yellow onion
6 cloves peeled, whole cloves of garlic
¼ C olive oil
2 t dried oregano
2 t fresh lemon zest, divided
2 (14 oz.) cans of white beans, rinsed and drained
2 C of clear homemade mushroom broth, or 2 C of organic clear mushroom broth from a carton, or 2 (14 oz.) cans of clear organic mushroom broth.

Directions:
1. Place the whole cloves of garlic in a ramekin, or small microwave safe bowl. Heat the garlic on high in the microwave for about 30 seconds.
2. In a large frying pan, place the microwaved garlic cloves along with the mushrooms and onions, the dried oregano, and 1 teaspoon of the lemon zest. Sauté all of these ingredients with ¼ cup of olive oil until the mushrooms just start to brown, about 5 minutes, over medium heat.
3. Place half of the browned mushroom mixture into a medium sized sauce pan or stock pot, making sure to add the garlic cloves. Add the clear mushroom broth and the rinsed and drained white beans. Use a stick blender or an immersion blender to blend all of the ingredients until smooth. Add the rest of the mushroom mixture to the pot and blend again leaving some of the mushroom bits intact for a slightly chunky texture. If you do not have a stick blender or an immersion blender, you can blend the soup in batches in a regular blender or a food processor, but you will need to use a little bit of the clear mushroom broth to get the mixture to whirl around properly.
4. Once the soup is blended to your liking, add 1 teaspoon of fresh lemon zest, heat through, and serve.

This recipe makes about 6 servings.

Salads

Photograph © Courtesy of Rhino Entertainment Company

Jessica Cramer Jones

When I was just a few weeks old I gained my first stamp in my passport. It read "Japan," and so started my incredible adventures both culinary and otherwise with my Dad! His job took him all over the world from the tender age of 10. My school friends would often comment "Wow. Your Dad is away a lot. Don't you miss him?" Of course I missed him like crazy, but before cell phones, text messages, e-mail, and Skype I had learned to deal with it! (Don't ask me how. I guess kids adapt!)

So what's this got to do with a cookbook I hear you ask...Well just imagine when you are Davy Jones of The Monkees touring the world for months at a time, you usually eat breakfast, lunch, and supper in a different restaurant in a different state or even a different country every day!

When it came to missing my Dad, there was a wonderful trade off. When school holidays came around, I actually got to go to the office with him every day! By the time I was 9 years old, I had eaten breakfast in every state in America at least twice!

Photograph © Courtesy
of Daryl Goldfarb

Dad's day to day schedule was jam packed, so at times our choice in eatery was limited. Sometimes we were at 30,000 ft., sometimes we were rocking around in the tour bus, maybe we had stopped at a roadside diner or we were lucky enough to be in a 5 star hotel restaurant, but just like other families all over the world, our meal times were an important time for us to be together.

Family and friends will all agree when it came to dinner time, my father was the most generous man I have ever known. He loved to gather everyone together and treat them to a feast. He was always excited when we were heading to a city or town where he knew "This Great Little Place." In fact, Dad could have written his own book, "Great Little Places To Eat On The Road"!

When he reached a city, he had to explore. He would check into a hotel and would usually take 10 minutes to make a cup of English tea, and then he would put on his sneakers and off he went. Dad would often talk to me about his "Gypsy Spirit" and these city hikes were how he captured a small sense of the freedom he felt being out in the countryside at home with his horses and his family. You see, it takes one to know one!

When you are on tour, the inside of a tour bus, hotel, airplane, and venue can be all you see for months if you don't take the time to stretch your wings. After 50 years of being in the travelling circus we call show business, Dad was a pro at keeping "healthy" on the road. Part of taking care of yourself is avoiding the trap of relying on fast food. Dad had it down to a fine art. Many of his friends and family can recall chasing him around the streets of some far off land weaving in out of alleys and thoroughfares in search of some "Great Little Place" he went to 10 years ago. Like a hound dog in pursuit of a scent there was no stopping him. All you could do was follow in blind faith as he miraculously navigated his way through the streets. In his pursuit of the "Great Little Places," Dad may have made a couple of detours over the years, but our journey always ended with a feast!

Dad loved what he called "Clean Food" which meant FRESH, healthy, simple, and nutritious ingredients cooked with love and care. Yes, he knew all "The Great Little Places," BUT what you really want when you are a long way from home is some good old fashioned home cooking.

I could tell you so many stories about all the meals in all the cities and backwaters all over the world that I shared with Dad, but what I really want to share with you is what I would like to cook for him if he popped by for supper now — good clean food that I know he would love.

Mum always tried to make Dad's homecoming a surprise, but little did she know that from a young age I had figured out her secret! Old fashioned ginger beer (non alcoholic) and beetroot would always appear in the fridge prior to Dad's return! He loved to make sandwiches when he got back from the horses, so the fridge would be bursting with lovely fresh green salad leaves and a rainbow of fruit and veg. Here are some recipes inspired by my dad's love of these fiery and colourful ingredients.

Photograph © Courtesy of Lawrie Haley

Davy, Anita, and Jessica with Lawrie Haley

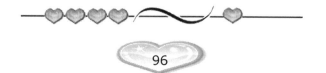

Daddy's Ginger Salad

Contributed by Jessica Cramer Jones, Davy's Daughter
Hampshire, UK

Ingredients:
fresh root ginger
1 small/medium red cabbage
1 kg of carrots
sunflower seeds

For the Dressing:
1 T canola oil or light olive oil
half a lime, squeezed
a little less than a desert spoon of apple cider
    vinegar
1 t honey

unbleached rock salt – a much tastier and
    healthier option to regular table salt as it still
    has trace minerals in it. Put it in a pestle and
    mortar or a rock salt grinder.
fresh ground black pepper
sprig of coriander

(Dad would really appreciate it if the
ingredients were organic or locally sourced
wherever possible.)

Directions:
1. You will need a large salad bowl. First, take the red cabbage and remove the very outer leaves and the very bottom white stalk which can be a little woody.
2. Then use a grater or food processor to grate the raw cabbage. Take care not to grate it too fine or too thick – imagine a chunky slaw!
3. Now peel the carrots and grate them into the bowl with cabbage. The quantities above are estimates. Sometimes I like a little more carrot and sometimes a little more cabbage.
4. Cut a few inches of ginger off the main stem and peel it, and then use a fine grater to grate it into the bowl. Dad and I LOVE ginger so I can handle quite a kick of it in my salad, but add just a little to start and build it up to *your* liking!
5. Mix all the ingredients and dressing together, and to finish, add a really good sprinkling of sunflower seeds and a sprig of coriander for colour.
6. When it comes to the dressing, mix up what tastes good to you and have fun experimenting with the flavours.

Depending on the time of year, the cabbage and carrots can really vary in sweetness, so I always make the dressing a little different every time! You really don't need a lot of oil; it's just a dash to help move the other ingredients around the bowl. Raw veg is really good for you, and like Dad, I eat most of my veggies raw throughout the day. The great thing about this salad is it goes really well with most meat and fish so your non-vegetarian guests will love it too! It keeps in the fridge for a few days, and I always take some to work for lunch or add it to the menu for supper the following night. I also put it in sandwiches with cheese like a fancy coleslaw, and that really hits the hunger spot after a hard day on the ranch!

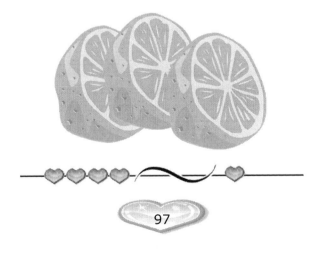

Ruby Slipper Salad

Contributed by Jessica Cramer Jones, Davy's Daughter
Hampshire, UK

This salad is a real Broadway show stopper, and it's got all the razzle dazzle of the great man himself! Its name is inspired by the beautiful ruby colours of the pomegranate seeds, beetroot, and raspberries, proving there is no place like home cooking! I have never had to put a dressing on this salad because of the sweetness of the fruit and richness of the cheese. The flavours are a perfect balance and so people often ask me what the delicious dressing is! For best results keep the cheese in a cold fridge until you are ready to serve your meal. This will ensure the cheese crumbles rather than coats the salad.

Ingredients: mixed baby leaf salad leaves 1 fresh beet 3 ripe pears fresh pomegranate seeds from at least 1 whole fruit (and/or raspberries) soft and crumbly garlic and herb cheese (Boursin or equivalent)	If you can't get hold of a soft crumbly garlic cheese, you could try to marinate some feta cubes in garlic and herbs overnight or use a crumbly blue cheese. It's not quite as scrumptious but will do the job!

Directions:
1. If you are removing the seeds from a pomegranate, this can take a while, so get this done first and don't wear white!
2. Peel and slice at least 3 pears.
3. Then place the salad leaves in a large salad bowl.
4. Grate some fresh beetroot into the leaves and toss.
5. Crumble the cheese into the leaves and very very gently toss, being careful not to break down the cheese crumbles.
6. Place the pears on top of the leaves, sprinkle the raspberries and the pomegranate seeds on top, and just gently pull through some of the rich green leaves and white cheese for a real feast for the eyes.

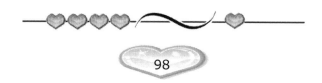

Dad's Daydream Potatoes

Contributed by Jessica Cramer Jones, Davy's daughter
Hampshire, UK

After a long day at the stables, Dad was not afraid of a carb or two. He took plenty of exercise, so faddy diets were not his thing, so let's roll out some potatoes to go with our meal, and we must not forget some good quality protein for a healthy finale! When you are a vegetarian, you need make sure you include plenty of vegetable based proteins in your diet. California avocados were one of Dad's absolute favourites. Talia, Sarah, and Dad used to pick them straight from the trees in Santa Barbara where my sisters grew up, so they are a firm favourite amongst all the Jones girls!

Ingredients:	
small or medium good quality salad potatoes	2 avocados
olive oil	juice of 1 lemon
rock salt	fresh basil leaves
pepper	

Directions:
1. First you need to "marinate" your avocados while everything else cooks. Peel and slice the avocados into thick slices and drench them with fresh lemon juice. Be careful to remove the lemon seeds as the marinade will become part of the dressing later on. Grind fresh black pepper over them and leave them to stand.
2. Now, leaving the skin on, quarter or halve the potatoes depending on their size.
3. Bring them to the boil and cook until they are just right. Not too soft and not too hard! Drain them and place them back in the pan. Pour olive oil over them and don't hold back on the rock salt and fresh ground pepper!
4. Place a lid on the potatoes and gently shake the sauce pan until the potatoes start to crack and split and all the lovely dressing starts to soak in. The culinary term is a "crushed potato." In essence, it's not neat and tidy like boiled potatoes, but it's not quite mashed either.
   It's delicious! Don't be afraid if they look a bit like they have been dropped or over cooked. The flavours will make up for it, and once the avocados are placed on top they will look table ready.
5. Spread your potatoes out on a serving plate. Now fan out the avocado slices on top in whatever pattern best reflects your favourite Monkees tune!
6. Pour over the remaining lemon marinade, grind a little more pepper, and decorate with your basil leaves or whatever tickles your fancy!

After all is said and done, grab your coats. We are going for ice cream! Dad was not one for desserts after a meal. However, when it came to sweet treats he was always excited to take us all out for ice cream! He loved all the classic flavours in a waffle cone. Ice cream "a la Davy" is best enjoyed with your family by the beach in the sunshine.

Keep smiling. Keep healthy.
Thank you for supporting the DJEMF and Dad's beautiful herd!
Big Love Always,
Jessica Jones x x x

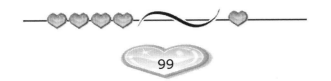

Kale Salad

Contributed by Karen Valentine
Star of Room 222

*Black kale, sometimes called lacinato, is the most tender of the kale family,
yet it's hardy enough to marinate in a lemon dressing. I find it more delicious when
allowed to sit for at least an hour, which makes it a great make-ahead salad.*

Ingredients:

4-6 C black kale leaves, loosely packed, sliced
   or torn, midribs removed (removing ribs is
   a must)
juice of 1 lemon
3-4 T extra-virgin olive oil

1-2 cloves garlic, mashed
salt & pepper, to taste
hot red pepper flakes, to taste
⅔ C grated Pecorino cheese
½ C fresh bread crumbs (optional)

Directions:

1. Let the garlic sit in the oil while you are prepping the kale. Discard garlic or not, as per taste.
2. Whisk lemon juice, salt and pepper, and a generous pinch of hot red pepper flakes into the oil.
3. Add the kale and toss well. Add ⅓ of the cheese and toss again. Repeat. Let sit for at least 30 minutes (an hour is even better). Toss occasionally.
4. If using breadcrumbs, add and toss again, and top with remaining cheese.

We appeared in a segment of Love American Style titled "Love and the Elopement" (1970). Davy was such a joy. His totally charming personality, boundless energy, and delightful humor lifted everyone around him.

~ Karen Valentine

Photograph © Courtesy of Karen Valentine

Rebekka's Tomato Salad

Contributed by Rebekka Bishop
Toledo, Iowa, USA

Ingredients:
4-6 large tomatoes, peeled
1 stalk celery, thinly sliced
⅛– ¼ C thinly sliced onion rings (red or yellow)
½ C cider vinegar
¼ C sugar or 6 NutraSweet packets

½ C chickpeas (garbanzo beans)
1 t chili powder
½ t dried parsley flakes
salt to taste

Directions:
1. Cut peeled tomatoes into ⅛ inch thin wedges.
2. Add celery, onions, and chick peas.
3. In a shaker, combine all liquids and spices. Shake well.
4. Pour over veggies. Be adventurous. Sprinkle with a bit more salt and chili powder. Chill for at least 1 hour before serving.

Tofu Salad

Contributed by Connor Baer
Bellmawr, New Jersey, USA

Ingredients:
1 pkg. firm tofu
1 head lettuce
4 tomatoes, sliced

1 onion sliced
1 cucumber, sliced
3 green peppers, sliced

Directions:
1. Drain tofu and wrap in paper towel to remove moisture.
2. Cut tofu into cubes.
3. Mix tofu with the other veggie ingredients.
4. Serve immediately.

You can add many toppings to tofu salad—your favorite dressing, of course! Also, croutons of any flavor, nuts, seeds, vegan bacon bits, fruit… An easy and delicious meal for lunch or dinner!

Southern Potato Salad

Contributed by Nita Kayla Nelson
Dallas, Texas, USA

This recipe has been in my family forever.

Ingredients:
8 medium russet potatoes
5 boiled eggs
1 large jar of pimentos
1 medium yellow onion
2 stalks of celery
½ C chopped sweet pickles

¼ C of pickle juice
1 C of mayonnaise. (add more if needed)
1 t yellow mustard
1 T of salt (more or less to your taste)
garnish with paprika

Directions:
1. Peel potatoes and boil until fork tender.
2. Chop eggs and onions.
3. While still hot, add hard boiled eggs, onions, diced sweet pickles, diced celery, and pimentos.
4. Mix together.
5. Add pickle juice, mayonnaise, mustard, and salt.
6. Mix. Add more mayonnaise and salt if needed. Do not mash; it will be the consistency of very lumpy mashed potatoes.
7. Sprinkle with paprika and refrigerate for 2 hours.

French Dressing

Contributed By Darlene Haines
Crestline, Ohio, USA

Ingredients:
¾ C ketchup
½ C vegetable oil
½ C cider vinegar
½ C packed brown sugar
¼ C chopped onion
1 garlic clove

½ t Worcestershire sauce
¼ t salt
¼ t paprika
dash hot pepper sauce
iceberg lettuce

Directions:
1. Cut iceberg lettuce into wedges.
2. Combine first 10 ingredients in a blender and process until smooth.
3. Store in refrigerator in a tight-fitting jar.
4. Shake and serve on lettuce wedges.

Windowbox Gardening

You don't have to be a gardener with a huge plot of land and a large budget to grow your own fruits, vegetables, and herbs. Remember growing cress on damp cotton wool as a child? There are plenty of ways to have fresh home grown goodness in your diet, even if you don't have a garden. Here are some ideas:

1. Windowbox/windowsill gardening is a great idea. Chili peppers or tomatoes (dwarf varieties!) can easily be grown on a sunny windowsill.

2. Herbs — Fresh herbs brighten up a kitchen and make it smell good as well as being a great source of flavour and vitamins. Grow from seed or buy plants from your supermarket or garden centre. Take cuttings of bought plants and pop the cut ends in a jar with a little water to root them for new plants and to keep your herb box going all year round.

3. Bean sprouts can be grown in a jar so you have them fresh for your stir-fry.

4. Mushrooms — Mail order mushroom kits are available with everything you need for fresh 'shrooms, and this is much safer than picking them from the wild!

5. Potatoes — If you have a balcony or roof terrace you can grow potatoes. Use an old bucket or barrel filled with compost. It needs to be deep enough to get a good 1 ½ - 2 feet of soil, but will produce a good crop. Potatoes will grow from any supermarket spud that is allowed to grow "eyes", but it's best to buy "chitted" seed potatoes, which are prepared specially, from your garden centre.

6. A tiny pop-up plastic greenhouse on a balcony or patio is enough to grow tomatoes, courgettes, peppers, and cucumbers outdoors.

7. A strawberry planter looks attractive and produces much tastier fruit than a supermarket can provide! Start with a few plants and when they start to produce "runners", (long whippy stems with leaves at the end), pin the new leaves down onto the surface of a pot of compost with a piece of bent wire hooked over the stem, and they will root and become new plants. Once your new plant roots you can trim the long stem away.

8. Radishes, spring onions, chives, cress, lettuces, dwarf beans, and baby carrots can be grown in pots to add to your summer salads.

9. And don't forget to add some flowering plants to your window boxes and container gardens to attract the insects that pollinate the plants. Grow lavender alongside your herbs; the leaves can be infused in hot water for a soothing drink, and marigolds grown with tomatoes will keep pests away.

~ Andrea Gilbey

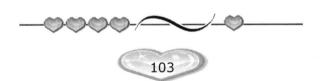

Lentil Salad

Contributed by Kim Briggs
Atlanta, Georgia, USA

Ingredients:
1 can garbanzo beans (drained)
1 package precooked lentils
8 oz. cherry tomatoes, halved
1 medium cucumber, chopped
½ C of fresh Italian parsley, chopped

½ C of fresh green onions, chopped
juice of one lemon
3 T olive oil
salt and pepper to taste

Directions:
Just mix it all together in a bowl and serve or refrigerate. This one is really easy to customize as well, so feel free to play with the ingredients.

Quinoa Taco Salad

Contributed by Karen Brostrom
Romeoville, Illinois, USA

Ingredients:
1 C quinoa
I can of black beans
mild, medium, or hot salsa
sliced black olives

fresh cilantro
avocado, cut into small pieces
romaine lettuce

Directions:
1. Prepare quinoa according to package instructions.
2. In a separate dish, heat black beans. Combine quinoa and black beans.
3. Portion out servings and add desired amount of salsa, black olives, avocado, and cilantro.
4. Mix together and serve on a bed of romaine lettuce.

If serving less than four portions at a time, keep the quinoa/black bean mixture separate from the other ingredients so that it can be heated again before adding the rest.
This recipe is gluten-free, dairy-free, and soy-free. If preferred, sour cream or shredded cheese can be added. It could also be eaten as a wrap in a soft tortilla or as a taco in a hard shell.

Makes about 4 servings

Horseradish Potato Salad

Contributed by Celine Allan
Dallas, Texas, USA

Ingredients:
2 to 2 ½ pounds small red potatoes
sea salt to taste
¼ C fruity tasting extra virgin olive oil, as needed
4-6 T apple cider or rice vinegar
1 smallish red onion, finely diced

2 T prepared horseradish
sea salt and fresh ground black pepper
2 T chopped fresh parsley
1-2 t dill, to taste
1 t caraway seeds (optional)

Directions:
1. Wash and cut up the red potatoes. Toss them into a pot of salted fresh water. Bring the water to a boil and simmer the potatoes until they are fork tender. Drain well.
2. Pour the cooked potatoes into a large bowl. While the potatoes are still warm, sprinkle with sea salt and drizzle with extra virgin olive oil and vinegar. Toss to coat and to soften the edges of the potato pieces a bit.
3. Add the diced onion and horseradish and toss to distribute. Taste and season with more sea salt and plenty of fresh ground pepper. Add the chopped parsley, dill, and caraway. Mix.
4. Taste test. Add more olive oil or vinegar, sea salt or herbs.
5. Serve warm (so yummy!) or cover and chill. Remember that chilling the potato salad will subdue its flavor considerably. Always season more vigorously if serving chilled. Taste test after chilling and add more seasoning if needed.

Serves 6 to 8

Cranberry-Pineapple Holiday Salad

Contributed by Colleen Johnson
St. Louis, Missouri, USA

This is one of my family's holiday favorites. As long as I can remember this festive salad has been on our table for each Thanksgiving and Christmas dinner. ENJOY!!

Ingredients:
1 bag coarsely ground fresh cranberries
20 oz. can crushed pineapple (drained well)
¾ C sugar
1 pint whipping cream

½ t vanilla
¾ bag vegetarian mini marshmallows
½ C chopped pecans or walnuts (optional)

Directions:
1. The night before, combine cranberries, pineapple, and sugar and refrigerate.
2. The next day, whip cream (add ½ teaspoon vanilla) until it forms peaks.
3. In a large bowl, fold whipped cream, mini marshmallows, and nuts into cranberry pineapple mixture and refrigerate before serving.

"Chicken" Salad

Contributed by Michele Allison
Long Valley, New Jersey, USA

Ingredients:
1 C hot water
2 C dry TVP (textured vegetable protein)
mayonnaise of your choice
1 stalk of celery, chopped
4-6 carrots, minced in food processor

1 onion, chopped
½ green pepper or cucumber, chopped
   (optional)
salt and pepper

Directions:
1. Pour hot water into bowl of TVP. Stir and let stand for 5 minutes to allow it to reconstitute. It will double in size.
2. Add mayonnaise and all the veggies.
3. Season.

Linguini Salad

Contributed by Leanna Mattson
Kennewick, Washington, USA

Ingredients:
linguini noodles
2 tomatoes
1 medium onion

Good Seasons Italian Dressing Mix
olive oil
Johnny's Salad Elegance

Directions:
1. Boil linguini 10 minutes (not any longer). Rinse with cold water.
2. Squeeze juice from the tomatoes and dice meat of the fruit.
3. Dice onion.
4. Mix Good Seasons dressing with olive oil instead of vegetable oil and mix with 1/2 jar of Johnny's Salad Elegance.
5. Toss in bowl and marinate overnight, tossing occasionally.

Cucumber Salad

Contributed by Donna Corbin
New Port Richey, Florida, USA

Ingredients:
5 peeled and sliced cucumbers
1 C mayonnaise
½ C red wine vinegar
½ t salt

¼ t pepper
4 t dill
¼ t oregano

Directions:
1. In a small bowl stir together mayonnaise, vinegar, dill, oregano, and salt.
2. Stir the mixture into cucumbers and chill.

Carrot Raisin Salad

Contributed by Paula Schmidt
Canton, Pennsylvania, USA

Ingredients:
4 C fresh carrots, finely shredded
1 (20 oz.) can of crushed pineapple with juice
1 C raisins

¾ C mayonnaise
1 T sugar
½ T fresh lemon juice

Directions:
1. Chill all ingredients except sugar for at least 30 minutes.
2. Dissolve the sugar in the pineapple, then combine everything gently in a large bowl.
3. May be refrigerated for up to 72 hours.

Serves 8

NOTE: Fresh carrots are the secret to making this recipe a success!

Easy Red Pepper and
Sweet Corn Pasta Salad

Contributed by Andrea Gilbey
Cheshunt, Hertfordshire, UK

Ingredients:
1 handful pasta shells (cooked)
1 sweet red pepper, chopped into ½" pieces
1 can sweet corn
1 small white onion or 2 shallots, chopped
1 T white wine vinegar
1 T lemon juice

½ T sunflower oil
ground black pepper
dried oregano
dried basil
pinch of salt (optional, to taste)

Directions:
Mix everything in a bowl, serve, eat! Makes enough for 2 people.

Sweet Papa Gene's
Bread and Butter Pickle Salad

Contributed by Ginny Fleming
New Albany, Indiana, USA

Ingredients:
lettuce
bread and butter pickles
2 t juice and spice from the bottom of pickle jar
4 peeled and unseeded cucumbers
half head of cauliflower
1 large floret broccoli

3 small sweet bell peppers
mayonnaise
sugar
sunflower seeds
1 small sweet onion (optional)

Directions:
1. Shred lettuce in large bowl.
2. Peel, remove seeds, and dice 4 medium cucumbers.
3. Halve cauliflower head; dice.
4. Dice 1 large broccoli floret.
5. Seed and dice 3 small sweet bell peppers (red, green, yellow – for display).
6. Optional: 1 small sweet onion – dice finely.
7. Dice jar of sliced bread and butter pickles – Set aside with juice and spice from the bottom of jar.
8. Add ½ cup of sugar to 1 cup of mayonnaise. Add pickles and juice.
9. Pour mayonnaise/pickle mixture over the combined salad. Lastly, garnish salad's top with sunflower seeds. Allow mixture to "seep" through the salad. Lightly toss minutes before serving.

Serves 10 to 12

Three Bean Salad

Contributed by Celine Allan
Dallas, Texas, USA

Ingredients:
1 can cannellini beans, rinsed and drained
1 can kidney beans, rinsed and drained
1 can garbanzo beans, rinsed and drained
½ red or sweet onion, chopped
1 C fresh, finely chopped flat-leaf parsley
1 T fresh finely chopped rosemary

Dressing:
⅓ C apple cider vinegar
⅓ C granulated sugar
¼ C olive oil (using really good olive oil makes
   a big difference)
1 ½ t salt
¼ t black pepper

Directions:
1. Combine first six ingredients in a bowl.
2. Mix dressing ingredients well.
3. Add dressing to bowl and gently mix.
4. Cover and put in fridge to chill. The colder the better before you serve it.

Combine salad with cold pasta, cherry tomatoes, and feta cheese
for another version that is fabulous.

Halloumi Salad
(With Houmous Dressing)

Contributed by Debbie Sanderson
Berkshire, England

Ingredients:
2 pitta breads, cut in strips
2 T of a good olive oil
250g pack halloumi
bag of mixed salad leaves
420g tin butter beans (drained and rinsed)
handful of fresh mint leaves, chopped

For the dressing:
50g houmous
50g natural yogurt
1 T lemon juice

Directions:
1. Preheat oven to 200° C, fan 180° C, gas mark 6. Put pitta strips on a sheet pan and drizzle over half the oil and season. Toss together then cook in the oven until crisp (approx. 8 minutes).
2. Heat a griddle pan over a high heat and cut halloumi into ¼" slices. Brush both sides with remaining oil and griddle for 4 minutes, turning once until cheese has charred lines on both sides.
3. In a large serving bowl, put leaves, pitta strips, beans, mint, and halloumi and toss together.
4. In a small bowl, stir together yogurt, houmous, and lemon juice. Season to taste. Drizzle this over the salad and serve.

Serves 4

Cool Quinoa Salad

Contributed by Suzanne Gee
Las Vegas, Nevada, USA

Ingredients:

1 ½ C uncooked quinoa	¼ C chopped fresh mint leaves
½ C pine nuts lightly toasted	⅛ t sugar
2 C English cucumber, peeled and finely diced	salt and pepper to taste
¾ C Roma tomatoes, seeded and finely diced	3 avocados diced
½ C shredded carrot	¼ C olive oil
½ C red onion, finely chopped	1 lemon juiced and zested
½ C chopped fresh parsley	

Directions:

1. Bring 2 quarts salted water to a boil. Add quinoa, cover, and reduce heat to medium. Simmer 12 to 14 minutes or until quinoa is tender yet still retains a bite.

2. While cooking quinoa, preheat oven or toaster oven to 250° F. Take pine nuts and spread in a thin layer on an ungreased, unlined cookie sheet. Toast in oven, removing to shake and toss every minute or so. The pine nuts are done when you start to smell them. The time will vary, so watch very carefully and never leave oven. Nuts burn quickly! Should take about 5 minutes. Remove from oven and set aside.

3. Drain quinoa and rinse under cold running water. Drain again. Set aside for 5 minutes, then fluff with a fork. Add in pine nuts, cucumber, tomatoes, onion, carrots, parsley, mint, sugar, salt, and pepper. Mix well, then fold in avocados, oil, lemon juice, and lemon zest. Taste and add more salt and pepper if needed.

Nice side dish or light lunch served with tortilla chips and a cold beer or ice tea.
Serves 6 to 12

Yummy Walnut, Apple, and Grape Salad

Contributed by Susan Gerald
Raleigh, North Carolina, USA

Ingredients:
¼ C chopped walnuts
2 C cubed apples
1 C halved seedless grapes
¼ C chopped celery

⅓ C sour cream
⅓ C plain yogurt
1 T lemon juice

Directions:
1. Combine walnuts, apples, grapes, celery, and lemon juice.
2. In another bowl, mix sour cream and yogurt.
3. Fold into fruit/nut mixture.
4. Refrigerate.

Macaroni Salad

Contributed by Lyn Tomkinson
(from my daughter, Vicki Patchen)
Finksburg, Maryland, USA

Ingredients:
2 eggs
4 T cornstarch
¾ C cider vinegar
1 C water
2 C sugar
½ t salt
¼ t pepper
1 t prepared mustard

1 small can evaporated milk
1 pint mayonnaise
1 lb. macaroni
1 stalk celery
1 red onion
1 green pepper chopped
1 large carrot

Directions:
1. Beat the two eggs; mix in cornstarch, vinegar, and water.
2. Boil until thick.
3. Add sugar, pepper, salt, and mustard.
4. When cool, not cold, add milk and mayonnaise.
5. Cook macaroni.
6. Add celery, onion, pepper, carrot, and dressing.
7. Sprinkle with paprika.

Ann's Bountiful Barley Salad

Contributed by Ann Moses
Associate Editor of Tiger Beat Magazine January 1966—June 1966.
Feature Editor of Tiger Beat Magazine July 1966—January 1968

Ingredients:	
2 C vegetable broth	1 carrot shredded
1 C Quaker quick cook barley	
½ red bell pepper, seeded and chopped into ½ inch cubes	Dressing:
	3 T fresh lemon juice
¼ - ½ large English cucumber, peeled, seeded, and thinly sliced	6 T olive oil
	½ t salt
2 T chopped fresh basil	½ t coarsely ground pepper
½ - 1 C baby spinach, roughly chopped (or Arugula)	

Directions:
1. Bring vegetable broth to a boil and then add quick cook barley. Reduce to low and cook about 20 minutes until all liquid is absorbed and barley is tender.
2. Pour into a bowl, immediately toss with dressing, then stir in remaining ingredients. Serve warm or room temperature.

Photograph © Courtesy of Ann Moses

Ann Moses with Davy

My time spent with Davy was always warm, friendly, and professional but one time was very different. For a few months I had been dating, even talking of marriage and a family with my British superstar boyfriend, "M", my first true love. On our last night together after he and his group spent a week taping a TV show in Hollywood, "M" broke up with me. He lied about "why" he was breaking up, but I was devastated, embarrassed, and heartbroken. I told no one; I was too hurt.

Two days later I was back at work and scheduled to go out to do my "I Visit The Monkees" column for Tiger Beat. When I entered The Monkees sound stage, Davy was sitting with Peter and a couple of their friends in directors chairs between scenes.

Photograph © Courtesy of Ann Moses

Davy spotted me and waved me over. I sat down with them, saying quiet "hellos."

Immediately, Davy took me by the hand and said, "Come with me," as he led me to his dressing room. Once alone, he put his hands on my shoulders and looked into my eyes. "What's wrong?" he asked. "I can tell you're really upset." I couldn't keep the tears back any longer. I told him how my boyfriend had broken up with me, and that was when he drew me into a hug as I sobbed on his shoulder.

After a couple of minutes I composed myself and Davy sat down beside me. "I don't know who the bastard is," he said, "but he's the loser, not you. You are a beautiful lady and someday you will find the man that's worthy of you."

Hearing those words from Davy, in his sincere and big-brotherly way, I believed what he said and my heart lifted just a little. Each time I thought back on how he had been so caring and thoughtful to me, to care about my feelings, it made my heart heal a little more each day. And it made a place in my heart for Davy, one of the most generous and kind men I would ever know.

~ Ann

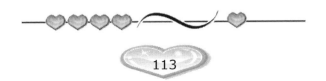

German Potato Salad

Contributed by Jennifer Stevens
Hoffman Estates, Illinois, USA

I saw Davy Jones perform at Epcot Flower Power Festival. At the time, I was going through one of the darkest times of my life and it was my birthday weekend. I knew Davy was performing and told my husband that all I wanted to do for my birthday was to see Davy. We got in line about two hours before the show. Davy was so wonderful towards all the fans. He did not hesitate to pose for a picture during the show with whomever wanted one. The smile on his face was from ear to ear and seeing his enthusiasm and love of life made me forget my problems for a time. I will never forget him and will always be thankful for the happiness he brought to my life during a time when I almost forgot what it was like to smile and laugh.

I've been a vegetarian for over 25 years. I've been making this potato salad for my family for years. Even the non-vegetarians tell me that this is the best potato salad they ever had.

Ingredients:	
2 C water (divided)	¼ t pepper
1 C apple cider vinegar	1 t celery seed
1 medium onion, chopped	2 T cornstarch
4 T sugar	3 T imitation bacon bits
1 t salt	8 pounds potatoes

Directions:
1. Cook, peel, and slice potatoes. Place in 9x13 inch baking dish.
2. Bring 1 ¾ cups of water, the cider vinegar, sugar, salt, pepper, and celery seed to a boil.
3. Add chopped onion. Slowly simmer until onion is glossy, about 30 to 45 minutes.
4. Mix cornstarch with ¼ cup of water and add to onion/liquid mixture to thicken.
5. Pour over potatoes. Sprinkle with imitation bacon bits.
6. Serve hot or cold.

Serves 10

Skinny Broccoli Salad

Contributed by Linda Mathers
Drumbo, Ontario, Canada

Ingredients:	
2 heads of broccoli, chopped	½ C green olives, chopped
1 head of cauliflower, chopped	1 C chopped tomato
½ C each of red and green peppers, chopped	1 C shredded Cheddar cheese
½ C red onions, chopped	1 C ranch dressing or your choice

Directions:
Toss all ingredients with the dressing and let sit 1 hour.

My Favorite Tortellini Salad

Contributed by Megan Bartlett
Keene, New Hampshire, USA

Ingredients:
1 bag tri-color tortellini, cooked and cooled to room temperature
1 (8 oz.) block Monterey Jack cheese, diced into small cubes (It's tempting to try an Italian cheese but I found them to be a little too salty for this recipe.)
1 large tomato, chopped
1 large onion, chopped

1 large red pepper, chopped
1 large green pepper, chopped
parsley, garlic powder, basil, and oregano to taste
1 T olive oil (It's tempting to add more oil, however the tomato will give off enough water to make the dressing *just* right.)

Directions:
Toss everything together and chill thoroughly before serving.

German Cole Slaw

Contributed by Beth Landry
Houston, Texas, USA

Ingredients:
1 large cabbage head shredded
1 small onion finely chopped
salt
1 C cooking oil

1 C sugar
1 C vinegar
1 t celery seed
1 T prepared mustard

Directions:
1. Mix cabbage and onion in large container (glass jar) and salt well.
2. Combine oil, sugar, vinegar, and celery seed, and bring to a boil.
3. Add mustard.
4. Pour immediately over cabbage and onion mix.

Prepare at least 24 hours before serving. Will keep in refrigerator for 1 month and remains crisp and delicious to the last cupful. It can be easily stored in a gallon glass container.

Photograph © Courtesy of Michael G. Bush

Middle Eastern Chick Pea Salad

Contributed by Madelyn Warkentin
Fullerton, California, USA

Ingredients:
¼ C fresh lemon juice
peel of 1 lemon, cut into strips
2 T olive oil
1 minced garlic clove
2 red peppers, cut into wide strips
3-½ C cooked brown rice
1 (15-oz.) can garbanzo beans, drained and
   rinsed

24 cherry tomatoes, halved
1 C pitted Kalamata olives
1 cucumber, peeled, deseeded, and diced
2 T chopped fresh parsley
¼ C finely diced red onion

Directions:
1. Preheat broiler. In a bowl, combine lemon juice, lemon peel, olive oil, and garlic. Set aside.
2. On a baking sheet, place red peppers and broil until skin bubbles and starts to turn black. Remove peppers from broiler and place in a covered bowl for 5 minutes. Remove outer skin, then dice peppers.
3. In a large bowl, combine rice, beans, tomatoes, olives, cucumber, parsley, onion, and peppers and toss with dressing. Depending on your preference, you can include the lemon peel in the salad or discard.

The British Tradition
of Tea

Photograph © Courtesy of Michael G. Bush

Photograph© Courtesy of Talia Jones Roston

Photograph© Courtesy of Talia Jones Roston

Tea

"There are few hours in life more agreeable than the hour dedicated to the ceremony known as afternoon tea."

~ *Henry James*

The tradition of afternoon tea is surprisingly not as old as most people would expect. Although tea drinking first became popular in England in the 1660s during the reign of King Charles II, it wasn't until the year 1840 when the tradition was actually launched by a hungry Duchess. Because the aristocracy generally had a late evening meal at around 8 o'clock, Anna Marie Stanhope, the 7th Duchess of Bedford and one of Queen Victoria's ladies-in-waiting, found herself suffering from a "sinking feeling" at about 4 o'clock in the afternoon. She initially asked her servants to bring her tea and a light snack privately in her boudoir, but she later began to invite friends to join her for a time of snacks and socializing. These gatherings proved to be so popular that other social hostesses began to pick up the practice, and afternoon tea quickly became respectable enough to move from private rooms into drawing rooms. Traditional afternoon tea generally consists of dainty sandwiches, scones, cakes, and pastries along with tea poured from teapots into china cups, but it can also be as simple as cookies and a mug of tea.

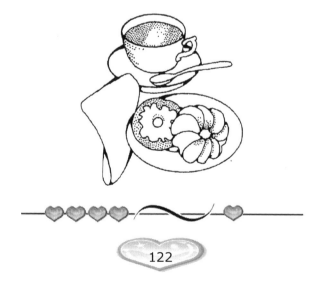

You Can Take the Boy Out of England
But You Can't Take England Out of the Boy

During his *Oliver!* days in the 60s, tea was a big part of David's life. Straight from England, of course, David did not like the taste of American teas. He enjoyed the robust and strong flavor of the English tea. There were two British grocers that he shopped at, one in Manhattan and one further downtown in Greenwich Village, and that's where he would buy his tea and his English biscuits and other foods from his country. I was already a tea drinker before I met David, because of my dad who was also English. I drank American teas, but, after meeting David and tasting his English tea, I fell in love with it. David made me a "cuppa" when he would have one, and of course, I drank it like he did with sugar and milk. However, he did make a modification to his cuppa by adding many of his favorite English biscuits, and he would wait until they soaked up all of his tea and then he would mash them and mix them until it looked like a strange type of oatmeal. Now David loved to share, and whenever he would make his concoction, he wanted to share it with me. I, however, was quite satisfied with my cup of English tea with milk and sugar, without the biscuits. I felt that if it tasted like it looked, I wanted no part of it. He would take his spoon with the "oatmeal" type of mixture on it and hold it to my mouth and tell me that all I needed was one taste and I would love it. I held out for quite a while, making a face and holding my hand to my mouth whenever he would offer a taste of the mixture, and he would eventually give up and laugh his head off. Then, one day, I finally gave in and closed my eyes tight and opened my mouth to the waiting spoon, and yes, to my surprise, it was quite good. So, after that, sometimes a "cuppa" with David was just a cup of English tea with milk and sugar, and other times, it was a concoction of biscuits, milk, sugar, and tea that looked like "mush" but tasted a lot like English heaven, especially when sharing it with such a terrific boy! And he would smile proudly to see his friend enjoying the "mush" mixture just like him. So if you are ever in a grocery store that offers ethnic foods and you find English biscuits, or if you are in New York City where there are still English grocers, grab a package of English Digestive biscuits and melt them into your tea and think of David!!! I still make the mixture and dream of days gone by!

~ Jody Proetta

Afternoon tea is, to my mind, one of our best traditions. We stop, we sit, we eat, we are civilized, and usually the pleasure of the occasion means everyone is filled with bonhomie. Here are the recipes for my scones and one of the cakes I love to bake.

~ Anita Pollinger-Jones

Carrot Cake

Contributed by Anita Pollinger-Jones, Jessica and Annabel's mother
Hampshire, UK

Ingredients:	Icing:
butter for greasing	4 oz. (110 gms.) of salted butter at room
7 oz. (200 gms.) plain flour	temperature
1/2 t salt	2 fl oz. (60 mls.) semi- skimmed milk at room
1 t bicarbonate of soda	temperature
1 1/2 t baking powder	1 t good quality vanilla essence
2 t cinnamon	1 t good quality orange essence
8 fl. oz. (225 ml.) vegetable or corn oil	1 lb. (500 gms.) icing sugar
8 oz. (225 gms.) of light or dark brown sugar	zest of one large orange
3 eggs	
10 oz. (275 gms.) shredded carrots	
zest and rind of one large orange (no pith as this will make it bitter)	

Directions:
1. Prepare an 8 inch cake tin (oil and line with grease proof paper).
2. Pre-heat oven to 170° C (fan 150° C, gas mark 3).
3. Sift together flour, salt, bicarbonate of soda, baking powder, and cinnamon. Whisk the oil and sugar together in a large bowl. Beat in the eggs one at a time until the mixture resembles mayonnaise. Fold in the flour and then the carrots and then the orange zest.
4. Pour mixture into the prepared tin and bake in the center of the oven for 1 ½ hours until well risen and firm. Insert a skewer into the middle which should come out clean. Remove the cake from the oven and let it sit for 10 minutes, then cool on a wire rack.
5. In a large mixing bowl, beat the butter, milk, vanilla, and orange extract and half the icing sugar until smooth. Gradually add the remainder of the sugar until smooth and creamy, then stir in the orange zest.
6. Smooth over your cake and enjoy!

Make a pot of tea and some delicate sandwiches if you are feeling really peckish.
Take some time out with your friends because everything stops for tea.

124

Jessica Cramer Jones, Anita Pollinger-Jones, and Annabel Jones at Grenville Hall

Photograph © Courtesy of *The News*, Portsmouth, UK

Scones

Contributed by Anita Pollinger-Jones, Jessica and Annabel's mother
Hampshire, UK

Ingredients:	
2 lbs. (900 gms.) self raising flour	4 oz. (100 gms.) caster sugar
8 t baking powder	4 eggs
6 oz. (175 gms.) softened butter	18 oz. (500 gms.) milk

Directions:
1. Pre-heat oven to 170° C (fan 150° C, gas mark 3).
2. Put flour, baking powder, and butter in a processor until a crumble-like texture, then add sugar and gently mix.
3. Beat eggs together and make up to a pint with the milk. Set aside 3 tablespoons egg/milk mix for glazing. Add the egg and milk. Mix until you have a soft dough. Much better that the dough is wetter than dry as this will make better scones.
4. Turn the dough onto a lightly floured surface and flatten to a thickness of ¾ to 1 inch. Use a 2 inch round cutter (I use a wine glass) to cut the dough into circles.
5. Arrange on the prepared baking tray and brush tops with set aside egg/milk mixture. Bake in pre-heated oven for 10-15 minutes until the scones are well risen and slightly golden.
6. Serve warm. Split in half and spread with strawberry jam and whipped cream. I also like to add finely chopped strawberries.

Enjoy!

These can be frozen, but give them 5 minutes in the oven to refresh and warm.
Scones are never so good left over to the next day, but if you store them in an
airtight container and reheat they are still pretty good!

125

Photograph © Courtesy of Rhino Entertainment Company

Vegan Blueberry Lemon Scones

Contributed by Amanda Grace Wilkins
Woodstock, Vermont, USA

Ingredients:
2½ C unbleached organic flour
⅓ C cane sugar
3 t baking powder
¼ t salt
½ C cold vegan margarine (one stick - Earth
    Balance is the best)

1 C organic blueberries
zest and juice from one organic lemon
½ C spring water

Directions:
1. Preheat oven to 425° F.
2. Put all dry ingredients in a separate bowl.
3. Add lemon juice to water and chill in fridge.
4. Cut vegan margarine into tiny chunks and work into dry mix, working into dough until tiny pieces are left in mix (be sure not to overwork dough, though).
5. Add blueberries to dry dough mix.
6. Add water/lemon juice mix to the dry dough, being sure again not to over mix. It should form into thicker, moist dough at this point, however sometimes mine still is a tad dry and I add a teaspoon or two more to make it doughier. Just be sure NOT to make the dough runny.
7. Form dough into ball and place in fridge for around 15-20 min.
8. Take out of fridge and place onto floured surface. Flatten ball of dough into a circle, being sure that the thickness is around 1-½ inches.
9. Cut into wedges, sprinkle with a little cane sugar, and place onto greased baking sheet.
10. Bake for 15 minutes at 425° F (convection or regular oven).

Now you're ready to enjoy!! Great with a cuppa (tea or coffee!)
Side note: it only really makes around 8 scones if they come
out big enough, so I ALWAYS double the recipe.

Beavertown Tea Party

While we may not remember what year the War of 1812 was, we will never forget May 17, 1993 when David Jones invited us to his house for tea. We asked what time we should be there and he replied, "Anytime. I'll be there all day." Despite the fact we had absolutely no idea whatsoever exactly where David lived (aside from Beavertown, Pennsylvania), we were somehow transported effortlessly to his house by the grace of God. Of course, being Americans, we lacked the knowledge of England's traditional afternoon tea-time by arriving at 10:00 o'clock in the morning. However unprepared (greeting us at the door in a bathrobe), David was still a courteous host and asked us if we would like our tea with milk and sugar. We said we would like ours plain. He looked at us as if we were from the moon and replied, *"You cawn't drink it like thaught."* We said, *"Okay, fine. Make it whatever way you want to make it."* We remember it tasted very good, and when Bonnie told him that, his facial expression conveyed the words "of course it does."

For months after that it was a joke between David's sister Hazel and us about the uncivilized American way of drinking tea and reminders of American tea parties. (We do remember the Boston Tea Party!)

A cup of tea has never tasted the same since.

~ Bonnie Borgh and Cindy Bryant

Grand Strawberries

Contributed by Suzanne Gee
Las Vegas, Nevada, USA

Ingredients:	
16 oz. fresh strawberries, hulled and cut in half	¼ C white sugar
1 lemon juiced and zested	⅛ t of salt
1 T Grand Marnier Liqueur	

Directions:
Place strawberries in a bowl. Pour lemon juice and liqueur over strawberries, then add sugar, salt, and lemon zest. Stir gently to combine. Cover and let sit at room temperature for at least 1 hour but not more than 3 hours.

Lovely with shortbread cookies and a hot cup of tea or coffee.

Serves 6

Peter's Perfect
Watercress Toasties

Contributed by Lucille Ryder
Westhampton Beach, New York, USA
(originally printed in a 60s teen magazine as a Peter Tork recipe)

Ingredients:
2 loaves bread	2 (8 oz.) pkgs. cream cheese
1 C milk	3 bunches watercress

Directions:
1. Combine the milk and the cream cheese until smooth and creamy.
2. Spread the bread with the cream cheese mix.
3. Top each with watercress and roll up from the top right corner to the bottom left corner and hold together with a toothpick.
4. Put in 350° F oven and heat for 5 minutes.

Scones for Two

Contributed by Jerri Keele
Salem, Oregon, USA

Ingredients:
½ C all purpose flour	1 T currants or coarse chopped raisins
½ t baking powder	1 T coarse chopped dried cranberries
1 T (or less) sugar	⅓ C whipping cream
½ t salt	

Directions:
1. Preheat oven to 400° F.
2. Mix dry ingredients.
3. Add cream and mix just until dough forms.
4. Turn onto floured board, flour your hands, and knead 4-6 strokes.
5. Flatten to 4 inch square about ¾ inch thick.
6. Cut into 4 triangles (corner to corner).
7. Bake about 12 minutes until golden brown.
8. Serve warm with jam or fruit, or cream.

Makes 4 scones

Quick Caribbean Bite

Contributed by Suzanne Gee
Las Vegas, Nevada, USA

Ingredients:	
guava shells (in syrup), guava paste, or guava jelly	low-fat or non-fat cream cheese saltines

Directions:
Spread a thick layer of cream cheese on saltines and cover with generous portion of guava.

Enjoy this super easy taste sensation with a cup of hot tea or coffee.

"Music mingles souls."

~ Davy Jones

Mike's Teacakes

Contributed by Lucille Ryder
Westhampton Beach, New York, USA
(originally printed in a 60s teen magazine as a Mike Nesmith recipe)

Ingredients:	
1 ⅔ C sifted cake flour	1 can fudge frosting
1 ½ t baking powder	1 C water
¼ t salt	2 eggs, well beaten
⅓ C shortening	⅔ C milk
I C sugar	1 t vanilla

Directions:
1. Sift flour, baking powder, and salt together.
2. Combine shortening with sugar until fluffy and then add eggs.
3. Add flour mixture alternately with milk and water in small amounts to shortening and sugar.
4. Add vanilla.
5. Fill greased muffin tins ⅔ full.
6. Bake in a 350° F oven for 15 to 18 min.
7. When cool, put frosting on top and decorate.

Makes 24 cakes

Potato Cakes/Scones

Contributed by Hazel Wilkinson, Davy's sister
Manchester, UK

Ingredients:	
1 dessert spoon (2 ½ t) hot milk	1½ oz. margarine/butter
8 oz. cooked potatoes	good pinch of salt
2 oz. plain flour	

Directions:
1. Mash potatoes with milk, salt, and margarine. Beat until smooth.
2. Add flour to make a stiff dough.
3. Roll out thinly.
4. Cut into rounds.
5. Bake for about 10 minutes or cook on a griddle.

Serve with butter while hot.

The Ceremony of Tea, English Style

1. Boil water.
2. Before kettle is completely boiled, pour some hot water into your teapot and swirl it around to warm the pot. Empty the pot.
3. Spoon loose tea into the warm pot - 1 teaspoon for each person who will drink the tea, and "one for the pot", to get the correct strength.
4. Stir, place lid on pot, cover with hand knitted tea cosy made by Granny in garish shades of leftover wool, and allow to "mash" (brew) for 5 minutes.
5. Enter into debate with nearest and dearest as to whether the milk goes in first or last, by which time said tea is stewed to "builders' tea" strength.
6. Pour, add milk and sugar to taste, sip, (with pinkie finger crooked) and utter "aaaaaaahh!"

~ Andrea Gilbey

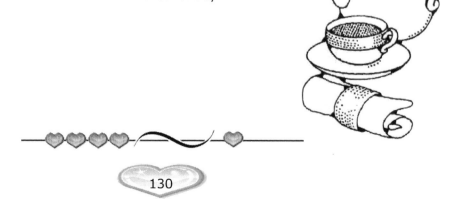

Main Dishes
and Casseroles

Photograph © Courtesy of Janice Ausbrooks Jennings

Tasty No Pastry Slimming Quiche

Contributed by Beverley Barber, Davy's Niece
Cheshire, UK

I'm a quick and easy cook, so my recipe is very simple.

Ingredients:	
400 g low fat cottage cheese	roasted veg of your choice
3 eggs	

Directions:
1. Whisk together.
2. Add anything you like. My favorite is roasted veg.
3. Pour into flan dish or tart pan.
4. Bake in the oven at 180° C for 40 minutes.

Davy and Beverley
beside a narrow boat
with a familiar name

Photograph © Courtesy of Beverley Barber

Wednesday Night Special

Contributed by Pam Patrick
Pleasanton, Kansas, USA

Ingredients:	
1 medium sized onion, roughly chopped	1 can cream of potato soup (or any other you like)
2 medium sized potatoes, sliced	
1 can chopped spinach, drained	3 T milled flax seed
1 can red beans, drained	cheese

Directions:
1. Sauté potatoes and onions until soft.
2. In a 9x13 inch glass baking dish, place beans, spinach, and soup.
3. Sprinkle flax seeds over the top.
4. Place onion and potatoes on top and sprinkle cheese on the very top.
5. Bake in 350° F oven for 25 minutes until heated thoroughly.

My Favorite Meal

Contributed by Caroline Boyce
Wife of singer/songwriter Tommy Boyce
Nashville, Tennessee, USA
http://www.officialboyceandhart.com/
http://carolineboyce.wordpress.com/

Salad

Ingredients:	
a mixture of arugula, frisée, radicchio, butterhead lettuce, and spinach	avocado
	crumbled feta cheese
chopped apple	thin sliced almonds that I've roasted in a toaster oven
chopped roasted pecans	
dried cranberries	choice of salad dressing (I love poppy seed)

Directions:
1. Toss lettuce and spinach with apple, pecans, cranberries, avocado, and feta cheese.
2. Top with thin sliced roasted almonds.
3. Use salad dressing of choice.

Roasted Veggies

Ingredients:	
sweet potatoes	coconut oil
asparagus tips	fresh ground pepper
baby carrots	parsley
green beans (sometimes)	turmeric
a variety of flavored olive oils, i.e. basil, dried tomato, garlic etc.	pear
	cinnamon

Directions:
1. Peel and slice sweet potatoes, asparagus tips, baby carrots, and sometimes green beans.
2. Mix a variety of flavored olive oils in a bowl and include a bit of coconut oil.
3. Add in fresh ground pepper, parsley, and turmeric.
4. Roll the veggies in the mixture. Vary the oil mixture with each veggie so they don't have the same taste.
5. Place each in its own uncovered casserole dish and bake at 350° F for around 1½ hours. (Asparagus usually cooks more quickly.)
6. Quarter slice a pear longwise, rub with cinnamon, and bake in separate dish with veggies until cooked through. (Great thinly sliced or diced on the side.)
7. You can also add pine nuts.

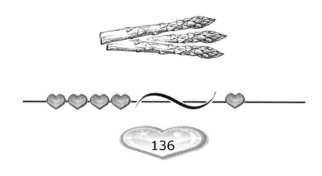

Baked Squash
(a family tradition)

Ingredients: any variety squash	1 T. brown sugar

Directions:
1. Slice squash in half and clean out seeds; do not peel.
2. Put 1 tablespoon of brown sugar in the cleaned out cavity.
3. Wrap in tin foil lightly twisting the gathered corners for easy opening.
4. Bake at 350 degrees until easily penetrated by fork.
5. Cool and then scoop out into bowl and stir.

I'm a lazy cook so I like to prepare enough to last me a few meals and just reheat various portions, except of course salad. I'm also blessed with a double oven stove so I can be broiling in the smaller oven and baking in the larger oven.

~ Caroline Boyce

Caroline

Caroline and Tommy

Photographs © Courtesy of Caroline Boyce

Zucchini Casserole

Contributed by Cindy Bryant
Muscatine, Iowa, USA

Davy appeared on TNN's Country Kitchen with Florence Henderson in March, 1991, and shared this delicious recipe. I received this recipe from Country Kitchen after Davy's appearance and some of the details were sketchy. There was no indication of how the zucchini was cut. I have sliced it and diced it. It really is your choice. It didn't say how the mushrooms were to be cut. Sliced works best. The original recipe said ½ cup of oil which I assumed was a typo, so use whatever you need to sauté the vegetables. This is a delicious meatless main course or side.

Ingredients:

2 T Wesson butter-flavored oil	14 oz. can tomatoes (chopped)
2 medium zucchini (chopped)	½ C grated Parmesan cheese
2 garlic cloves (chopped)	1 C sour cream
8 oz. fresh mushrooms (sliced)	1 T chopped or slivered almonds
1 C dark bread crumbs (can use whole wheat or	1 t paprika
pumpernickel bread crumbs)	

Directions:
1. Pre-heat oven to 350° F.
2. Sauté zucchini with garlic and set aside in a bowl.
3. Sauté mushrooms.
4. Add zucchini, garlic, and mushrooms together with bread crumbs, tomatoes, sour cream, almonds, and paprika.
5. Pour into glass baking dish.
6. Add Parmesan cheese on top.
7. Bake for 30 minutes at 350° F.
8. Serve on noodles.

"I do believe, not to get too far out here right now, that this opportunity that I've been given to be this celebrity that people know is only the first stage of my life because I'm going to be afforded the opportunity to help and care for people that I haven't even met yet. I just feel that something else is waiting for me there."

~ Davy Jones

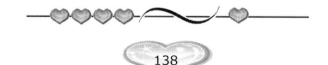

Vegan General Tso's "Chicken"

Contributed by Shelley Calissendorff
Pullman, Washington, USA

Ingredients:

8 oz. seitan chopped into one inch cubes	⅓ C sugar
¾ C cornstarch	2 t Chinese rice wine or dry sherry
3 T sesame, canola, or safflower oil	1 T sesame oil
⅓ C soy sauce (I use tamari)	1 T minced fresh ginger
3 T rice vinegar	2 T minced fresh garlic
3 T water	5 green onions (scallions), sliced
8 small, dried, red chili peppers, according to taste (I use red pepper flakes. 1/4 t = about 2 chili peppers. 8 makes this dish about 2.5 - 3 stars. Adjust according to your desired spiciness level preference.)	1 T cornstarch
	2 T water

Directions:

1. In a small bowl, whisk together soy sauce, rice vinegar, water, sugar, sesame oil, and Chinese rice wine or dry sherry. Set aside. Make sure to dissolve sugar (especially if you're using raw sugar or turbinado sugar).
2. Put cornstarch on a plate. Add seitan cubes, toss, roll, whatever it takes to coat them.
3. Add 3 tablespoons of oil to large frying pan and heat to medium-high. Add seitan cubes and brown until crispy. Remove from pan and drain on paper towels.
4. Add the remaining 1 tablespoon of oil to pan. Add red chili peppers, ginger, and garlic. Stir-fry on medium heat for about 2 minutes or until aromatic, being sure not to burn garlic. Pour in soy sauce mixture.
5. Quickly whisk 1 tablespoon of cornstarch and 2 tablespoon of water and add this to the pan, stirring to thicken sauce. As soon as the sauce thickens, remove from heat and add seitan cubes and sliced green onions.

Serve with rice and steamed broccoli.

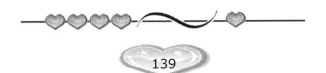

Shepherd-less Pie

Contributed by Cindy Bryant
Muscatine, Iowa, USA

Ingredients:

2 lbs. potatoes	1 green pepper, chopped
3 T sunflower oil or margarine	2 t vegetable yeast extract
2 T extra virgin olive oil	2 carrots, coarsely grated
4 oz. mushrooms, chopped	2 bay leaves
salt and ground black pepper to taste	2 garlic cloves
2 (14 oz.) cans adzuki beans, drained	1 t dried mixed herbs
1 large onion, chopped	dried breadcrumbs or chopped nuts to sprinkle
2 ½ C vegetable stock	

Directions:
1. Boil the potatoes in the skins until tender, then drain, reserving a little of the water to moisten them.
2. Peel the potatoes and mash them well, mincing in the olive oil and seasoning. (Potatoes are easier to peel when boiled in their skins. This also preserves vitamins.)
3. Gently fry the onion, pepper, carrots, and garlic in the sunflower oil or margarine for about 5 minutes until they are soft.
4. Stir in the mushrooms and beans and cook for a further 2 minutes, and then add the stock, yeast, bay leaves, and mixed herbs. Simmer for 15 minutes.
5. Remove the bay leaves and empty the vegetables into a shallow ovenproof dish. Spoon on potatoes in dollops and sprinkle with the crumbs or nuts. Broil until golden brown.

Serves 6 to 8

Bubble Pizza

Contributed by Bonnie Musser
Milroy, Pennsylvania, USA

Ingredients:

2 tubes buttermilk biscuits	2 C cheese (mozzarella, Parmesan, Romano, or provolone)
15 oz. sauce (pizza or homemade)	

Directions:
1. Press buttermilk biscuits into 13x9 inch pan.
2. Pour sauce over biscuits.
3. Add cheese and any other toppings you like (mushrooms, basil, onion, peppers, oregano, etc.).
4. Bake according to tube directions.

Lynda's Curry

Contributed by Lynda Moore, Davy's sister
Norfolk, UK

I cooked this for David every visit for 40 years.

Ingredients:
1 T sunflower oil	4 potatoes, chopped
1 onion, chopped	broccoli florets, chopped
1 T cumin seed	cauliflower florets, chopped
1 t coriander	1 t turmeric
2 cloves garlic, chopped	1 tin chopped tomatoes
various vegetables	2 T tomato puree
4 carrots, chopped	1 cup water or vegetable stock

Directions:
1. Pour sunflower oil into pan.
2. Add onion, stir until soft.
3. Add cumin seeds and garlic.
4. All all the vegetables gradually and stir.
5. Add turmeric to add color and stir.
6. Add the tin of chopped tomatoes and the tomato puree, and stir.
7. Add the cup of water or stock and simmer for 20-30 minutes.
8. Check vegetables until they are soft and cooked.
9. Leave the vegetables to marinate in the sauce and warm later. Serve.

Asian Stir-Fry

Contributed by Pam Patrick
Pleasanton, Kansas, USA

Ingredients:
1 T coconut or safflower oil	¼ C thin red bell pepper strips
1 ½ t toasted sesame oil	1 small head of bok choy, chopped into bite sized
2 cloves of garlic	chunks
1 T grated fresh ginger	1 T Bragg Liquid Aminos (or soy sauce)
1 carrot, cut in thin diagonal slices	
½ C broccoli florets	

Directions:
1. In large wok, heat oils on high. Add garlic, ginger, and carrot. Cook, stirring well, for 1 minute.
2. Add broccoli, stir, and cook 5 minutes.
3. Add remaining veggies. Reduce heat to medium and cook until done.
4. Turn off heat. Add Bragg Liquid Aminos. Stir well.

Serves 4 to 6

She Can't Find Her Quiche

Contributed by Paul Petersen
Star of The Donna Reed Show
http://www.minorcon.org/

Ingredients:
1 unbaked pastry shell	1 C milk
1 medium onion, sliced thin	1 T salt + generous dash of nutmeg (ground, of
1 heaping T of all-purpose flour	course)
4 eggs, beaten	1 ½ C shredded Swiss cheese
1 C light cream	

Directions:
1. Set oven to 450° F.
2. Line your pastry shell with foil and dried beans (to prevent swelling and shrinkage) and bake for 5 minutes.
3. Remove from the oven and carefully remove foil and beans, then return pastry shell to the oven for another 5 minutes.
4. While pastry shell bakes, get your onions tenderized in a skillet (butter or coconut oil), then mix all your ingredients in a large bowl.
5. Reduce heat to 325° F.
6. Pour mixture into the warm pastry shell. Cover crust edges to prevent over-browning.
7. Bake for 45—50 minutes until your filling sets. (Test for that in the center of the quiche.)
8. Let stand for 10 minutes, then slice and serve.

Photograph © Courtesy of Paul Petersen

Optional: For extra flavor, cook tempeh-bacon (crumble when crisp) with your onion slices and add a bit more salt to your mixture.

Serves 4 hearty eaters

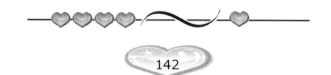

Eggplant Panini with Pesto

Contributed by Dawn Hoffman
Marengo, Illinois, USA

Ingredients:
1 large eggplant, about 12-14 oz
kosher salt to taste
olive oil spray
12 oz. French bread (or baguette), cut into 4
    pieces

4 slices part skim mozzarella cheese
2 T skinny pesto
8 thin slices of tomato

Directions:
1. Slice the eggplant into ¼ inch thick slices. Place the eggplant slices on a paper towel and season with salt. Set aside about 30 minutes. This will help draw some of the moisture out of the eggplant. Pat the eggplant dry with paper towels.
2. Preheat panini grill. Lightly spritz eggplant with olive oil. Season with salt and pepper. When the grill is hot, grill eggplant about 7-8 minutes, turning once half way through. Set aside.
3. Slice the bread open and place 3 slices of grilled eggplant, 1 slice of mozzarella, ½ tablespoon of pesto, and 2 slices of tomatoes on each sandwich.
4. Close and lightly spray the top of the bread with oil. Place on a panini press and close until the cheese melts and the bread is toasted.
5. Cut in half diagonally and eat immediately.

Mozzarella Salad Sandwich

Contributed by Ellen Donati
Burlingame, California, USA

Ingredients:
½ lb. mozzarella cheese
sun-dried tomatoes (desired amount)
green onions (desired amount)
4 t white vinegar

¼ t pepper
⅛ t salt
¼ C olive oil
4 crusty rolls

Directions:
1. Cut cheese into very thin slices and put in a bowl.
2. Cut sun-dried tomatoes into slivers and add to cheese.
3. Shake vinegar, salt, and pepper in a small jar until salt dissolves.
4. Add olive oil and shake again.
5. Add this dressing to the cheese and toss.
6. Fill rolls with the cheese salad.

Zucchini And Goat-Cheese Tart

Contributed by Pamela Richardson
Chicago, Illinois, USA

Ingredients:

Crust:
5 oz. (100g) flour
1 pinch of salt (I use sea salt—makes a slight but lovely difference)
4 oz. (125 g) chilled butter

Filling:
3 eggs
1 lb. (500 g) fresh goat cheese
1 T Herbs de Provence (more or less to taste)
1 t fresh grated nutmeg (fresh is awesome)
salt and pepper to taste
2 T olive oil
1 onion, chopped
2 zucchini, sliced thick
2 T fresh basil, chopped
½ C Gruyere cheese

Directions:

To prepare crust:
1. Put flour and salt into a bowl and cut in the butter (I usually use my fingers; could also use 2 knives or a fork.) Blend well.
2. Add a little water and blend quickly into a ball.
3. Place on lightly floured surface and knead with the heel of your hand, pushing dough away from you. (Don't overly knead the dough because the warmth of your hands will heat the butter and make the dough too chewy.)
4. Form dough into a ball, sprinkle with a little flour, and refrigerate for 2-3 hours or overnight.
5. Remove from refrigerator and roll out on a flat surface.
6. Preheat oven to 400°F (205°C).
7. Place dough into buttered tart dish, prick the bottom with a fork, place a sheet of buttered wax paper on top, and weigh dough down with pie weights (TIP: You can use dried beans for this purpose, but that's wasteful because the beans are then unsuitable for eating. Rice is a better substitute, if you don't have pie weights, because it can still be used after for other recipes.)
8. Bake the crust for 8-10 minutes.

To prepare filling:
1. Mix the eggs, goat cheese, Herbs de Provence, nutmeg, salt, and pepper.
2. In a pan, sauté the onion in oil till translucent, about 2 minutes.
3. Add zucchini, basil, salt, and pepper. Cook for 8 minutes, until tender.
4. Remove from heat, discard liquid, set aside.
5. Lower oven heat to 350°F (180°C).
6. Place half the egg mixture in the crust, top with zucchini and onion, and cover with the remaining egg mixture.
7. Sprinkle with Gruyere, place in the oven and bake for 30-35 minutes.

Vegetarian Nasi Goreng

Contributed by Andrea Gilbey
Cheshunt, Hertfordshire, UK

I work in handfuls for the main ingredients as this is a very "loose" recipe that can be adjusted to taste. You can of course use fresh vegetables, but for a quick meal frozen works fine and is just as nutritious.

Ingredients for 2 people:
a handful of long grain rice
2 oz. cashew nuts
a handful of frozen mixed vegetables (peas, carrots, sweet corn, broccoli, cauliflower)
4 mushrooms, sliced
1 vegetable stock cube
1 T sunflower oil

1 level t cumin
1 level t turmeric
½ level t ground coriander
1 clove garlic, crushed
chili paste to taste
black pepper
boiling water

Directions:
1. Heat the oil gently in a flat based pan. Add the spices, garlic, chili, vegetables, and nuts, and toss them gently in the oil to flavour them. Do not add salt! The stock cube is salty enough.
2. Add the rice and stock cube and top up with enough boiling water to cover all the ingredients.
3. Bring to the boil, then reduce the heat and simmer until all the water is absorbed and the rice is cooked.

Garlic-Toasted Tomato
Sandwiches

Contributed by Darlene Brushwood
Lexington. North Carolina, USA

Ingredients:
3 oz. fresh feta cheese, crumbled
¼ C mayonnaise
2 T minced chives
flaky sea salt
freshly ground pepper

6 slices of garlic-rubbed grilled country bread
2 pounds mixed heirloom tomatoes and cherry tomatoes cut into different sizes
extra-virgin olive oil for drizzling on tomatoes
radish sprouts for garnish

Directions:
1. In a medium bowl, mash the feta with the mayonnaise and chives and season with salt and pepper.
2. Spread the mayonnaise on the toasts and top with the tomatoes.
3. Drizzle with olive oil and season with sea salt.
4. Top with radish sprouts and serve right away.

Total time: 30 minutes   Servings: 6

Stuffed Zucchini

Contributed by Jody Proetta
Putnam Valley, New York, USA

This is a vegan recipe that I use as a main dish or a side dish. It can be either.
It will make 3 main dish servings or 6 side dish servings.

Ingredients:
3 large zucchini	salt and pepper to taste
2 T of vegan grated cheese	1 ½ C of cooked brown rice
2 T of extra–virgin olive oil	1 C vegetarian refried black or pinto beans
¾ C of chopped onion	¾ C mild salsa
1 small red pepper, chopped	fresh basil leaves chopped fine, to taste
1 small green pepper, chopped	vegan sour cream
2 cloves of elephant garlic, finely chopped	shredded vegan Cheddar cheese

Directions:
1. Pre-heat oven to 350° F.
2. Lightly oil a shallow baking dish and place it to the side.
3. Halve zucchini lengthwise . Scoop out the flesh of the zucchini and chop it into small pieces. Place in a small bowl.
4. Rub your zucchini shells with some olive oil, salt, and pepper. Place them in the preheated oven for 15 minutes at 350° F.
5. In a large frying pan, place a tablespoon of the olive oil, the chopped zucchini, chopped red pepper, chopped green pepper, chopped onion, and garlic. Add salt and pepper to taste. Sauté vegetables until soft.
6. Add rice, refried beans, and 2 tablespoon of vegan grated cheese, salsa, and basil leaves.
7. Take zucchini shells out of the oven and spoon the vegetable/refried beans mixture into the shells.
8. Place back in the oven for 30 minutes until zucchini shells are fork tender.
9. Top with shredded vegan shredded Cheddar and place back in the oven until cheese is melted.
10. Remove from the oven and add a scoop of vegan sour cream to taste on top of shells. Enjoy!

If this is used as a main dish I will serve this with a romaine lettuce salad with tomato and onion and some chopped apple with green and black olives and a good homemade dressing.

"I make it as tough as I can
for the next act coming on.
They'd better be good if they're following me."

~ Davy Jones

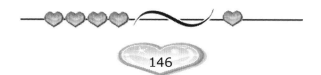

Vegetarian Bean Wraps

Contributed by Jennie Gomes
Vancouver, British Columbia, Canada

Ingredients:
1 can cooked black beans, drained/washed	vegetables of your choice
¼ C Greek yogurt	1 clove garlic, minced
½ C cooked and drained spinach	¼ C grated sharp Cheddar cheese
1 package Lipton's dry onion soup mix	1-2 whole wheat tortillas
¼ C salsa	

Directions:
1. Sauté minced garlic in skillet on low heat with ½ t butter or oil. Add cooked spinach and combine so that the spinach is mixed with garlic. Set aside.
2. In a saucepan, cook black beans and ½ package of dry onion soup mix on low heat until dry onions are soft. Turn off heat and set aside. (The longer you let the beans sit, the tastier they will be!)
3. Build your tortilla by first adding the cooked black beans, then top with spinach/garlic mixture. Add the salsa, vegetables, and a dollop of Greek yogurt. Sprinkle the top with grated cheese and roll.

Potatoholic's Cheating One Pot Dinner

Contributed by Andrea Gilbey
Cheshunt, Hertfordshire, UK

Ingredients:
1 small potato	1 can of leek and potato soup
½ of a parsnip	bread crumbs
½ of a sweet potato	Parmesan cheese (or any preferred hard cheese,
a handful of broccoli florets	grated)
a handful of cauliflower florets	

Directions:
1. Slice the potato, sweet potato, and parsnip thinly, and lightly cook until tender but not soft.
2. Break the cauliflower and broccoli into small pieces and cook as above.
3. Layer half the sliced root veggies in the bottom of an ovenproof dish, add the cauliflower and broccoli, and pour ¾ of the soup in.
4. Layer the rest of the root veggies on top, pour over remaining soup, and sprinkle the top with bread crumbs and grated cheese.
5. Bake in the oven at 180°C/250°C/gas mark 4 for 35 minutes until top is crispy.

This recipe is adaptable to whatever veggies you have. Try mushrooms and tomatoes instead of cauliflower and broccoli, and use a tomato based vegetable soup.

Spicy Curried Couscous with Veggies

Contributed by Suzanne Gee
Las Vegas, Nevada, USA

Ingredients:

½ C raisins (plumped in 2 C water)
½ C almond pieces, lightly toasted
1 ¾ C water or vegetable stock (If you use Israeli couscous, increase to 2 C)
1 C uncooked couscous
1 ½ C small broccoli and cauliflower florets (steamed with 2 T water)
2 T olive oil
½ C finely chopped scallions or shallots
1 t fresh ginger minced
1 medium clove of garlic minced
2 T white wine vinegar

⅓ C shredded carrot
½ t coriander
½ t cumin
½ t turmeric
¼ t crushed red pepper
¾ t salt
1 T honey
1 (15-oz.) can garbanzo beans (chickpeas), drained and rinsed
1 lime juiced
1 C crumbled feta cheese
½ C cilantro chopped

Directions:

1. Add raisins to 2 cups boiled water and set aside to plump.
2. Preheat oven or toaster oven to 250° F. Spread almond pieces in a thin layer on an ungreased, unlined cookie sheet. Toast in oven, removing to shake and toss every minute or so. The almonds are done when you start to smell them. The time will vary, so watch very carefully and never leave oven. Nuts burn quickly! Should take about 5 minutes. Remove from oven and set aside.
3. Bring water or stock to a boil. Gradually stir in couscous. Remove from heat; cover and let stand 5 minutes, then fluff with a fork.
4. In a microwave safe cooking dish (with a lid), add broccoli, cauliflower and 2 tablespoons of water. Cover and cook in microwave for 2-3 minutes depending on how tender you like your veggies. set aside.
5. Set sauté pan (large enough to hold all ingredients) on medium heat and add olive oil. After a minute, add scallions or shallots and stir until lightly brown.
6. Add garlic and ginger and stir constantly until you smell the garlic (about a minute). Don't let garlic burn!
7. Add vinegar, then carrots, coriander, cumin, turmeric, crushed red pepper, salt, lime juice, honey, and garbanzo beans. Stir well and leave on heat until everything is heated through.
8. Add broccoli and cauliflower, couscous and raisins (drained and patted dry on paper towel). Stir well to incorporate all ingredients.
9. Fold in feta cheese then taste and add more salt if needed.

When serving, add almonds and cilantro.
Great with some toasted naan bread and a gin and tonic or lemonade.
Serves 4

Cheese and Onion Quiche

Contributed by Bobbi Boyce
Nashville, Tennessee/London, UK

I never knew David to eat pastry much.
He wasn't a quiche person, but he did love this one.

Ingredients:	
pastry crust, homemade or frozen	2 large free range eggs
large onion	½ C milk
Cheddar cheese	your choice of herbs

Directions:

1. Grease a quiche dish lightly. Either make enough short crust pastry to cover it or use frozen. Line the dish with short crust pastry.
2. Slice and dice a large onion. Sauté the onion in a little oil until transparent and cover the pastry with it.
3. Grate mature Cheddar cheese until it covers the onion thickly.
4. Beat two large free range eggs with a half cup of milk.
5. Pour the mixture over the cheese.
6. Sprinkle some mixed herbs over the cheese.
7. Bake in oven on gas mark 4/180° C (350° F) for about 25 minutes or until the mixture is set.

You can eat it hot or cold, but David liked it cold.

Photograph © Courtesy of Bobbi Boyce

Mushroom Paprika

Contributed by Jackie Price
Cabo San Lucas, Mexico

Here is one of my favorite recipes from when I lived in Hungary.
I absolutely love anything with mushrooms and this dish hits the spot for me. Enjoy!

Ingredients:
2 lbs. fresh mushrooms, quartered or sliced	1 green pepper, diced
2 T oil	1 (15 oz.) can chopped tomatoes
1 onion, finely chopped	8 oz. (1 C) sour cream
3-4 cloves garlic, minced	salt to taste
1-2 T paprika, depending on taste	pepper to taste

Directions:
1. Fry the finely chopped onion in the oil until soft and transparent.
2. Remove from the stove and sprinkle with the paprika and stir to coat.
3. Add the mushrooms and garlic; salt and pepper to taste.
4. Add the diced green pepper and the can of chopped tomatoes (juice and all). Return to heat.
5. Stew covered over medium heat in its juices for about 20-30 minutes. At the end of this time, remove the lid and continue cooking until most of the juices evaporate.
6. Add sour cream toward the end of cooking time. (More or less sour cream may be added depending on your tastes.)
7. Serve over noodles or rice.

Serves 4 to 6

Low-Fat Eggplant Casserole

Contributed by Janice Jennings
Huntsville, Alabama, USA

Ingredients:
1 T olive oil	2 large tomatoes, diced
1 eggplant, cubed	1 ½ t all-purpose seasoning or Italian seasoning
1 C whole mushrooms	1 t salt
½ C tomato juice	1 onion, diced

Directions:
1. Preheat oven to 350°F and prepare vegetables.
2. In medium bowl, combine olive oil, eggplant, mushrooms and seasoning.
3. Spread into 9x13 inch casserole dish and bake for 30 minutes.
4. Mix onion, tomatoes, tomato juice, and salt. Pour over baked eggplant mixture.
5. Return to oven for additional 30 minutes.
6. Cool a little before serving. Enjoy!!!

Artful Dodger's (David Jones) Grilled Cheese Sandwich

Contributed by Jody Proetta
Putnam Valley, New York, USA

Back in the 60s, during his Broadway days, David prided himself on his grilled cheese sandwiches which I was honored to have shared with him. He would take a big gob of real butter and put it into a frying pan, and then take some white bread and put cheese on it, and then a layer of baked beans, and then sliced tomato, and then some ketchup. He'd then close the sandwich and butter the outside of the bread, and then he'd place it into the frying pan with a small plate on top to cover it. I must say, it was pretty good once it was finished. After he left Broadway and went on to bigger things, I still made and ate his sandwiches. Now that I am a lot older and a vegan, I confess I still eat his grilled cheese, but a bit of a healthier version and a totally vegan version. One of my favorites -- oh, memories of days gone by, with my recipe as follows:

Ingredients:
1 whole grain brown rice cake
2 slices of vegan Cheddar cheese
2 thin slices of large red tomato
1 can of fat-free refried beans (fat free refried black beans from the health food store if you have access)

4 green pimento stuffed olives, sliced
a few slices of chopped onions, optional
salsa (takes the place of ketchup)

Directions:
1. Place your rice cake on a microwave safe plate.
2. Open your can of fat free refried beans and spread a good amount on your rice cake.
3. Next, put your two slices of vegan cheese on the rice cake.
4. Then spread out your green olives on the cheese slices .
5. Next sprinkle your onions if you want to use them.
6. Lastly top with your tomato slices.
7. Place your David concoction into the microwave oven and cook on 50% for 1 minute. Three-quarters of the way through stop your oven to take a peek to make sure it is not overcooking. If the cheese is not totally melted, continue until the cheese is totally melted.
9. When done, scoop some salsa onto your plate and put some on your rice cake with every bite. The salsa takes the place of David's ketchup.

This tastes really good and is a healthy version of David's delicious grilled cheese from the 60s. Enjoy and think of days gone by. I like to listen to the songs from Oliver! and drink tea when I eat this treat.

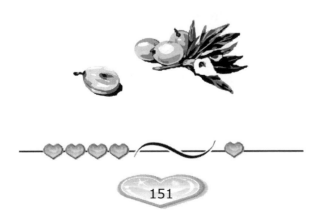

Polenta Pizza

Contributed by Debbie Sanderson
Berkshire, UK

Ingredients:
750 ml. strong veg stock
175 g. instant polenta (dry)
40 g. freshly grated Parmesan cheese
75 g. tomato puree
1 ½ T extra virgin olive oil
1 ½ t dried oregano

125 g. ball buffalo mozzarella, torn roughly into pieces
200 g. of veg antipasti (e.g., roast peppers, sun blush tomatoes)
large handful rocket leaves to garnish

Directions:
1. Preheat oven to 220° C, gas mark 7.
2. Line a large sheet pan with parchment. Put stock into a large pan. Bring to a boil and stir in polenta. Stir continuously for 5 minutes until mixture thickens.
3. Stir in the Parmesan; season well.
4. Tip onto prepared sheet pan and shape to make a 12 inch diameter circle. Leave this to cool while you get on with the toppings.
5. In a small bowl, put tomato puree, oil, and oregano and stir together with a tablespoon of water to make a smooth sauce. Spread this evenly over the polenta base, leaving a border of approximately ¾ inch.
6. Scatter over the mozzarella and your chosen antipasti.
7. Cook in oven for 15 minutes or until cheese is brown and bubbling.
8. Scatter over the rocket leaves. Cut into wedges and serve.

Photograph © Courtesy of Michael G. Bush

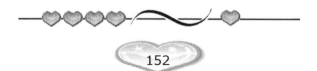

Minton's Veggie Casserole

Contributed by Marian Allen
Corydon, Indiana, USA

Ingredients:
¼ C melted butter or margarine
½ to 1 C crushed Ritz crackers
2 cans mixed vegetables, drained
1 can sliced water chestnuts (or raw celery if you don't like water chestnuts)
1 C mayonnaise (NOT SALAD DRESSING OR MIRACLE WHIP!!!)

1 to 2 T Worcestershire sauce (not necessarily vegan, so beware)
½ C shredded cheese (I like more, and I use sharp Cheddar)
whole Ritz crackers

Directions:
1. Grease casserole dish. Mix butter and crushed crackers and press into bottom of dish and partly up sides.
2. Mix veggies, water chestnuts, mayo, and Worcestershire sauce. Add other seasonings to taste, such as salt, pepper, minced onion. Layer mixture, cheese, and whole Ritz crackers.
3. Cover and bake at 350° F for 30 minutes, then uncover and bake for another 5 to 10 minutes until top is brown and bubbly.

Even better left over!

Pumpkin Soufflé

Contributed by Nicole Jesson
Brooklyn, New York, USA

Ingredients:
12 oz. cooked pumpkin
¼ C butter, melted
½ C flour
½ C sugar

2 C milk
3 large eggs
dash each - salt, cinnamon, nutmeg, ginger

Directions:
1. Separate eggs. Let eggs and pumpkin stand at room temperature for 30 minutes.
2. Grease a 1½ qt. soufflé dish and lightly sprinkle with flour; set aside.
3. In a large bowl, combine the egg yolks, milk, pumpkin, butter, sugar, and spices.
4. In a large bowl with clean beaters, beat egg whites until stiff peaks form.
5. With a spatula, stir a fourth of the egg whites into squash mixture until no white streaks remain.
6. Fold in remaining egg whites until combined.
7. Transfer to prepared dish.
8. Bake at 350° F for 55-60 minutes or until the top is puffed and center appears set. Serve immediately.

Yellow Squash Taco Sauté

Contributed by Jody Proetta
Putnam Valley, New York, USA

Ingredients:

olive oil for frying pan (I usually use about 2 T. You can use a little more if needed.)

2 large cloves of elephant garlic, minced (5 cloves of regular garlic if you can't find elephant garlic)

7 yellow squash, cubed (This makes about 5 C)

1 package of shredded mozzarella flavor vegan cheese (will use probably half of this package depending on how cheesy you want your taco)

1 large red onion chopped

1 jar of salsa, mild (or medium if you like it spicy)

½ C of water

1 lemon

sprinkle of sea salt and pepper for taste

crispy taco shells

Directions:

1. Sauté your onion and garlic until the onion and garlic are translucent and soft.
2. Add your water and squash and steam/sauté until the squash is nice and tender, turning with a wooden spoon when needed. You can cook until soft if you prefer. The water should be partially evaporated from the heat so it is not watery. Do not cook on high temperature, just hot enough to be able to sauté/steam with good control.
3. When done, add your lemon juice to taste and salt and pepper.
4. Warm crispy taco shells in the oven.
5. Take a crispy taco shell, and using a slotted spoon to scoop up some of your squash mixture, scoop onto a crispy taco shell and add some shredded mozzarella vegan cheese.
6. Place in microwave for a few seconds to melt the cheese and place some salsa on top.

Enjoy!!!!

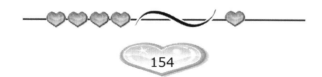

Classic Mock Meat Loaf

Contributed by Marian Allen
Corydon, Indiana, USA

Ingredients:

9 slices (8 oz.) whole wheat bread
2 C walnuts
3 large eggs
3 medium onions, diced
1 small green bell pepper, diced
1 small celery rib, minced
1 small bunch parsley, chopped

⅔ C canned crushed tomatoes or 16 oz. can diced tomatoes WELL-DRAINED
1 ½ T oil
1 t poultry seasoning
1 t salt
pepper

Directions:
1. Toast the bread slices either in the toaster or on a baking sheet placed under the broiler. Let cool.
2. Preheat the oven to 375° F. Generously butter a 9x5 inch loaf pan, then line the bottom with wax paper and butter the paper.
3. Tear up the toasted bread slices and make crumbs out of them in a food processor. Set aside.
4. Process the walnuts until finely ground and mix into the bread crumbs. Combine the eggs and onions in the processor and process until fine but not liquefied. Stir into the bread crumbs. Place the green pepper, celery, parsley, tomatoes, and oil in the processor and grind until fine but still with some texture. Stir into the loaf mixture along with the poultry seasoning, salt, and pepper. Mix this all very well until evenly moistened. (The mixture may be prepared to this point and refrigerated up to 8 hours in advance.) Scrape it into the prepared loaf pan and smooth over the top. Cover the loaf with foil.
5. Bake 1 hour and 20 minutes or until a knife inserted in the center of the loaf comes out dry. Let sit 5 minutes, then run a knife all along the sides of the loaf to help loosen it. Unmold the loaf onto a platter and remove the wax paper. Let the loaf cool 20 minutes or so before slicing it. It's best to serve the loaf warm and the gravy hot. Serve with mushroom gravy (recipe below).

Mushroom Gravy
(to go with Mock Meatloaf)

Contributed by Marian Allen
Corydon, Indiana, USA

Ingredients:

4 T butter
2 C (8 oz.) thinly sliced mushrooms
¼ C flour
2 ½ C vegetable stock or bouillon

¼ C dry red wine
2 T soy sauce
pepper to taste

Directions:
Sauté mushrooms in butter, stir in flour, and cook. Stir in liquid and heat until thick.

Carrot, Tofu, and Pineapple
Stir Fry

Contributed by Marian Allen
Corydon, Indiana, USA

Ingredients:

2 T olive oil
1 clove garlic, minced (or a bunch of garlic
    powder, if you're like me)
2 medium carrots, sliced
concentrated vegetable broth
the larger regular-sized can of pineapple chunks
    (with juice)

1 package extra-firm tofu
2 T soy sauce
2 t sesame oil
1 t ground ginger
½ t crushed red pepper (or ground)

Directions:

1. First off, don't throw out the pineapple juice!
2. Press the tofu. In case you haven't ever done that, all you have to do is put it on some paper towels on a flat surface and put something kinda heavy on it, like a big cookbook, for about ten or fifteen minutes.
3. Heat oil in skillet over med-high heat.
4. Add garlic and carrots. Stir-fry for 4 to 5 minutes. Add a few tablespoons vegetable broth, all the pineapple juice, and the tofu, and sauté for 5 to 10 minutes (ten is probably best).
5. Add soy sauce, sesame oil, ginger, red pepper, the pineapple, and a few more tablespoons of vegetable broth. Heat 3 to 5 minutes. (Personally, I like to add the pineapple five minutes after I put in the tofu, but it depends on how soft you want the pineapple to be.)
6. You can serve it over either rice or noodles. We found some plain ramen noodles, and it was really good with those, but I think authentic Asian noodles would be much, much better. If it looks like it needs to be saucier at any point, you can just add more vegetable broth and some more soy sauce.

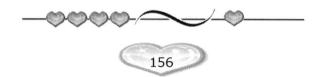

**Davy and
Valerie Kairys Venet
on *The Monkees***

Photograph © Courtesy of
Rhino Entertainment Company

Comfort Food

I remember that when I was very young and working (or not working) as a struggling actress, my roommate and I would have hot Shredded Wheat for dinner. This was a wonderful comfort food when we were broke, which was most of the time. Hot Shredded Wheat—one or two Nabisco large Shredded Wheat biscuits (depending on how hungry you are). Butter. Salt and pepper. Place Shredded Wheat biscuits in a bowl and place a pat of butter on top of each biscuit. Pour hot milk on the butter and biscuit. Salt and pepper as desired. If it's a hot day then just create your own recipe for "lemonade."

With Love,
Valerie Kairys Venet

Photograph © Courtesy of Valerie Kairys Venet

"Glorious" Mushroom Bourguignon

Contributed by Karen Steele
Marstons Mills, Massachusetts, USA
www.gloriastavers.com

Ingredients:

2 T olive oil	2 C vegetable broth
2 T butter, softened	2 T tomato paste
2 pounds portabella (or crimini) mushrooms in ¼-inch slices (save the stems for another use)	1 t fresh thyme leaves (or ½ t dried)
	1 ½ T all-purpose flour
	1 C pearl onions, peeled (thawed if frozen)
½ carrot, finely diced	egg noodles, for serving
1 small yellow onion, finely diced	sour cream and chopped chives or parsley for garnish (optional)
2 cloves garlic, minced	
1 C full-bodied red wine	

Directions:

1. Heat the 1 tablespoon of the olive oil and 1 tablespoon of butter in a medium Dutch oven or heavy sauce pan over high heat. Sear the mushrooms until they begin to darken but not yet release any liquid — about three or four minutes. Remove them from pan.
2. Lower the flame to medium and add the 2ⁿᵈ tablespoon of olive oil. Toss the carrots, onions, thyme, a few good pinches of salt, and several grinds of black pepper into the pan and cook for 10 minutes, stirring occasionally, until the onions are lightly browned. Add the garlic and cook for just one more minute.
3. Add the wine to the pot, scraping any stuck bits off the bottom, then turn the heat all the way up and reduce it by half. Stir in the tomato paste and the broth. Add back the mushrooms with any juices that have collected, and once the liquid has boiled, reduce the temperature so it simmers for 20 minutes or until mushrooms are very tender. Add the pearl onions and simmer for five minutes more.
4. Combine remaining butter and the flour with a fork until combined; stir it into the stew. Lower the heat and simmer for 10 more minutes. If the sauce is too thin, boil it down to reduce to the right consistency. Season to taste.
5. To serve, spoon the stew over a bowl of egg noodles, dollop with sour cream (optional) and sprinkle with chives or parsley.

Serves 4

"My family is a part of my life and everything is all a mixture of enjoyment."

~ Davy Jones

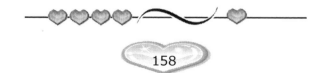

Fantastic Spaghetti Squash
with Tomato Sauce

Contributed by Susan Ritter
Philadelphia, Pennsylvania, USA

When my younger brother Kenneth was in his teens, he and his buddy Mark sent away for spaghetti squash seeds advertised in the back of a comic book by The Fantastic Seed Company. (Yes, they also ordered Amazing Sea Monkeys, but that's another story.) We'd mistakenly thought the actual plants were called "fantastics" especially as they rapidly grew to overtake the entire back garden, so we came to call the squash "fantastic."

Ingredients:
1 average-sized spaghetti squash
1 large onion (we preferred Vidalia)
1 clove garlic, crushed
olive oil
1 small can tomato paste

1 small can stewed plum tomatoes
½ chopped green bell pepper
salt and pepper to taste
shredded provolone cheese

Directions:
1. Pierce rind of spaghetti squash (i.e., "fantastic") in several places with fork. Set squash on foil-lined baking sheet in 350° F degree oven for 45 minutes.
2. Turn squash over, and continue to bake for an additional 25 minutes or until rind smooshes in when pressed.
3. While squash is baking, prepare tomato sauce.
4. Cover bottom of heated skillet with about 1 tablespoon of olive oil; add chopped onion, pepper, and crushed garlic. Stir for about 2 minutes, then drain on plate lined with paper towel.
5. In a medium saucepan, combine tomato paste and pear tomatoes. Simmer and stir while adding the onion, pepper, and garlic mixture. Continue to stir while adding oregano, basil leaf, salt, and pepper to taste. Simmer, covered, stirring occasionally, while squash is baking.
6. Remove baked squash from oven and discard seeds. Pull "spaghetti" strands free from rind with a fork, placing them in a casserole dish. Ladle desired amount of sauce over spaghetti squash and toss lightly with fork. Sprinkle with grated provolone cheese, and place casserole in oven (350 °F) until cheese melts (about 3 minutes).

Serves 4 to 6

Lunch in New Jersey

In 1976, my best friend and I spent the day with David and Tommy Boyce. They were awesome tennis players. They treated us to lunch at a New Jersey diner. David ordered two glasses of milk, sides of vegetables, and rice pudding. We drove around the area and visited a farmers' market. David bought Jersey tomatoes, apples, oranges, cherry apple cider, and a cucumber.

I had the pleasure and honor of cooking for David in 1977. He loved the fruit salad which had grapes, cantaloupe, apple, orange, grapefruit, watermelon, and banana. I also added a small can of fruit salad to sweeten it up. David asked me to pack up the leftovers for him.

David was performing at The Riverboat, a club in the Empire State Building, with Micky and Coco for a week in 1977. I invited David to New Jersey for lunch during the week. He accepted and asked for the train schedule.

The day arrived but David did not. I stood on the platform paralyzed. He stood me up! I waited for the next train. No David. I returned home and my parents were gone. They had received a call from David explaining that he missed the train, ran from NY PENN to NY Port Authority, and took a bus to my town. My parents picked him up, then they drove to the train station. David hopped out looking for me before they returned to the house where we all met up. How did we survive without mobile phones!

Anyway, we had a great afternoon! He loved looking at the photos I had of him, Talia, and Sarah in my room. David explained he overslept because he was up most of the night with Harry Nilsson! When I drove him into NYC for his evening show, he had his head on my shoulder as he took a snooze.

~ Michele Allison

Grilled Cheese

Contributed by Michele Allison
Long Valley, New Jersey, USA

David liked grilled cheese. Here's a variation:

Ingredients:	
2 slices sourdough bread	3 slices provolone
roasted red pepper pesto	butter

Directions:
1. Spread pesto on the inside of the bread.
2. Arrange provolone between bread.
3. Pan fry in butter until cheese is melted.

"Chicken" Marsala

Contributed by Michele Allison
Long Valley, New Jersey, USA

Ingredients:
1 box "Quorn Naked Chicken"
fresh mushrooms, sliced
butter
olive oil

Marsala wine (about 1-2 C)
flour
paprika, garlic powder, salt, and pepper

Directions:
1. Take "chicken" out of freezer and let sit on counter.
2. Place mushrooms in frying pan and cook over medium heat until they start to brown.
3. Add salt and pepper and remove from pan.
4. Add oil to pan.
5. Mix dry seasonings into flour.
6. Dip the "chicken" into flour mixture and sauté.
7. When browned on both sides, remove "chicken."
8. Add Marsala wine to pan and deglaze.
9. Put the "chicken" and mushrooms back in and cook another few minutes so they can absorb the wine.

Debbie's Corn Casserole

Contributed by Debbie Maldonado
McAllen, Texas, USA

Ingredients:
1 (15 ¼ oz.) can whole kernel corn, drained
½ C butter, melted
1 (14 ¾ oz.) can cream-style corn
1 -1 ½ C shredded Cheddar cheese
1 (8 oz.) package corn muffin mix (I recommend Jiffy)

1 C sour cream
optional: one egg, diced green chilies, diced onion, diced red bell pepper

If adding the onion, peppers, or chilies, sauté in the ½ cup butter then add to the mix.

Directions:
1. Preheat oven to 350° F.
2. In a large bowl, stir together the 2 cans of corn, corn muffin mix, sour cream, and melted butter.
3. Pour into a greased casserole dish. Bake for 45 minutes or until golden brown.
4. Remove from oven and top with Cheddar.
5. Return to oven for 5 to 10 minutes or until cheese is melted.
6. Let stand for at least 5 minutes and then serve warm.

S.A.G. Paneer

Contributed by Susan Olsen
Star of The Brady Bunch

Probably my favorite food on the planet is Indian food. Sag paneer, or Palak paneer, means "spinach and cheese." It is one of my favorites. Its appearance can be a little off putting to some, but if you like spinach and you like curry, you will love this. S.A.G. stands for "Screen Actors' Guild". I'm just being cheeky with the title.

Ingredients:
1 t curry powder
½ t nutmeg
sea salt
¼ t black pepper
3 T vegetable oil
1 t sesame oil
1 T Sriracha sauce
12 oz. Indian cheese (paneer) cut into 1 inch cubes* (If you want to go vegan, you may substitute with extra firm tofu.)
1 ½ T coconut oil (or more vegetable oil)
1 pound (16 oz. package) spinach, finely chopped with a knife or in food processor

1 medium white onion, finely chopped (about 8 oz.)
1 (1 inch thumb) ginger, peeled and minced (about 1 T, or 1 T ginger puree found in some grocery stores – you can use less but don't use more - it can take over the dish.)
4 cloves garlic, minced
½ t garam masala (I've made it without and liked it just as well.)**
½ C plain Greek yogurt, stirred until smooth

Directions:
1. In a large bowl, whisk together the curry powder, cayenne, 1 teaspoon salt, 3 tablespoons vegetable oil, 1 teaspoon sesame oil, and 1 tablespoon Sriracha.
2. Gently drop in the cubes of paneer and gently toss. Let the cubes marinate while you get the rest of your ingredients together and prepped.
3. Place the spinach in a microwave safe container and nuke it for a couple of minutes to wilt it. This is just to lower the volume and make it easier to manage. Then transfer to a food processor to puree until finely chopped (about five pulses) or you can chop it very finely with a knife.
4. Place a large nonstick skillet over medium heat and add the paneer as the pan warms. In a couple of minutes give the pan a toss; each piece of paneer should be browned on one side. Fry another minute or so. Then, using a slotted spoon or spatula, remove the paneer from the pan onto a plate or back into the bowl it marinated in. Try to keep as much of the spicy oil in the pan as possible.
5. Add 1½ tablespoon coconut oil to the pan. Add the onions, ginger, and garlic. Now here's the important part: sauté the mixture until it's evenly toffee-colored, which should take about 15 minutes. This is where the flavors of the dish are developed. If you feel like the mixture is drying out and burning, add a couple of tablespoons of water.
6. Add the 2 teaspoon lemongrass (optional) and the garam masala. Sprinkle a little water to keep the spices from burning (if you haven't already). Cook, stirring often, 3 to 5 minutes.
7. Add the spinach and stir well, incorporating the spiced onion mixture into the spinach. Add a little salt and ½ cup of water, stir, and cook about 5 minutes with the lid off.
8. Turn the heat off. Add the yogurt, a little at a time to keep it from curdling. Once the yogurt is well mixed into the spinach, add the paneer. Turn the heat back on, cover and cook until everything is warmed through for about 5 minutes. Serve.

* Paneer is available in Asian markets but you can make your own! Then you can say you've made your own cheese and people will be so impressed with you. See the recipe on the next page.
**Garam masala is available at online or at some specialty retailers.

Homemade Paneer

Contributed by Susan Olsen
Star of The Brady Bunch

Ingredients:	
8 C whole milk cheese cloth	3-4 T of lemon juice (Have more on hand; it may be needed.)

Directions:
1. Line a colander with a double layer of cheesecloth and set it in your sink.
2. In a large (preferably non-stick) pot, heat the milk to a gentle boil. Stir frequently to avoid scorching.
3. As soon as it comes to a boil, turn off the heat and add 3 tablespoon of lemon juice. Stir until milk separates into curds. If it doesn't seem to be separating completely, add another tablespoon of lemon juice. Stir in a motion that gathers the curds together rather than breaks them up. Don't be alarmed that the liquid is green and looks gross. This is the way it's supposed to be! At this point you have cottage cheese or Little Miss Tuffet's favorite dish: curds and whey.
4. Pour the mixture into the cheesecloth-lined colander. Gently rinse with cool water to remove the lemon flavor. When it's cool enough to handle, gather the corners of the cheesecloth into a bundle and squeeze out as much of the excess liquid as you can. Tie the cheesecloth to your kitchen faucet and allow the cheese to drain for about 5 minutes.
5. To press it into a solid cheese, set the bundle in the middle of a plate with a good lip to catch the liquid that will be squeezed out. Put another plate on top and press until the bundle has flattened into a 1 inch disk. Leave the plate on and weight it down with something heavy (like a few cans of tomatoes). Move to the refrigerator and let it sit for at least 20 minutes, an hour is ideal.
6. Then use it or wrap it in plastic wrap and refrigerate. It is best if used in a day or two.

Photograph © Courtesy of Susan Olsen

Spinach Quiche

Contributed by Trish Abbott
Belle Isle, Florida, USA

Ingredients:
1 nine inch deep dish pie crust	¼ t ground white pepper
1 package (10 oz.) frozen spinach (thawed)	¼ t ground nutmeg
¼ C sliced onion	1 ½ C half and half
3 oz. grated Swiss cheese	1 oz. grated Swiss cheese (additional for
4 whole eggs	the end)
½ t salt	

Directions:
1. Pre-heat oven to 400° F.
2. Prick bottom insides of pie crust all over with a fork.
3. Bake crust until light golden brown.
4. Remove crust from oven and reduce oven temperature to 375° F.
5. Squeeze all moisture from thawed spinach.
6. Chop spinach coarsely.
7. In a bowl, beat eggs thoroughly with seasonings (salt, pepper, nutmeg).
8. Add half and half; mix thoroughly.
9. Add spinach, onion, and Swiss cheese to custard and mix well.
10. Pour mixture into pre-baked pie shell.
11. Sprinkle with 1 oz. additional grated Swiss cheese.
12. Place on cookie sheet and bake until puffed and golden brown, approximately 45-60 minutes.
13. Allow to cool slightly before slicing and serving. Enjoy!

Mirza Ghassemi
(Persian Eggplant Casserole)

Contributed by Marian Allen
Corydon, Indiana, USA

Ingredients:
2 medium eggplants	½ t salt
2 medium onions, peeled and chopped	¼ t peppercorns
8 cloves garlic, peeled and chopped	1 tomato, peeled and chopped
¼ C butter or margarine	4 eggs, lightly beaten
1 t turmeric	

Directions:
1. Roast eggplants in a 400°F oven until brown on the outside and soft on the inside. Cool and peel and mash with fork.
2. Sauté the onions, garlic, and turmeric until onions are brown.
3. Add the eggplant pulp and sauté briefly, stirring well. Add the salt and pepper.
4. Stir tomato into the eggplant. Cook over a low heat for 5 minutes.
5. Pour eggs over the eggplant. When the eggs start to set, stir briefly and serve.

Serves 6

Mjuddara
(Palestinian Lentils And Rice)

Contributed by Carrie Ann Dressler
Shamokin, Pennsylvania, USA, and Ramallah in the West Bank

Ingredients:	
2 C brown lentils	3 t cumin
1 C rice	1 ½ t pepper
4 C water approximately	onions
3 t salt	olive oil

Directions:
1. Rinse lentils under hot tap water.
2. Cover and cook the lentils in enough water to cover them by about ¼ of an inch (approx. 2 cups) for 10 minutes or until all water is absorbed.
3. Run rice under hot water for a minute or two.
4. Add to lentils when the lentils finish initial cooking.
5. Add spices and enough water to cover the entire mixture by ¼-½ inch (about 3-4 cups).
6. Bring to a rapid boil, lower heat, cover and cook for approximately 10-12 minutes (I usually check after 8 minutes) or until most of the water is absorbed.
7. Add oil from the onions (instructions to follow) and cook on low for another 2-3 minutes.
8. Onions: Slice and cook in as much extra virgin olive oil as you like (usually about ⅓ of a cup or so) until light golden brown.
9. Pour the oil over the lentils and rice. Serve onions on top.

Note: This is delicious served with an Arab salad of finely chopped cucumbers and tomatoes served with a little salt and pepper, olive oil, and fresh lemon juice. This dish has become a family favorite!

"I've worked hard and lived an extraordinary life. I've travelled the world and met many famous people, but I'm at my happiest when I come back home...home to my family, my girls. Home to my friends. Home to my fans. Because at home my life is replenished and I never come up empty. I'm given the love and inspiration to keep giving back."

(Daydream Believin' © David Jones 2000)

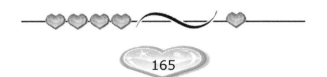

Cheesy Eggplant Casserole

Contributed by Yolanda Valenzuela
Walnut Creek, California, USA

Easy go-to comfort food when the weather gets cooler,
but just because it's comforting doesn't mean it has to be high in fat and calories.

Ingredients:	
¼ t salt	1 clove garlic, minced
2 small to medium eggplants, peeled and sliced, about ½ inch thickness	1 t dried Italian seasoning
	2 C no-salt added tomato puree
1 T olive oil	1 (14-oz.) can no-salt added diced tomatoes
¼ C green onions, chopped	¼ C all-purpose flour
1 medium onion, coarsely chopped	olive oil cooking spray
1 bell pepper (red or green) diced	2 C low-fat cottage cheese
½ C mushrooms, sliced	1 ¼ C shredded, low-fat mozzarella cheese

Directions:
1. Preheat oven to 350° F. Sprinkle salt over eggplant and set aside.
2. Heat oil over medium-high heat in a large skillet. Sauté onions, pepper, mushrooms, and garlic until tender, about 3-4 minutes. Add seasoning, tomato puree, and diced tomatoes and bring to a boil. Reduce heat and simmer about 22 minutes.
3. Coat eggplant with flour, front and back. Coat skillet with cooking spray and heat over medium heat. Add eggplant slices in batches and cook, covered, until browned, turning once about 3-5 minutes per side. Transfer to plate.
4. In a 7x11 inch casserole dish, spread about 1 cup of sauce. Add a layer of eggplant. Top with 1 cup of cottage cheese, more sauce and ½ cup mozzarella. Repeat again, placing a layer of sauce on top. Sprinkle with remaining mozzarella.
5. Bake uncovered, about 30 minutes. Let stand 5 minutes before serving.

Makes 6 servings

"...when I go out to the refrigerator, I do three minutes (entertaining) when the light goes on."

~ Davy Jones

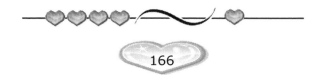

Daydream Believer Shepherd's Pie

Contributed by Buffy Ford Stewart
Angel Rain
San Anselmo, California, USA

(Buffy Ford Stewart was the inspiration for her husband John Stewart's song "Daydream Believer,"
and in 2010 she and Davy recorded a beautiful new version of the song together.)

This recipe is a favorite dish in my family. My husband John Stewart requested
this dish every Thanksgiving and Christmas! Your family will too!!!!

Ingredients:	
1 package of Gimme Lean veggie ground meat style	5 russet potatoes
1 package frozen organic mixed veggies	nutmeg (just a bit in the potatoes after they are mashed!)
1 can organic lentil soup	salt, pepper, cream, butter, and nutmeg to taste
tamari sauce	
olive oil	

Directions:
1. Skin and boil potatoes.
2. Put some olive oil and the package of Gimme Lean into a large skillet. Brown it until it looks like ground beef.
3. Add the frozen veggies and some tamari sauce (just a few squirts!)
4. Mix and add one can of lentil soup.
5. Mix and add a bit of salt and pepper.
6. When the potatoes are done, mash with butter, cream, salt, pepper, and a bit of nutmeg. The nutmeg makes it really special!
7. When the potatoes are mashed and perfect, put all the ingredients from the skillet into a casserole dish and cover the top with the mashed potatoes. Put pats of butter on top.
8. Sprinkle with nutmeg, salt, and pepper and bake for 30 to 35 minutes in a 350°F oven.

Buffy with Lucy

Photograph by Henry Diltz © Courtesy of Buffy Ford Stewart

It's Nice to be Tofu

Contributed by Daryl Goldfarb
Lynnwood, Washington, USA

This is my favorite meal. It has a delicious cheesy or chicken-y taste and is simple to make! The hardest part of making this dish is not eating it all while cooking it! It goes great with mashed potatoes, veggies, or salad.

Ingredients:
1 package (16 oz.) very firm tofu (packaged in shrink wrap rather than in tub of water)
3 eggs
nutritional yeast flakes, large or small flakes OK
canola or other vegetable oil

garlic powder and salt to taste
paper towel on a cookie sheet to drain oil
larger frying pan

Directions:
1. Dry the tofu and cut into ½ inch slices.
2. Beat the eggs until mixed.
3. Pour a layer of yeast onto the plate and mix in the garlic powder and salt.
4. Begin heating about ½ inch of the oil in the pan.
5. Dip each tofu slice in the beaten eggs to coat, then lay them in the yeast "breading" until coated, and then turn with fork to get both sides and the edges.
6. When the oil is hot, lay the slices in the pan. You can lay as many pieces in the pan as will fit (really big pans work great).
7. When the bottom sides are brown, usually in just a couple of minutes (lift carefully to check), turn over with fork. When both sides are golden and crispy, remove with fork and drain on paper towels.

Tips:
Nutritional yeast is NOT the same thing as yeast used for baking. It has a lovely, cheesy taste and is great on veggies, pasta, and sprinkled on popcorn!

You may have to add oil to the pan periodically depending on how much you start with, how hot it gets, and how much is absorbed. Don't use olive oil as it shouldn't be used with high heat.

I prefer sea salt as it does not have the astringent after-taste of iodized salt.

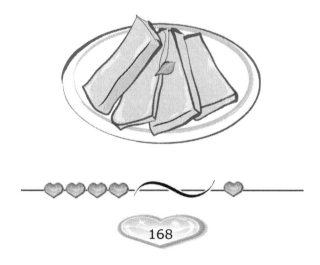

Photograph © Courtesy of Michael G. Bush

"A lot of people go days without having someone hug them or shake their hand. I get that all the time."

~ Davy Jones

Pasta

Photograph © Courtesy of Rhino Entertainment Company

Vegan Chicken-less Noodles

Contributed by Heather Dahman
Fort Wayne, Indiana, USA

This vegan version of chicken and noodles uses Edwards and Sons Not-Chick'n Bouillon which is my all time favorite vegan chick'n broth. You may be able to find it at your local grocery store in the natural foods section or you can purchase it online. The noodles are the Kroger brand eggless noodles. You may find something similar at your store, or you can even make your own which I've been known to do when time permits. The gravy is also a great base for a chicken-less pot pie, or use less flour for a chicken-less gravy to top your mashed potatoes.

Ingredients:

1 pkg. egg-free noodles, cooked per package directions	1 T vegan butter
	¼ C diced celery
2 T unbleached all-purpose flour	2 cubes Not Chick'n Bouillon
1 C rice or soy milk	½ t poultry seasoning
1 C water	black pepper

Directions:
1. Melt butter in large skillet.
2. Add diced celery. Cook celery until it becomes tender and almost transparent.
3. In a shaker bottle, add 1 tablespoon flour and the cup of water. Shake until well combined and lump free.
4. Add flour/water mixture to skillet.
5. Stir to combine with water mixture.
6. Add poultry seasoning and one Not-Chick'n bouillon cube. Mix until fully melted.
7. Cook over medium high heat stirring occasionally to keep lump-free until desired consistency.
8. Toss with cooked egg-free noodles and add remaining bouillon cube.
9. Mix on low heat until bouillon is completely melted and mixed thoroughly.
10. Pepper to taste.

Optional Add-Ins:
Vegan chicken strips or TVP for protein, chickpeas, diced carrots, peas

Note: The bouillon has plenty of salt so there is no need to salt these noodles.

Nonna's Baked Ziti

Contributed by Nanci Iannone
Malibu, California, USA

Ingredients:
1 lb. any tubular pasta - ziti, rigatoni, mezza rigatoni
3 C prepared Italian tomato sauce
1 lb. small diced mozzarella - fresh is the best, but packaged is okay; shredded will work in a pinch.

8 oz. part skim ricotta (do not use low fat - no no no!)
¾ C grated Parmesan (Reggiano Parmesan if you can find it)
black pepper and salt to taste
red pepper flakes to taste if you roll that way!

Directions:
1. Salt water and boil one pound of any tubular pasta - ziti, rigatoni, mezza rigatoni - 2 minutes LESS than the box calls for.
2. When pasta's done, fold into cheese mixture.
3. Grease a casserole dish lightly with olive oil (the spray olive oil works great for this) and then spoon your pasta and cheese mixture in.
4. Bake at 400° F for 30 minutes.

HEAVEN! And people think you slaved over a hot stove for HOURS!!!

Roasted Red Pepper Rotini

Contributed by Bonnie Borgh
Bettendorf, Iowa, USA

Ingredients:
1 box whole wheat rotini
1—12 oz. jar roasted red peppers, sliced
4 C fresh baby spinach or frozen spinach
1 C creamy Caesar or creamy peppercorn/ Parmesan dressing

shredded Parmesan to taste
cracked pepper and salt to taste
1 can black olives (optional)

Directions:
1. Cook pasta according to package directions.
2. Add cooked spinach, red peppers and dressing, stirring frequently until heated through.
3. Add black olives.
4. Top with Parmesan cheese, cracked pepper, and salt.
5. Bake at 350° F.

Good served hot or cold.

Zucchini Lasagna

Contributed by Tina Howard
Longview, Texas, USA

Ingredients:

2 large zucchini	1 egg
1 T salt	1 (15 oz.) container low-fat ricotta cheese
1 small green bell pepper, diced	2 T chopped fresh parsley
1 onion, diced	1 (16 oz.) package frozen chopped spinach,
1 C tomato paste	thawed and drained
1 (16 oz.) can tomato sauce	1 pound fresh mushrooms, sliced
¼ C red wine	8 oz. shredded mozzarella cheese
2 T chopped fresh basil	8 oz. grated Parmesan cheese
1 T chopped fresh oregano	1 ½ t ground black pepper
hot water as needed	

Directions:
1. Preheat oven to 325° F (165° C). Grease a deep 9x13 inch baking pan.
2. Slice zucchini lengthwise into very thin slices. Sprinkle slices lightly with salt; set aside to drain in a colander.
3. To prepare the sauce, stir in black pepper in a large skillet over medium high heat for 5 minutes. Add in green pepper and onion and stir in tomato paste, tomato sauce, wine, basil, and oregano, adding a small amount of hot water if sauce is too thick. Bring to a boil; reduce heat and simmer sauce for about 20 minutes, stirring frequently.
4. Meanwhile, stir egg, ricotta, and parsley together in a bowl until well combined.
5. To assemble lasagna, spread ½ of the sauce into the bottom of prepared pan. Then layer ½ the zucchini slices, ½ the ricotta mixture, all of the spinach, followed by all of the mushrooms, then ½ the mozzarella cheese. Repeat by layering the remaining sauce, zucchini slices, ricotta mixture, and mozzarella. Spread Parmesan cheese evenly over the top; cover with foil.
6. Bake for 45 minutes. Remove foil; raise oven temperature to 350° F (175° C.). Bake until cheese begins to brown.
7. Take out of oven and let sit for 15 minutes before serving.

Daydream Believer Lasagna

Contributed by Peggy Hanson
Seattle, Washington, USA

Ingredients:	
4 Italian Field Roast veggie sausages	feta, mozzarella, or soy cheese
1 tube polenta	pesto pasta sauce

Directions:
1. In a 9x13 inch pan, pour a thin layer of pasta sauce.
2. Next cut polenta into 8 half-inch slices and place in the pan.
3. Spread these with pesto. Cut a veggie sausage in half crosswise, and then lengthwise.
4. Put ½ sausage on top of each polenta slice.
5. Pour pasta sauce over this and top with your choice of cheese.
6. Cook at 350° F for 25 minutes. Cool 5 minutes before serving.

Serves 6

Spinach Lasagna

Contributed by Bonnie Borgh
Bettendorf, Iowa, USA

Ingredients:	
1 lb. pkg. lasagna noodles (whole wheat are good)	1 lb. ricotta cheese
1 pkg. frozen chopped spinach	1 egg beaten
1 lb. shredded mozzarella cheese	1 (8oz.) can pizza or tomato sauce
	8 oz. grated Parmesan or Romano cheese

Directions:
1. Cook noodles and drain. Rinse with cold water.
2. Boil or microwave frozen spinach.
3. Combine mozzarella cheese, ricotta cheese, and egg in a bowl. Add cooked spinach.
4. Arrange a layer of noodles in bottom of a greased 13x9x2 inch casserole dish. Place ½ of spinach mixture over noodles.
5. Add another layer of noodles and spinach mixture and top with another layer of noodles.
6. Pour sauce over noodles. Sprinkle with Parmesan cheese. Bake until bubbly and light brown.

Serves 8

Spinach Cheese Manicotti

Contributed by Cheryl Belle
Brandywine, Maryland, USA

Ingredients:
1 pound dry ziti pasta	1 ½ C sour cream
1 onion, chopped	6 oz. mozzarella cheese, shredded
2 (26 oz.) jars spaghetti sauce	2 T grated Parmesan cheese
6 oz. provolone cheese, sliced	

Directions:
1. Preheat oven to 350° F (175° C).
2. In a large bowl, combine ricotta, spinach, onion, and egg. Season with parsley, pepper, and garlic powder.
3. Mix in 1 cup of mozzarella and ¼ cup of Parmesan.
4. In a separate bowl, stir together spaghetti sauce and water.
5. Spread 1 cup of sauce in the bottom of a 9x13 inch baking dish.
6. Stuff uncooked manicotti shells with ricotta mixture and arrange in a single layer in the dish.
7. Cover with remaining sauce. Sprinkle with remaining mozzarella and Parmesan.
8. Bake in preheated oven for 45 to 55 minutes or until noodles are soft.
   If refrigerating overnight, do so after step 3. Remove from the refrigerator 30 minutes before baking.

Cajun Mac and Yease

Contributed by Anita Williams Weinberg
Seattle, Washington, USA

Ingredients:
16 oz. package of elbow macaroni or ziti pasta	1 ½ t salt
½ C flour	1 ½ t garlic powder
½ C margarine	1 pinch of turmeric
2 T soy sauce	1 pinch of cayenne pepper
1 C nutritional yeast	about 1 T of red pepper flakes
3 ½ C boiling water	½ to 1 T mustard

Directions:
1. Bring 4 quarts of water to a boil, add salt to taste, and add macaroni.
2. Melt the margarine over low heat. Beat in flour with a wire whisk. Continue to beat over medium heat until mixture is smooth and bubbly.
3. Whip in boiling water. Add salt, garlic powder, turmeric, cayenne, pepper flakes, soy sauce, and mustard to the liquid.
4. Let the sauce cook until it thickens and bubbles. When this happens, beat in the nutritional yeast. If the sauce is too thick, add more water.
5. When macaroni is cooked, drain and add the sauce. Serve immediately.

I sometimes stir in shredded vegan mozzarella cheese until it is melted for a creamier version.

Lemon Kale Pasta

Contributed by Suzanne Gee
Las Vegas, Nevada, USA

Ingredients:

2 T / ¼ C / ⅛ C olive oil
1 T salt
4 oz. uncooked linguini or fettuccine (fresh or dry)
2 C walnut pieces, lightly toasted
½ C onions or scallions, chopped
1 large garlic clove. minced
¼ C dry or semi-dry white wine
8 oz. kale, cleaned and chopped
¼ C shaved carrots
¼ C shaved red cabbage

¾ C pasta water
¼ C balsamic vinegar
½ t celery seed
1 t hot pepper flakes
1 medium lemon, juiced and zested
salt and pepper to taste
½ C non-fat or low-fat plain yogurt
1 T fresh oregano, chopped (1 t if dried)
2 T fresh sage, chiffonade or chopped (1½ t if dried)
shaved Parmesan to taste

Directions:
1. Cook pasta according to package directions, adding 2 tablespoons of olive oil and 1 tablespoon of salt to boiling water. Stir occasionally while cooking pasta to keep from sticking together. Before draining pasta, reserve ¾ cup of the pasta water and set aside. Never rinse pasta with tap water when draining!
2. Preheat oven or toaster oven to 250° F. Spread walnut pieces in a thin layer on an ungreased, unlined cookie sheet. Toast in oven, removing to shake and toss every minute or so. The walnuts are done when you start to smell them. The time will vary, so watch very carefully and never leave oven – nuts burn quickly! Should take about 5 minutes.
3. Remove from oven and set aside.
4. Set a large sauté pan (big enough to hold all ingredients including cooked pasta) on medium heat.
5. Add ¼ cup of olive oil and wait a minute. Add chopped onions/scallions and keep moving until light brown. Add minced garlic and keep moving for about a minute or until you start to smell the garlic. Be very careful not to burn the garlic!
6. Add white wine and turn up heat so it simmers. Cook down for a minute and then add kale, carrots, cabbage, pasta water, balsamic vinegar, celery seed, hot pepper flakes, lemon zest, and juice. Salt and pepper to taste.
7. Turn heat on high and when the liquid starts to simmer again turn back down to medium. Continue simmering to cook down liquids for about 5 minutes.
8. Add pasta, remaining olive oil, yogurt, oregano, and sage. Mix well until all ingredients are incorporated and heated through. Taste and add more salt and pepper if needed.
9. When serving, add toasted walnuts and shaved Parmesan.

Great with some crusty bread and a glass of white wine or sparkling water.

Makes 4 to 6 servings

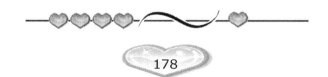

Pasta with Lentils

Contributed by Carl Giammarese of the Buckinghams

Ingredients:	
1 large can whole tomatoes	½ - ¾ t sugar
½ cup cooked lentils	oregano and basil to taste
2 cloves of chopped garlic	olive oil
1 large onion, chopped	pasta of your choice

Directions:
1. In a large skillet, heat olive oil on medium, then add the onion and garlic.
2. Once the onion starts to brown a little, add the whole tomatoes. Chop the tomatoes and mix well with the onions.
3. Sprinkle basil and oregano and let it cook down on medium until it starts to thicken.
4. Then add a ½ - ¾ teaspoon of sugar to taste. Simmer on low with lid on skillet for another 10-15 minutes.
5. Turn stove off and let it set another 5 minutes.
6. Last, fold in the lentils and pour over pasta of your choice. You can sprinkle grated cheese if desired.

The Buckinghams had a lot of fond memories performing many concerts through the years with Davy. He was a true talent and an inspiration. We performed together in 2012 on Paul Revere's "Where The Action Is" cruise. His performance was exceptional, but I remember one morning on the cruise when he had us rolling on the floor during a question and answer session for our fans. His wit and humor were beyond compare. We all miss him deeply.

This is a pasta recipe that goes back many years from my Sicilian grandmother Sarah. When my family first came to the United States from Sicily in the early 1900's, they struggled and couldn't afford meat very often for their family, so they had many different pasta recipes with vegetables. This is one of my favorites of many that we still enjoy all the time.

I hope you enjoy,
Carl Giammarese

Photograph © Courtesy of Carl Giammarese

Cashew and Noodle Casserole

Contributed By Darlene Haines
Crestline, Ohio, USA

Ingredients:
2 oz. mushrooms, canned	1 C water and mushroom broth
1 C celery, chopped	1 C cashews
1 C onion, chopped	3 oz. chow mein noodles
¾ t oil	1 T soy sauce
1 can of cream of mushroom soup	

Directions:
Combine and bake in a casserole pan at 350° F for an hour.

Vegetable Penne

Contributed by Janet Litterio
Homer Glen, Illinois, USA

Ingredients:
1 sweet onion, sliced	olive oil
1 bell pepper, sliced	salt and pepper to your taste
1 medium zucchini, sliced (I've used yellow squash—works well)	½ pint cherry tomatoes
chopped garlic to your taste	¼ C white wine
½ pound mushrooms sliced, I use cremini, but buttons will be good. Use as many as you like.	12 oz. whole grain penne or whatever pasta you prefer
	½ C pasta water reserved
	freshly grated Parmesan cheese to garnish

Directions:
1. Sauté veggies in a pan in the olive oil and the garlic until a bit soft, but not mushy.
2. Season with salt and pepper.
3. Deglaze with the white wine.
4. Cook penne/pasta according to package directions. Drain. Toss cooked/drained penne into the Veggies adding the reserved pasta water if needed to moisten.
5. Garnish with Parmesan and fresh basil when plated.

Pasta con Broccoli

Contributed by Sharon Kenney Currran
St. Louis, Missouri, USA

I fell hard for Davy that first night The Monkees premiered.
As a little girl, how I wished I was there on the beach with him during
"Saturday's Child" in the "Monkee vs. Machine" episode. I think of him every day.

Ingredients:
4 oz. fettuccine or linguini
1 C whipping cream
2 T butter
½ t minced garlic
2 T tomato sauce

½ C broccoli
¼ C mushrooms
¼ C Parmesan

Directions:
1. Cook noodles until half done (4 minutes). Drain.
2. Add cream, butter, garlic, tomato sauce, and broccoli. Boil over medium heat.
3. Stir in mushrooms.
4. Remove from heat. Add Parmesan.
5. Serve immediately.

One Pot Simply Delicious Pasta

Contributed by Janet Litterio
Homer Glen, Illinois, USA

Ingredients:
12 oz. pasta (I use linguine)
1 can (15 oz.) diced tomatoes with liquid
1 medium sweet onion, cut in julienne strips
4 cloves garlic, thinly sliced
½ t red pepper flakes
2 t dried oregano leaves

2 large sprigs basil, chopped
4 ½ C vegetable broth (regular broth and NOT
   low sodium)
2 T extra virgin olive oil
Parmesan cheese for garnish

Directions:
1. Place pasta, tomatoes, onion, garlic, and basil in a large stock pot. Pour in vegetable broth. Sprinkle on top the pepper flakes and oregano. Drizzle top with oil.
2. Cover pot and bring to a boil. Reduce to a low simmer and keep covered. Cook for about 10 minutes stirring every 2 minutes or so. Cook until almost all liquid has evaporated.
3. Season to taste with salt and pepper, stirring pasta several times to distribute the liquid in the bottom of the pot. Serve garnished with Parmesan cheese.

Vegan Mac and Cheese

Contributed by Kim Graul
Wilkes-Barre, Pennsylvania, USA

Ingredients:
1 ½ lbs. macaroni pasta

Vegan Cheese Sauce:
1 ½ C nutritional yeast
1 ½ C unsweetened nondairy milk
½ C veggie oil
1 C water

⅓ C soy sauce
12 oz. block of firm tofu
1 T paprika
1 T garlic powder
1 T salt
1 t mustard

Directions:
1. Preheat oven to 350° F. Boil water in a large pot and cook pasta according to directions on package.
2. Add all of the vegan cheese sauce ingredients in a blender and process until smooth. Once pasta is cooked, drain and put it in a baking pan. Pour the cheese sauce over the pasta.
3. Bake until top of the pasta looks slightly browned and crispy, about 15 minutes.

You can also add vegan bread crumbs to the top to make an extra crispy top and bake a few minutes

Food Glorious food

Daniel Jones

You are what you eat
I'm Pasta

Image © Courtesy of David T. Jones Estate

Veggie Lasagna

Contributed by Kathy Lawler
South Windsor, Connecticut, USA

Ingredients:
1 T canola oil	1 carton of ricotta cheese
1 ½ lbs. ground soy with veggies	1¾ C blue cheese or Gorgonzola cheese, crumbled
2 small onions, chopped	½ C minced parsley
2 celery ribs, chopped	3 C shredded skim mozzarella
2 garlic cloves	2 C white cheese
1 can tomatoes	1 medium eggplant (instead of pasta)
1 bottle of soy barbeque sauce	
½ C water	
1 ½ t Greek seasoning	

Directions:
1. Bake one medium eggplant. When cooled, peel and slice thinly. (Use in lieu of pasta.) Set aside.
2. Mince garlic. While using a wooden spoon, squish garlic, adding just a bit of salt (very old secret to enhance the garlic's flavor).
3. Over medium heat, add garlic to vegetable oil, allowing garlic to slowly merge into the oil.
4. Add prepared eggplant. Simmer until tender, about 1 hour.
5. Add tomatoes, water, barbeque sauce, and Greek seasoning.
6. Add cheeses, egg, and parsley into a separate bowl.
7. In a 13x9 inch pan, spread sauce; layer eggplant and cheese. Repeat layers and bake covered at 350° F for 20 minutes. Bake 20 minutes uncovered. Allow to sit for 15 minutes. Serve.

Penne with Sun-dried Tomatoes and Feta Cheese

Contributed by Janet Hartman
Beaufort, North Carolina, USA

Ingredients:
3 garlic cloves, minced	1 t dried basil
⅓ C chopped or julienned sun-dried tomatoes	4 oz. crumbled feta cheese
1 ¾ C vegetable broth	8 oz. penne pasta
½ C sliced olives	
1 t dried parsley	

Directions:
1. Combine the first six ingredients in a small saucepan and simmer for 10 to 15 minutes. (Dry-packed tomatoes take longer than those packed in oil.) While the sauce simmers, cook penne per package directions.
2. When penne is cooked, drain and divide between two bowls. Spoon sauce over top and add the feta.
3. Serve immediately. The sauce is thin, so eat with a spoon to get every last drop!

Serves 2

Pesto Pasta

Contributed by Erica L. Shames
Founder and Publisher of
Susquehanna Life Magazine

I've been using the basil from my summer garden to make pesto pasta for my family since my mother introduced me to the dish years ago. It's a family favorite and, for variety, I sometimes leave out the pine nuts for a completely different, more earthy flavor. Enjoy!

Ingredients:	
3-4 C fresh basil leaves, washed and dried (squeeze out the water with your hand)	2-3 garlic cloves, put through a press
	½ to 1 C extra virgin olive oil
½ C Parmesan cheese, the fresher the better	1 ½ to 2 lbs. pasta, depending on how saucy you
½ C Romano cheese, authentic and sharp	like your pasta
⅓ C pine nuts, toasted	

Directions:
1. Boil pasta in 2 to 3 quarts of water until al dente (approx. 10 minutes).
2. While the pasta is cooking, toast the pine nuts by placing them in a skillet on medium-high and stirring them around until a golden brown. (Watch closely or they will burn.)
3. Combine the basil leaves, cheeses, garlic, pine nuts, and finally olive oil in your food processor until smooth. Do not over-mix or it will become dry and pasty. Taste test to make sure each ingredient is equally represented. If not, add a little more of what's missing and mix again.
4. When pasta is done, drain and place into a large bowl.
5. Add pesto, a little at a time, until it covers the pasta with just the right amount of sauce.

Pair with salad and garlic bread for an incredibly tasty summertime meal.

The Interview

Photograph © Courtesy of Erica Shames

Davy and Erica

We rang Davy Jones' doorbell to interview and photograph him for the Spring 2007 issue of Susquehanna Life magazine. He answered the door in his undershirt, apologized for the pile of dishes in the sink, and led us into the living room of his Spruce Farm home in Beavertown, PA -- a 40 minute drive from my home in Lewisburg, Pennsylvania.

He remarked about eating his vegetarian dinner last night in front of the TV -- alone. "How can that be?" he quipped. "I'm a star!" The kidding and sarcasm in his voice was apparent. What a wonderfully kind, down to earth person was Davy Jones. We had a wonderful time interviewing him, photographing him, and reminiscing with him.

He showed us Monkees memorabilia, let us visit with his prized thoroughbred racehorses, and when finally I was back in my car getting ready to leave for home, Davy told me to wait a minute and ran back into the house. When he came outside again, he ran up to my car and pulled out of his pockets a bunch of CDs -- "More of The Monkees," a Christmas CD, and others -- as well as armfuls of tee-shirts and books. He said, "I'll give you the CDs if you promise to listen to them on the way home!"

How could I refuse? It was a treat to meet and interact with Davy Jones.

~ Erica L. Shames

Roasted Butternut Penne
with Pistachio Pesto

Contributed by Madelyn Warkentin
Fullerton, California, USA

I used a brown rice penne (gluten free) but you can use whole grain pasta as well. The pesto can be made a few days in advance and kept in a covered container in the fridge. Extra pesto can be mixed with a bit of water and more lemon juice for a delicious salad dressing.

Ingredients:	
2 lbs. (one large) butternut squash, peeled, seeded, and cut into 1" pieces	For pistachio pesto:
2 t extra virgin olive oil	2 small cloves of garlic
2 t smoked paprika	zest and juice of one Meyer lemon
1 t sea salt	⅓ C toasted, unsalted pistachio nuts
bit of freshly grated nutmeg	I C packed fresh basil
8 oz. of brown rice, quinoa, or whole wheat penne pasta	2 T Italian flat-leaf parsley
	½ C grated Parmesan, plus more for garnish
	¼-⅓ C extra virgin olive oil
3 C well chopped baby spinach or Swiss chard	few pinches of salt and pepper

Directions:
1. Preheat the oven to 450° and set a large pot of salted water to boil.
2. On a large jelly roll baking sheet, toss the butternut cubes with the olive oil (enough to coat), smoked paprika, salt, a grate of nutmeg, and toss to coat. Bake for about 20 minutes or until edges are slightly charred.
3. Cook the pasta according to instructions. Reserve 1 cup of the cooking water for later.
4. For the pesto, add the garlic, lemon zest, and juice to the processor and pulse a few times to break down.
5. Add the pistachios, basil, parsley, and parmesan, and run the processor to mix, about 30 seconds.
6. Drizzle in the olive oil and a few pinches of salt and pepper until combined.
7. Taste and add more salt if desired. If it seems too thick you can add a splash of water or oil to thin it out a bit.
8. In a large mixing bowl, combine the pesto, greens, drained pasta, and 1/2 cup of the reserved pasta water and toss gently. The warm pasta and water will wilt the greens perfectly. Add more water if needed.
9. Garnish with a fresh grate of cheese, pepper, and any chopped basil and parsley.

Zucchini Pasta

Contributed by Beth Pinterich
Berwick, Pennsylvania, USA

Ingredients:	
1 box pasta of your choice, cooked according to directions 2 T olive oil 3 T butter 1 small onion, chopped	minced garlic (as much as you like) 2-3 sliced zucchini chopped tomato (optional) Parmesan cheese

Directions:
1. In a large frying pan, heat olive oil and butter.
2. Add onion and garlic and sauté a few minutes.
3. Add zucchini and cook until it begins to get tender.
4. If you would like to add tomato, do so now.
5. Add pasta and stir until heated through.
6. Serve topped with Parmesan cheese.

"Oh my goodness gracious!"

~ Davy Jones

Perogi Lasagna

Contributed by Bonnie Musser
Milroy, Pennsylvania, USA

This is so easy.

Ingredients:	
lasagna noodles onions, caramelized, as many as you want	mashed potatoes (instant work fine) your favorite cheese

Directions:
1. Cook lasagna noodles according to package, drain, and cool.
2. Layer noodles, caramelized onions, and mashed potatoes as many times as you have ingredients for in a buttered casserole dish.
3. Top with your favorite cheese.
4. Bake at 350 °F until the cheese is bubbly and golden.

Rose Marie's Lasagna

Contributed by Rose Marie
Star of The Dick Van Dyke Show
and guest star on The Monkees

Ingredients:

lasagna noodles, cooked and drained
your own sauce, however and whichever way
    you make it
two pounds of ricotta cheese
4 eggs
¾ to 1 C grated Romano cheese
Lawry's flavored garlic salt, to taste

Lawry's flavored pepper, to taste
3 cloves of garlic pressed through garlic press
1 ½ T oregano
1 ½ T sweet basil
1 ½ T parsley
1 good sized mozzarella cheese, shredded

Directions:
1. Mix together the ricotta cheese, eggs, Romano cheese, salt, pepper, garlic, oregano, sweet basil, and parsley and refrigerate for one hour.
2. Spoon a layer of sauce on the bottom of a deep, square pan. Lay a layer of strips of lasagna one way along the pan. Dot three or more tablespoons of the ricotta mixture along lasagna and spread evenly. Sprinkle some Romano cheese on top. Spoon over this sufficient sauce to cover well.
3. Lay a layer of lasagna crosswise on top of sauce layer. Dot three or more tablespoons of the ricotta mixture along lasagna and spread as before. Sprinkle with Romano cheese and spoon sauce over this as before.
4. Repeat these two steps, alternating direction of lasagna, until you reach top of pan. Top layer should finish with sauce. Sprinkle the mozzarella cheese on top of final layer.
5. Bake for one hour at 300° F.

Ma's Spinach Kugel

Contributed by Michele Allison
Long Valley, New Jersey, USA

Ingredients:

16 oz. egg noodles
8 oz. butter, softened
16 oz. sour cream

2 envelopes onion soup mix
1 t black pepper
4 (10 oz.) boxes frozen spinach

Directions:
1. Cook the noodles.
2. Mix all ingredients.
3. Bake 1 hour at 350° F.
4. To serve, cut into individual pieces (like lasagna).

Macaroni and Cheese
with Broccoli

Contributed by Elyse Kopel
Neponsit, New York, USA

Ingredients:	
1 lb. elbow macaroni	2 C shredded sharp Cheddar cheese
2 ½ C whole milk	½ C Parmesan cheese
2 heads broccoli florets	bread crumbs
3 T butter	salt and pepper to taste
3 T flour	butter to grease pan

Directions:
1. Pre-heat oven to 425° F.
2. Boil 1 lb. macaroni to "al dente".
3. Blanch broccoli florets and put aside.
4. Heat 2 ½ cups milk until hot, then turn off heat.
5. Heat 3 tablespoons butter until foamy over low heat.
6. Add 3 tablespoons flour and mix until mixture turns light brown.
7. Add milk little by little and stir as sauce thickens and looks like heavy cream.
8. Add 2 cups Cheddar cheese to pot and stir until creamy. Put macaroni in a bowl.
9. Add ½ cup Parmesan cheese.
10. Add sauce and broccoli.
11. Add salt and pepper to taste.
12. Grease 9x11 inch baking dish with butter.
13. Put mixed ingredients into baking dish.
14. Top mixture with thin layer of bread crumbs.
15. Place in oven and bake at 425° F for 7 - 10 minutes or until bread crumbs brown.

"The kind of love and affection I've gotten from being Davy Jones of The Monkees is crazy. You don't believe what my life is like. I wake up in the morning and I go

'I love my life!' "

~ Davy Jones

Side Dishes

Photograph © Courtesy of Rhino Entertainment Company

Peter's Harvest Applesauce

Contributed by Peter Tork

When he's not on the road at harvest time, Peter picks his own apples and makes a big batch of applesauce, freezing some to serve at Thanksgiving, lightly sweetened with his homemade maple syrup!

Ingredients:	
8 apples, scrubbed, cored, and chopped	¼ t cinnamon
1 C water	1 t vanilla extract
1 t lemon juice (or orange juice)	

Directions:
1. Mix water, lemon, cinnamon, and vanilla extract in large sauce pan.
2. Add chopped apples to the water mixture and stir. The citrus juice prevents the apples from turning brown. (Leave skins on the apples for a heartier sauce.)
3. Simmer at low setting until apples are soft.
4. Remove from heat and mash or blend for a smoother texture.

This recipe serves 4 as a side dish or light dessert and is tasty warm or cold with an extra dab of maple syrup for extra sweetness. Double the recipe to guarantee leftovers. Freeze leftovers to serve at a future feast!

**Davy, Peter, and Micky
"The Monkee Walk"**

Photograph © Courtesy of Michael G. Bush

Oven Baked Mixed Vegetables

Contributed by Andrea Gilbey
Cheshunt, Hertfordshire, UK

Ingredients for a side dish for two people:	
1 fist sized potato (peeled or not, depending on whether you like the skin)	1 medium onion, white or red as preferred
1 courgette / zucchini	1 T olive oil.
I red, orange or yellow sweet pepper (mix the colours for a pretty effect)	Mixed dried herbs
1 aubergine / eggplant	Salt and pepper to taste (Add a little more salt than you think you need as it helps draw the juices from the vegetables so they mix
2 medium tomatoes	together for a great flavor.)

Directions:
1. Preheat a baking sheet/tray in a moderate oven, 180° C / 350° F / gas mark 4.
2. Chop all the vegetables into dice sized pieces, but keep the chopped onion to one side.
3. Mix all the ingredients except the onion in a bowl, ensuring that all the pieces have a coating of oil.
4. Tip the vegetables onto the hot tray; it should sizzle!
5. Bake for 15 minutes, remove from the oven, add the onions, stir, and bake for another 10 minutes. (Putting the onions in halfway stops them from getting too burnt).

Eat!

Browned Butter Vegetables
with Almonds

Contributed by Theresa Archey
Oklahoma City, Oklahoma, USA

Ingredients:	
½ C butter	1 medium red bell pepper, chopped
1 t garlic salt	2 C chopped broccoli
1 t garlic 2 T sliced almonds	2 C chopped cauliflower
2 T white wine	1 t garlic pepper
1 medium onion, chopped	

Directions:
1. Melt butter in a skillet over medium-low heat. Season with garlic salt and garlic pepper.
2. Mix in almonds and cook until golden brown. Stir in wine, onion, red bell pepper, broccoli, and cauliflower.
3. Cook 5 minutes, or until vegetables are tender.

Baked Tempeh

Contributed by Pam Patrick
Pleasanton, Kansas, USA

Ingredients:
2 T apple cider vinegar
2 T Bragg Liquid Aminos (or soy sauce)
1 ½ t toasted sesame oil

1 ½ t pure maple syrup (or honey)
½ clove garlic, finely chopped
½ block of tempeh or tofu, cut into strips

Directions:
1. Mix first 5 ingredients well.
2. Arrange tempeh strips in single layer in glass baking dish and pour marinade over tempeh.
3. Marinate for at least 1 hour in refrigerator.
4. Preheat oven to 350° F and bake 20 minutes.
5. Turn pieces over and bake another 15 minutes more. If using tofu, you can fry in a skillet to make the slices crisper.

Breaded Tomatoes

Contributed by Ginny Fleming
New Albany, Indiana, USA

This is one of the simple country dishes my Grandma served every night I sat at her table.
The memory brought to mind with this old-fashioned "comfort food" is the evening
of February 9th 1964 — the night David and the cast of Oliver! joined the Beatles
on Ed Sullivan's stage. On this very night, the "Artful Dodger" was introduced nationwide,
and a few very lucky girls gazed into those magical, sparkly eyes. Little did they know the small
English lad "owning" the stage would grow into the man... David T. Jones.

Ingredients:
large can plain (or stewed) tomatoes
4 oz. butter (or to taste)
½ C sugar (or to taste)

1 t balsamic vinegar
4 to 6 bread slices, shredded
salt and pepper –season to taste

Directions:
1. Using a large sauce pan, heat tomatoes until bubbling (or boil down fresh – remove skin).
2. Add any options desired (minced onion, green peppers, etc.).
3. Add butter and sugar adjusting amounts to taste.
4. Add vinegar.
5. Allow to reduce only slightly; keep at gentle boil for five minutes.
6. One minute before serving, add shredded bread.
7. Serve immediately.

Photograph © Courtesy of William Russ

Rusty Russ' Rockin' Kale

Contributed by William Russ

Fast and easy...

(William Russ is an American actor and television director. He is perhaps best known for his role as Alan Matthews on the sitcom Boy Meets World. Russ is also notable for his roles in the television series Wiseguy, the soap operas Another World and The Young and the Restless, and the feature films Pastime and American History X.)

"Davy was a true gentleman and a thrill to meet."

Ingredients:	
olive oil, don't be stingy — good for you...	2 to 3 bunches of kale (or more) any kind from
2 t of chopped garlic, store bought is great	anywhere
2 red peppers, chopped or sliced	1 C (or more) vegetable stock
1 onion, chopped how ya feel	soy sauce, whatever ya need

Directions:
1. Just put on some Monkees on the Hi Fi...
2. Sautee the garlic, onions, and peppers in olive oil with some soy sauce till they turn a little brown and a little sticky.
3. Throw in the chopped kale, add veggie stock and/or a little water to blanche the kale, cover and let simmer for however long...Kale holds up really well to cooking.

If ya feeling it, throw some navy beans in and maybe some stewed tomatoes and flavor with a little hot pepper. Good as a soup or over brown rice...

Roasted Fennel

Contributed by Pam Patrick
Pleasanton, Kansas, USA

Ingredients:
1 large fennel bulb
1 T extra virgin olive oil

¼ t Himalayan salt (regular salt also works)

Directions:
1. Preheat oven to 350° F.
2. Remove greens and root end from fennel.
3. Cut bulb into chunky wedges.
4. Toss with oil and salt.
5. Place on baking sheet and roast for 25 to 35 minutes, until golden and tender.

Cuddly Cauliflower

Contributed by Peggy Harvey
Houston, Texas, USA

Ingredients:
1 large cauliflower
2 bay leaves
sea salt
1 stick butter
2 t English mustard (Colman's dry mustard)

⅓ C all-purpose flour
2 C milk
3 C grated red Leicester cheese (Cheddar cheese)

Directions:
1. Preheat your oven to 425° F.
2. Cut the cauliflower into small florets, put into a saucepan with the bay leaves, and cover with cold water. Add a sprinkling of salt and bring to a boil, then drain and refresh with cold water. Let the cauliflower drain again in a colander; pluck out the bay leaves and discard.
3. When the cauliflower is completely drained, put into an ovenproof dish in an even layer.
4. To make the cheese sauce, melt the butter in a heavy-bottom saucepan, then whisk in the mustard and flour, and cook over a gentle heat for about 5 minutes. Whisk in the milk off the heat, and then put it back on the heat and keep stirring until it becomes really thick and begins to bubble.
5. Sprinkle in all but a handful of the grated cheese and stir over the heat until it has melted into the sauce. Check the seasoning, then pour it over the cauliflower in the dish, and then scatter the remaining handful of grated cheese over the top.
6. Cook for 20 minutes or until the cauliflower is hot, the sauce is bubbling, and the cheesy top is slightly browned.

Rotel Corn

Contributed by Mickie McLaughlin
Jackson, Tennessee, USA

This dish is awesome. I get requests for it whenever
there's a potluck or holiday dinner, and someone always asks for the recipe.

Ingredients:	
2 cans white shoepeg corn (drained)	1 stick butter
1 can Rotel* (drained)	1 package cream cheese

Directions:
1. Put all ingredients into a microwave safe dish and heat until cream cheese and butter have softened.
2. Remove from microwave and stir until well blended.
3. Return to microwave and heat until the mixture is warm throughout.
4. Stir and serve.

May be used as a side dish or as a dip with tortilla chips.

*Rotel is a name brand of a variety of canned diced tomatoes.

Creamy Corn Casserole

Contributed by Linda Mach
Kewaunee, Wisconsin, USA

This is probably one of the easiest casseroles in my recipe box.
I love dishes that you can just dump and go!

Ingredients:	
½ C butter, melted	1 (15 oz.) can whole kernel corn, drained
2 eggs, beaten	1 (14.75 oz.) can creamed corn
1 (8.5 oz.) package dry corn bread mix	1 C sour cream

Directions:
1. Preheat oven to 350° F (175° C), and lightly grease a 9x9 inch baking dish.
2. In a medium bowl, combine butter, eggs, corn bread mix, whole and creamed corn, and sour cream.
3. Spoon mixture into prepared dish.
4. Bake for 45 minutes in the preheated oven, or until the top is golden brown.

Carlsbad Corn

Contributed by Rose Ann Gillett
Beech Grove, Indiana, USA

Ingredients:
2 cans un-drained white shoepeg corn
⅔ C Carnation evaporated milk
4 T butter
2 small cans of chopped green chilies
1 C Ritz cracker crumbs (+ ¼ C for topping)

⅔ C shredded Cheddar (+ ¼ C for topping)
2 T Parmesan (+ additional sprinkling for topping)
pepper to taste

Directions:
1. Stir ingredients in greased casserole dish.
2. Top with additional cracker crumbs and cheese.
3. Bake uncovered at 375° F for 45 minutes.

Davy's Mexican Potatoes

Contributed by Cathy and Tiffany DeFini
Mentor, Ohio, USA

Ingredients:
1 C oil
8 medium potatoes, sliced
1 large green pepper, diced
1 large red pepper, diced
1 medium onion, diced

1 McCormicks's brand taco seasoning mix
sour cream
shredded cheese
¾ C water (or whatever the taco seasoning mix you use calls for)

Directions:
1. In a nonstick frying pan, fry the potatoes with the oil (about 20 minutes). I like them on the soft side, but you can fry them until they are browned if you prefer, turning them over every few minutes with a spatula.
2. When done, remove from heat and drain oil from potatoes in a strainer. Set aside.
3. Using the same pan, sauté both peppers and onion with a little of the oil from the potatoes for about 5 minutes or so . They should be on the crunchy side.
4. Return potatoes to the pan and mix together.
5. Add the packet of taco seasoning and water. Stir well.
6. Cook on medium heat until all the water is absorbed into potatoes, peppers, and onions (about 5 minutes).
7. Remove from heat and place in dish.
8. Mix in sour cream and Cheddar cheese (as much as you like).

Bubble and Squeak

Contributed by Andrea Gilbey
Cheshunt, Hertfordshire, UK

This is a traditional dish for the day after Christmas Day (Boxing Day in the UK) to use up leftover vegetables, so it is a very flexible recipe, but generally equal quantities of greens and potatoes should be used. You can use half quantity of potatoes and half turnip, swede, or parsnip for extra flavour. The name is supposed to come from the sound it makes cooking as the steam escapes.

Ingredients (per person):
½ lb. potatoes, peeled and cooked until soft
½ lb. Brussels sprouts or cabbage cooked

1 small onion, finely chopped
a knob (1-2 T) of vegan butter substitute

Directions:
1. Mash potatoes and greens with butter substitute and stir in the chopped onions.
2. Pre-heat a heavy based frying pan on the highest setting, spread the mixture in and press down with a fork.
3. Cook until it catches very slightly, turn, break up the mixture, and press down again.
4. Cook and turn until everything is slightly crispy. (I like mine slightly singed at the edges!)

Tastes great with vegetarian sausages and pickle or chutney.

Creamed Potatoes

Contributed by Angi and Braeden Gonzalez
Jackson, Wisconsin, USA

Great for holidays

Ingredients:
5 lbs. of russet potatoes
6 oz. cream cheese, softened
1 C of sour cream
¼ C butter, softened

2 t onion salt
¼ t pepper
½ C Parmesan cheese

Directions:
1. Boil potatoes until tender; mash.
2. Combine potatoes, cream cheese, sour cream, margarine, onion salt, and pepper in a large bowl. Mix well.
3. Spoon into casserole dish. Sprinkle with Parmesan cheese.
4. Chill covered in refrigerator for several hours.
5. When ready to make, preheat oven to 350° F. Bake for 30 minutes or until cheese is brown.

Rita's Amazing Sweet Potatoes

Contributed by Georgeann Maguire
Mechanicsburg, Pennsylvania, USA

This recipe calls for a 13x9 baking dish to serve, but you can use 2 or 3 smaller baking dishes. Assemble and freeze before baking for smaller table gatherings.

Potato Ingredients: 5 lbs. sweet potatoes, boiled with skins on until fork tender 2 eggs (room temperature) ½ C sugar ½ can evaporated milk 1 stick of butter, melted 1 t vanilla	Topping Ingredients: 1 C packed dark brown sugar 1 stick of butter, softened/melted 2 ½—3 C chopped walnuts ⅓ C flour

Directions:
1. After boiling potatoes, drain water, and while hot, quickly peel the potatoes. (Use a fork to hold them.)
2. Put the peeled potatoes into a large bowl and keep them covered as you work. (Use a butter knife and the skins will slide right off.)
3. Put the rest of the potato ingredients in and blend with a mixer until thoroughly combined.
4. After spraying with non-stick spray, turn the potatoes into a 13 X 9 baking dish or evenly distribute potatoes into smaller dishes.
5. In a medium bowl, combine the topping ingredients and crumble on top of potatoes.
6. Cover with aluminum foil.
7. Bake at 350° F for about 35 minutes.
8. Take off foil and insert knife into center. Potatoes should be hot and sides of pan a little bubbly.
9. If not, keep foil off and bake about 10 minutes more, being careful not to burn the walnuts.

Enjoy!

Sweet Potato with Garlic-Tahini Filling

Contributed by Pam Patrick
Pleasanton, Kansas, USA

Ingredients: 1 large sweet potato 2 T sesame tahini 1 t miso paste	¼ t finely chopped garlic 1 t extra virgin olive oil

Directions:
1. Bake sweet potato until soft. Slice sweet potato in two long ways. Place on foil lined baking sheet.
2. Mix together tahini, miso, garlic, and oil and pour over sweet potato.
3. Bake at 400° F for 20-30 minutes. Can also be made with squash, but do not pre-bake.

Corn Fritters

Contributed by Bonnie Musser
Milroy, Pennsylvania, USA

Ingredients:
1 ¾ C flour	2 eggs beaten (or egg substitute)
2 t baking powder	1 14 oz. can creamed corn
2 t salt	1 C fresh corn
½ t black pepper	

Directions:
Mix ingredients. Drop by spoonful into greased pan. Fry both sides.

"Bump di bump di bum!"

~ *Davy Jones*

Garlic Veggies

Contributed by Pam Patrick
Pleasanton, Kansas, USA

Ingredients:
½ small head broccoli, cut into bite size pieces	1 t water
1 carrot, cut into thin diagonal slices	juice of ½ lemon
½ medium zucchini, cut into chunky half moons	1 or 2 cloves garlic, crushed (to taste)
¼ red bell pepper, cut into 1 inch strips	1 ½ t Bragg Liquid Aminos or soy sauce
2 t extra virgin olive oil	(optional)

Directions:
1. Heat oil in large sauté pan over medium-high heat. Add garlic and stir 15-20 seconds.
2. Add carrots and broccoli. Stir frequently for 1 minute.
3. Add water and cover for 1 minute.
4. Uncover and add zucchini and bell pepper. Cook, stirring, for a few minutes until almost tender.
5. Add lemon juice and aminos or soy sauce (if desired) and remove from heat. Veggies should be cooked, but still crisp.

Serves 1

Photograph © Courtesy of Michael G. Bush

Pickled Beets and Eggs

Contributed by Darlene Haines
Crestline, Ohio, USA

Ingredients:
6 or 8 eggs (hard boiled)	3 peppercorns
1 can beets (sliced works best)	¼ bay leaf
½ C vinegar	1 green pepper, sliced (optional)
½ C beet juice	1 small onion, sliced (optional)
2 T sugar	
½ t salt	

Directions:
1. Place the hard boiled eggs and sliced beets into a container.
2. Combine the remaining ingredients and bring to a rolling boil.
3. Pour over eggs and beets.
4. Let stand in refrigerator for at least 2 days. Serve cold.

Caponata

Contributed by Cindy Bryant
Muscatine, Iowa, USA

Ingredients:
1 medium eggplant (about 1 lb.), peeled and cut into ½ inch pieces	2 T capers, drained
	2 T balsamic vinegar
1 can (14 ½ oz.) diced Italian plum tomatoes, un-drained	3 cloves garlic, minced
	1 t dried oregano
1 medium onion, chopped	¼ t salt
1 red pepper cut into ½ inch pieces	⅓ C packed fresh basil cut into thin strips
½ C medium or hot salsa	Italian or French bread, toasted and sliced
¼ C extra virgin olive oil	

Directions:
1. Mix eggplant and tomatoes with juice, onion, pepper, salsa, oil, capers, vinegar, garlic, oregano, and salt in a slow cooker.
2. Cover and cook on low for 7-8 hours or until vegetables are crisp-tender.
3. Stir in basil. Serve at room temperature on toasted bread.

Coconut Collard Greens

Contributed by Pam Patrick
Pleasanton, Kansas, USA

Ingredients:
1 ½ t extra virgin olive oil
¼ yellow onion, diced
½ bunch collard greens, washed, stems
   removed, and cut into ½ inch strips

¼ C coconut milk
⅛ t salt (optional)

Directions:
1. Heat oil in large wok over medium-high heat. Add onion and sauté 10-15 minutes until golden brown and very soft.
2. Add collard greens and stir. Sauté another 10 minutes.
3. Add coconut milk and stir. Sauté another 10 minutes, or until greens are very tender.
4. Add salt.

Can use kale or spinach also.
Serves 1

Grilled Cabbage

Contributed by Nancy Bowman
New Albany, Indiana, USA

Ingredients:
1 head of cabbage
spray butter

Mrs. Dash (seasoning)
heavy duty aluminum foil

Directions:
1. Quarter and core the cabbage head.
2. Place each cabbage quarter in a separate sheet of foil.
3. Spray the cabbage with butter. Sprinkle each with Mrs. Dash.
4. Fold foil around the cabbage to form a sealed pouch.
5. Put the pouches on grill. Cook for approximately 45 minutes to one hour, turning frequently.

Baked Baby Potatoes

Contributed by Lyn Tomkinson
Finksburg, Maryland, USA

Ingredients:
1½ lb. potatoes in chunks	4 t thyme
2 T olive oil	2 t salt
8 cloves garlic, thinly sliced	ground black pepper
4 t rosemary	

Directions:
1. Preheat oven to 425° F.
2. In baking dish, toss potatoes and ½ the oil, garlic, rosemary, thyme, and ½ the salt. Cover with foil.
3. Bake for 20 minutes, then mix in veggies and remaining oil and salt. Cover and cook additional 15 minutes or until potatoes are tender.
4. Increase oven to 450° F, remove foil, and continue cooking 5-10 minutes until potatoes are lightly browned; season and pepper.

Zucchini Tots

Contributed by Grace Ilasi
New York, New York, USA

Ingredients:
1 C zucchini, grated	½ C seasoned bread crumbs
1 large egg	salt and pepper to taste
¼ medium onion, diced	cooking spray
¼ C reduced fat sharp Cheddar cheese, grated	

Directions:
1. Preheat oven to 400° F.
2. Spray mini muffin tin with cooking spray.
3. Grate zucchini into a clean dish towel. Wring all of the excess water out of the zucchini.
4. In a medium bowl, combine all of the ingredients and season with salt and pepper to taste.
5. Fill each muffin section to the top, pushing down on the filling so it is nice and compacted and the muffins don't fall apart when you remove them from tin.
6. Bake for 16-18 minutes or until tops are golden.
7. Use a plastic knife or rubber spatula around the edge of each tot to remove them from the tin.

Crunchy Corn Medley

Contributed by Darlene Burd
Nashville, Tennessee, USA

Ingredients:

2 C frozen peas, thawed	2 celery ribs, chopped
1 can (15-¼ oz.) whole kernel corn, drained	1 medium green pepper, chopped
1 can (15-¼ oz.) white or shoepeg corn, drained	½ C vinegar
1 can (8 oz.) water chestnuts, drained and chopped	½ C sugar
1 jar (4 oz.) diced pimientos, drained	¼ C vegetable oil
8 green onions, thinly diced	1 t salt
	¼ t pepper

Directions:
1. In a large bowl, combine the first 8 ingredients.
2. In a small bowl, combine vinegar, sugar, oil, salt, and pepper; whisk until sugar is dissolved.
3. Pour over mixture; mix well. Cover and refrigerate for at least 3 hours. Stir just before serving. Serve with a slotted spoon.

Curried Cauliflower

Contributed by Pam Patrick
Pleasanton, Kansas, USA

Ingredients:

1 T extra virgin olive oil	½ large head of cauliflower, stem removed, cut into large florets
½ to 1 t curry powder	½ t salt (or to taste)

Directions:
1. Preheat oven to 400° F. In a small nonstick sauté pan, heat oil over medium-low heat.
2. Add curry powder and stir for 15-30 seconds until fragrant (don't allow it to burn).
3. Place cauliflower in bowl and add oil/curry mixture and salt; mix well.
4. Arrange in single layer in a glass baking dish and bake 20 to 25 minutes or until tender, stirring gently a few times.

Serves 1

Curried Potatoes and Peas
(Alu Mattar)

Contributed by Marian Allen
Corydon, Indiana, USA

Ingredients:

¼ C (60 ml) ghee
1 T (15 ml) finely chopped fresh ginger
1 T (15 ml) finely chopped garlic
½ C (125 ml) finely chopped onion or shallots
salt to taste
1 t (5 ml) ground cumin
½ t (2 ml) turmeric
¼ t (1 ml) cayenne pepper, or to taste
2 - 10 oz. (280 g each) packages frozen green
    peas

1 large potato, peeled and cut into ½-inch
    (1 cm) cubes
1 C (250 ml) water
3 T (45 ml) finely chopped cilantro (coriander
    leaves)
3 medium tomatoes, finely chopped
½ t (2 ml) garam masala**

Directions:
1. Heat the ghee in a heavy pot over moderate heat until it is very hot. Add the ginger and garlic and cook for 30 seconds.
2. Add the onion and salt and cook, stirring frequently, until the onion is soft and golden brown, about 8 minutes.
3. Stir in the cumin, turmeric, and cayenne, followed by the tomatoes. Cook, stirring frequently, until most of the liquid has evaporated and the mixture forms a thick paste, about 5 minutes.
4. Add the peas and potatoes and stir to coat them with the tomato mixture. Stir in the water and bring to a boil, stirring frequently.
5. Reduce the heat and simmer covered for 10 minutes, until the potatoes are tender.
6. Sprinkle with chopped cilantro and garam masala and serve immediately.

Serves 4 to 6

Editor note:
*ghee is a type of clarified butter (you may substitute canola oil or olive oil).
**garam masala is a blend of spices that often includes cumin, cinnamon, coriander, cardamom, cloves, and nutmeg among others.
Both of these products are available online, or at some specialty retailers.

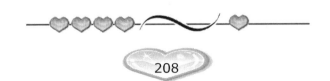

Marinated Carrots

Contributed by Debbie Garey
Chicago, Illinois, USA

Ingredients:	
5 C cooked carrots	½ C salad oil
1 medium sliced onion	1 C sugar
1 small bell pepper	1 t dry mustard
1 (10 oz.) can tomato soup	1 t salt
1 t black pepper	1 t Worcestershire sauce

Directions:
Mix together, cover tightly, and marinate over night.

Second Saturday Sweet Potatoes

Contributed by Marian Allen
Corydon, Indiana, USA

Ingredients:	
sweet potatoes	fresh or dried rosemary
honey	bread
vegan margarine	

Directions:
1. Bake sweet potatoes and cool. Can be done a day ahead.
2. Mix and warm equal parts honey and vegan margarine. Put in some fresh or dried rosemary and let sit for a couple of hours to infuse the liquid with the herb.
3. Toast some bread, cut or break into cubes, and toss with more melted margarine. Spread buttered toast cubes in bottom of baking dish.
4. Slice baked sweet potatoes thickly and place, one layer deep, over bread. Cut crosses in each potato slice. Spoon honey-butter over potatoes. Can be covered and refrigerated until ready to finish.
5. Bake, covered, at 350° F for 30 minutes.

Parsnips à la Beverlie

Contributed by Beverlie Tyler and Michael G. Bush
(Monkees photographer)

Ingredients:	salt
parsnips	pepper
olive oil	

Directions:
1. Cut parsnips julienne style.
2. Toss parsnips on a cookie sheet with olive oil, salt, and pepper.
3. Cook at 350 ° for 15-20 minutes.

And now for the story behind the recipes:

Spending so much time with David over the years you do have to eat! You can't eat at restaurants every day (especially in Beavertown!), and since I don't cook at all, I had to leave my large appetite in his hands. David was a very modest eater. He used to lecture me all time about cutting down the amount of food I ate on a regular basis, but I would logically explain to him that I was twice his size, and if he expected me to take a bullet for him, I had to keep up my strength! That being said, with him in charge in the kitchen I never had a bad meal! Whether we were in Beavertown or Florida, one of the things that was first on the menu was what he called his 50 bean soup. Here is Beverlie's version* of it which David enjoyed tremendously. Also, the first time I ever had parsnips was in Beavertown. I believe they came out of his own garden there and when he pulled these golden brown crunchy delights from the oven, I was hooked! Beverlie tried them for the first time during the Oliver! run in Miami and has been making them for me ever since...

Bon Appetit!!!
~ Michael G. Bush

*Beverlie's version of 50 Bean Soup can be found on page 79.

Photograph © Courtesy of Michael G. Bush

Micky, Peter, Davy, and Michael G. Bush

Lentil and Vegetable Medley

Contributed by Connie Gee
Las Vegas, Nevada, USA

Ingredients:	
2 ½ C water	4 t vegetable oil
1 (14 oz.) can vegetable broth	½ t salt
1 C lentils, washed and sorted	½ C chopped carrots
1 t chili powder	½ C chopped onion
½ t thyme, crushed	2 garlic cloves, minced
⅛ t cracked pepper	1 C chopped tomato

Directions:
1. In a medium saucepan over medium heat, heat water, broth, lentils, chili powder, thyme, and pepper to boiling.
2. Reduce to low; cover and simmer about 30-35 minutes until lentils are tender.
3. Meanwhile, in a large skillet, heat oil over medium-high heat.
4. Add carrot, onion, salt, and garlic and sauté about 7 minutes until tender.
5. Stir in tomatoes; cook about 2 minutes more.
6. Add vegetable sauté mixture to lentils and simmer uncovered for 2-3 minutes until heated through.
7. Taste and add more salt and pepper if desired.
8. Serve with white rice and top with non-fat plain yogurt.

Serves 4

Gorgonzola Baked Potatoes

Contributed by Helen Kensick
South Hadley, Massachusetts, USA

Ingredients:	
potatoes	chives
sour cream	Gorgonzola cheese

Directions:
1. Bake potatoes for 40 minutes at 375° F.
2. Scoop out contents of each and mix with sour cream, chives, and Gorgonzola cheese.
3. Put mixture back into shelled potatoes.
4. Bake for additional 20-30 minutes.

Photograph © Courtesy of Dawn Wells

Turnips

I am not a vegetarian but I adore veggies. Can't do a day without them. If you or your kids do not like turnips, my mother taught me to appreciate them by doing this... Shred the turnips and stir fry them with real butter, salt, pepper, and garlic salt. Kids will love them. Stir frying them shredded takes the strong taste away.

~ Dawn Wells
Star of Gilligan's Island

Zucchini Patties

Contributed by Bonnie Musser
Milroy, Pennsylvania, USA

Ingredients	
2 C grated zucchini	red pepper flakes and/or tabasco to taste
1 ½ C flour	2 eggs beaten (or egg substitute)
1 T minced onion	½ C grated cheese (Cheddar is best)
¼ t ground cumin	

Directions:
Mix all ingredients. Drop by spoonful into greased pan. Fry both sides.

Parmesan Crumb Coated
Brussels Sprouts

Contributed by Josh Kilmer-Purcell and Brent Ridge
Stars of the reality TV series, The Fabulous Beekman Boys
Cookbook authors and winners of the 21st season of CBS's Amazing Race
Sharon Springs, New York, USA

Ingredients:
1 ½ lbs Brussels sprouts, trimmed, halved
    through the stem end
2 T extra-virgin olive oil
2 cloves garlic, thinly sliced
½ t coarse salt

1 C grated Parmesan cheese
½ C Panko breadcrumbs
2 T unsalted butter, cut into bits

Directions:
1. Preheat the oven to 400° F.
2. Cook the Brussels sprouts in a large pot of boiling salted water until softened but not falling apart, about 5 minutes. (Timing will vary depending upon the size of the Brussels sprouts.) Drain well.
3. Place the oil and garlic in a 9x13 inch baking pan and roast until fragrant, about 5 minutes.
4. Add the Brussels sprouts and salt and toss to coat.
5. Toss together the Parmesan and breadcrumbs in a small bowl and scatter the mixture over the Brussels sprouts. Dot with the butter.
6. Bake until the crumbs are golden brown and the Brussels sprouts are tender and piping hot, about 15 minutes.

Note: The Brussels sprouts can be prepared through step 2 up to a day ahead. To store them, once they've been well drained, line a storage container with paper towels. Place the sprouts in the container and refrigerate.

Photograph © Courtesy of Beekman1802.com

**Brent Ridge and
Josh Kilmer-Purcell
The Beekman Boys**

Rice

Spanish Rice

Contributed by Cathy DeFini
Mentor, Ohio, USA

Ingredients:
1 C of rice	1 small can of tomato paste
1 medium onion, diced	oil to coat pan
1 large green pepper, diced	2 ½ C of water
5 bay leaves	1 t of red pepper flakes
3 cloves of garlic, sliced	

Directions:
1. Place enough oil in bottom of pan to coat (about 3 tablespoons) depending on size of pan you are using.
2. Sauté onions, green peppers, and garlic until soft.
3. Add whole can of tomato paste and bay leaves. Mix well while stirring.
4. Add 1 cup of rice and the water to the pan. Stir all ingredients well.
5. Place cover on the pan. After about 10 minutes, stir well, cover with lid, and simmer for 20 minutes.
6. Fluff with a fork and enjoy!!!

One Pot Curried Rice
With Vegetables

Contributed by Andrea Gilbey
Cheshunt, Hertfordshire, UK

Ingredients:
1 medium potato	½ t cumin
1 small onion	½ t turmeric
6 mushrooms	½ t ground coriander
4 oz./100g frozen mixed vegetables	1 t concentrated tomato puree
4 oz./100g long grain rice	1 vegetable stock cube
1 clove garlic, crushed	black pepper to taste
chili to taste	2 t mango chutney
¼ t ground ginger	

Directions:
1. Chop the potatoes into cubes and cook until soft but not disintegrating.
2. Drain potatoes and place in a heavy based frying pan.
3. Chop the onion and mushrooms and add these and all other ingredients to the potatoes.
4. Add boiling water until everything is just covered, bring to the boil, stirring, then reduce the heat and simmer until nearly all the water is absorbed, leaving just enough sauce to keep the dish moist.

Makes enough for 2 to 3 people as a main dish

Caribbean Rice and Peas

Contributed by Cindy Bryant
Muscatine, Iowa, USA

Ingredients:

1 ¼ C quick cook unconverted long-grain rice
¾ C gungo peas or red kidney beans, soaked
    and cooked but still firm
3 ⅔ C water

2 oz. creamed coconut, chopped
1 t dried thyme or 1 t fresh thyme leave
1 small onion stuck with 6 whole cloves
salt and ground pepper

Directions:
1. Put the rice and peas or kidney beans into a large saucepan with water, coconut, thyme, onion, and seasoning.
2. Bring to a boil, stirring until coconut melts. Cover and simmer gently for 20 minutes.
3. Remove the lid and allow to cook for 5 minutes to reduce down any excess liquid. Remove from heat and stir occasionally to separate the grains. Rice should be quite dry.

"You can put me in the basement or the penthouse; it doesn't matter to me."

~ Davy Jones

Okra and Rice

Contributed by Mary Villanueva
Corpus Christi, Texas, USA

Ingredients:

2 T olive oil
3-4 cloves of garlic
3 carrots, sliced
1 medium onion, sliced
½ bell pepper, sliced
4+1 C water

1 large bag of cut okra
2 C of white rice
salt (to personal taste)
2 habanero peppers, sliced (optional)

Directions:
1. Heat oil in a medium sized saucepan and sauté the garlic.
2. Add the carrots, onion, peppers, and 4 cups of water. Boil until carrots are medium soft.
3. Add the last cup of water and boil on high for 10 minutes.
4. Lower heat and boil on medium for another 10 minutes.
5. Serve with salt and butter if desired.

Brown Rice and Asparagus with Tofu

Contributed by Jody Proetta
Putnam Valley, New York, USA

Ingredients:

3 C of cooked brown rice
3 C of asparagus sliced diagonally into 1 inch pieces
2 large cloves of elephant garlic minced (4 cloves of regular garlic if you can't find elephant garlic)
1 large Vidalia sweet onion chopped (You can use red onion if you prefer.)

6 sun dried tomatoes cut into thin pieces
½ C of grated vegan Parmesan cheese (You can buy it already grated in container.)
olive oil for sautéing (I use about 2 T)
sprinkle of parsley and basil leaf to taste
sea salt and pepper to taste
2 half inch slices of tofu cut off of tofu block, cubed

Directions:
1. Sauté the onions and garlic until translucent and soft.
2. Add your tomatoes and asparagus and sauté' until tender. You may like it softer.
3. When done, turn off the heat and add your Parmesan cheese (add as much as you and your family like).
4. Stir into the asparagus mixture and add your salt and pepper to taste.
5. Take your cubed tofu and add this to your brown rice.
6. Warm up your already cooked brown rice and tofu in a large microwave safe bowl.
7. When the rice is nice and warm, add your asparagus mixture and sprinkle your parsley and basil on top for taste and garnish.

Makes a nice side dish, or for vegans and vegetarians a main meal!

Rice and Chili Casserole

Contributed by Jerri Keele
Salem, Oregon, USA

Ingredients:

3 C cooked rice
½ lb. sharp Cheddar cheese, grated
½ lb. Monterey jack cheese, grated

1 pint sour cream
1 can roasted green chilies (4 oz.)

Directions:
1. Mix all ingredients.
2. Bake at 350° F for 1 hour.

Angela's Vegetarian Risotto

Contributed by Angela Painter
Cheshunt, Hertfordshire, UK

Ingredients:
8 oz. Arborio rice	one litre of hot vegetable stock
two sticks of celery, finely chopped	grated Parmesan or other cheese to taste (can
one large onion, finely chopped	be omitted if vegan)
one garlic clove, finely chopped	chopped parsley or basil to taste
1 oz. butter and 2 T olive oil (or 3 T of olive oil	
if vegan)	

Directions:
1. In a large frying pan, heat the olive oil and butter until butter has melted.
2. Add the onions, celery, and garlic, and gently fry until transparent and soft and slightly sticky. This will take a good 10 minutes as you need them to cook well but not go brown.
3. Add the Arborio rice and dry fry until all the rice grains are covered in oil, about 2 minutes.
4. Add about one third of the hot stock, and stir until the stock has been absorbed.
5. Add the next third and continue as above.
6. Keep adding stock until the rice is cooked. This will take about 20 minutes or more as Arborio rice swells up much more than the usual rice we tend to use. Taste to check the grains are soft. You may need to add more stock (or if you have run out, hot water from the kettle!)
7. When cooked, add a third of your grated cheese and stir through. Season.

To serve: Place on warmed plates. Sprinkle over remaining cheese and chopped parsley or basil if required. Really good served with roasted tomatoes!
Serves 4

"Warming the Winter" Rice Pilaf

Contributed by Megan Bartlett
Keene, New Hampshire, USA

I like to make this in February, when it feels like the snow will never leave.

Ingredients:
4 T butter	salt
2-3 T olive oil	allspice
1 sweet onion, chopped	parsley
½ C pine nuts	2 ½ C hot, cooked rice (I prefer jasmine rice)
1 C dried cranberries	

Directions:
1. Sauté first three together until fragrant and the onion is translucent.
2. Stir in pine nuts and cranberries. Heat together until completely warmed through.
3. Season to taste with salt, allspice, and parsley.
4. Gently fold in rice.
5. Serve immediately.

Rice Noodles with Tofu and Broccoli

Contributed by Jody Proetta
Putnam Valley, New York, USA

Protein, fiber, vitamins---lots of good things!

Ingredients:
3 C broccoli florets
6 cloves of garlic minced
2 large red peppers cut into 1 inch pieces
4 T of regular soy sauce
2 t minced fresh ginger

4 T canola oil
3 medium shallots, sliced
1 package (14 oz.) extra firm tofu
1 package (8 to 10 oz.) wide rice noodles

Directions:

1. Place your rice noodles in a large bowl and cover with boiling water. Let them soak for about 30 minutes or until soft.
2. Cut your tofu crosswise into 2 pieces and each should be about 1 inch thick. Wrap each piece of tofu with paper towels. Place a cutting board on your counter and place your pieces of tofu side by side on the cutting board wrapped in paper towels. Put another cutting board on the top of the tofu. The pressure of the cutting board on the top will enable the tofu to release the moisture that is inside of it. Let the tofu sit like that for 20 minutes. Once tofu is done, cut tofu into little squares of bite-sized pieces.
3. Heat your oil in a wok or large skillet, add the tofu, and cook until browned over medium-high heat. Remove tofu from wok or skillet. The browning process should only take about 5 minutes.
4. Next, add your shallots, red pepper, garlic, and ginger, and stir fry for 3 to 4 minutes. Then add your broccoli and stir fry for a couple of minutes, and then cover and cook for a few minutes longer until broccoli is tender. Now drain your noodles which should be done by now and stir into your wok or skillet. Add tofu and your soy sauce. Stir fry about 8 minutes or until noodles are coated and flavors are blended. Enjoy.

You can substitute the rice noodles with brown rice if you wish.

Rice Salad

Contributed by Celine Allan
Dallas, Texas, USA

Ingredients:
1 C long grain rice (cook according to directions)
1 C finely chopped celery
½ C grated dill pickle
¼ C grated onion

T finely chopped bell pepper
1 small jar (2 oz.) pimento
2 hard boiled eggs grated
1 C mayonnaise

Directions:
Mix well. Chill thoroughly.

Rice and Spinach Pilaf

Contributed by Patricia Walsh
Arlington, Massachusetts, USA

Ingredients:
1½ C rice, Uncle Bens or similar
1 small onion, chopped
½ package frozen/fresh spinach

3 cubes vegetable bouillon
1 stick butter
2 cans vegetable broth

Directions:
1. Sauté onion in butter and add broth, bouillon, and spinach and bring to boil.
2. Add rice and simmer for 30 minutes.

Serves 4

Basic Risotto

Contributed by Megan Bartlett
Keene, New Hampshire, USA

Ingredients:
4-5 T butter
2-3 T olive oil
2 C Arborio rice (must be Arborio - anything
    else will lack the creamy texture)
vegetable stock (about 8 C)
2 T Marsala wine

2 oz. reduced fat (NOT fat free) cream cheese
    or ⅓ C shredded Parmesan cheese
1 T parsley
1 t salt (optional - skip if the stock is well
    salted)

Directions:
1. In a deep frying pan on medium/high heat, sauté the rice in the oil and butter.
2. When the rice is coated and lightly browned, add 1 cup of stock. (I use this amount for the first bit of liquid going in simply because the rice and pan will be so hot that much of it will immediately turn to steam.)
3. Reduce heat to medium.
4. Gently and continuously stir until stock is absorbed. Each time the stock is absorbed, add more at the rate of ½ cup at a time and keep stirring as it cooks.
5. Continue until rice is cooked through and the texture is creamy. (Expect to use 8 cups of stock, at least. If you run out of stock, it's okay to switch to water.)
6. When the rice is cooked and creamy, add Marsala wine, cheese, parsley, and salt.
7. Stir gently as cheese melts and alcohol evaporates.

This works as a brilliant base to any risotto recipe and can also be served as is. The best part of making risotto is its malleability; you really can add whatever tickles the fancy and harmonizes with the season. For spring and summer, I make the preceding. For fall and winter, simply switch out the peppers and asparagus with cubes of butternut squash and apples.

Risotto Primavera

Contributed by Megan Bartlett
Keene, New Hampshire, USA

Ingredients:
2 T olive oil
2-3 C chopped (favorite vegetables)
a pinch each of salt, garlic powder, and rosemary
1-2 t brown sugar

risotto (see recipe for "Basic Risotto" on previous page)
fresh Parmesan cheese

Directions:
1. In a separate pan, heat oil and veggies.
2. Sauté and season to taste with salt, garlic powder, and rosemary.
3. As it cooks, sprinkle it with brown sugar.
4. Cook slowly, allowing the sugar to caramelize the vegetables.
5. Gently fold vegetables into cooked risotto.
6. Garnish with freshly grated Parmesan cheese and a sprinkle of parsley.

I use a mixture of sweet onions, mushrooms, peppers, zucchini, and asparagus. It's tempting to add the veggies while cooking the rice - I tried it once, thinking it would add to the flavor. Essentially, it changed the flavor, but not for the better. Think sautéed onion vs. boiled onion... *Definitely* cook the rice separately.

Serve with a crisp salad and a baguette.

Vegetable and Rice Casserole

Contributed by Marian Allen
Corydon, Indiana, USA

Ingredients:
1 can cream of celery or cream of mushroom soup
1 can water
¾ C uncooked rice
½ t onion powder or chopped sautéed onion to taste

pepper
2 C frozen mixed vegetables or 2 cans mixed vegetables (drained) or any durn kind of cooked or semi-cooked vegetables you durn well please
seasonings to taste

Directions:
1. Grease a 2 quart shallow baking dish.
2. Mix all ingredients.
3. Cover and bake at 375° F for about 50 minutes. If desired, top with shredded cheese.
4. Let stand for 10 minutes. Stir and serve.

Munchie Burgers

Contributed by Christine Loch
Bedminster, Pennsylvania, USA

Ingredients:

1 T sunflower or peanut oil
1 ½ C finely chopped mushrooms (I use
    pre-sliced mushrooms to save time.)
2 C cooked brown rice
1 ½ C gluten-free panko bread crumbs
¾ C chopped walnuts (Walnuts are very soft and
    can crumble easily with a good rolling pin.)

4 eggs
2 T fruity marmalade (any type of pineapple or
    peach marinade would be great; try some
    interesting fruity vinaigrettes.)
a dash of salt and pepper

Directions:
1. Cook rice a few days before hand and let it sit in the refrigerator. This will allow the starches to slightly solidify and become nice and sticky.
2. Heat oil in a large, deep skillet and add mushrooms. Cook for just a few minutes (about 2 minutes) until they soften.
3. Remove skillet from heat and add rice, bread crumbs, walnuts, eggs, marmalade, salt, and pepper. Not everyone has a big, deep skillet, so transferring to a large ceramic bowl to mix is fine; you just want to retain as much warmth as possible so it mixes better. A plastic or metal bowl will cool too fast.
4. Make your burgers! Form the mixture into nice size burgers.
5. Place burgers in refrigerator for at least 30 minutes. I like to freeze them and grill as needed.
6. Grill Time!! Grill for 5 to 6 minutes on each side. Baste frequently with the oil. Grill some tomato slices and onions (in foil) alongside burgers. For the last few minutes of grilling try adding a slice of cheese on the burger.

Butternut Vegan Quick Brown Rice

Contributed by Jody Proetta
PutnamValley, New York, USA

Ingredients:

2 C of cooked brown rice
½ C vegan soy Parmesan cheese
1 (14.5 oz.) can vegan butternut squash soup

garlic powder
onion powder
sea salt and pepper to taste

Directions:
1. Place all ingredients in a large sauce pot and place oven burner on low/medium heat, stirring often until all ingredients are warmed well to hot.
2. Stir well once again before serving. I usually serve this with a veggie burger and a romaine lettuce salad. It is nice and quick—especially easy for busy working moms.

Black Beans and Rice

Contributed by Pam Patrick
Pleasanton, Kansas, USA

Ingredients:
¾ C cooked brown rice
½ C canned low sodium black beans
¼ t extra virgin olive oil
⅛ t chili powder

1 pinch ground cumin
¼ t ground coriander
1 t Bragg Liquid Aminos (or soy sauce)
salt (to taste)

Directions:
1. While rice is cooking, heat beans gently in saucepan until very hot.
2. Drain and return to pan. Add oil, spices, aminos, and salt. Stir well.
3. Gently fold beans into cooked rice.

Great with salsa and guacamole in a tortilla shell!
Serves 1

Last Train to Clarksville Rice

Contributed by Jerry Phares
Clarksville, Indiana, USA

Ingredients:
¾ C long grain rice
1¾ C V-8 juice (or other vegetable juice)

1 (15 oz.) can tomatoes and chilies (Ro-tel)

Directions:
1. Prepare rice as normal, using the vegetable juice instead of water.
2. While the rice cooks, heat up the tomatoes and chilies.
3. Add tomato mixture to cooked rice, stir and serve.

Note: Instant rice may be substituted, but increase amount to 1½ C, and use only 1½ C vegetable juice. Bring to a boil, stir, cover, remove from heat and let sit for 5 minutes. Fluff with fork, then add tomatoes and chilies.

Add vegetable juice if mixture is too dry. Heat, stirring constantly, if mixture is too loose.

Desserts

Photograph © Courtesy of Tiffany DeFini

On June 15, 2013, Annabel Jones was surprised with a cake for her upcoming 25th birthday at the Beavertown, Pennsylvania memorial for her father.

Rose Marie's Dream Cake

Contributed by Rose Marie
Star of the Dick Van Dyke Show and guest star on The Monkees

(This was Lucille Ball's favorite dessert. Rose Marie always fixed it
when Lucy and Desi came over for dinner.)

Ingredients:	
½ C Crisco	2 eggs
½ C butter	1 C white sugar
½ C brown sugar	1 C walnuts, broken in pieces
2 C flour	1 can coconut
¼ t salt	

Directions:
1. Cream butter and Crisco. Add brown sugar. Add flour and salt. Mix well.
2. Press dough into a jellyroll pan or shallow baking dish and bake in 325 degree oven for 15 minutes.
3. While this is baking, beat the 2 eggs and 1 cup of white sugar in mixmaster. Fold in 1 cup of broken walnut pieces. Spread this mixture over entire top of cake and sprinkle top with 1 can of coconut.
4. Bake another 15 minutes until brown on top.

Allow to cool and cut into squares. Serves many!

Photograph © Courtesy of Rhino Entertainment Company

Rose Marie with Davy in *The Monkees* episode "*Monkee Mother*"

Toffee Apple Rice Pudding

Contributed by Andrea Gilbey
Cheshunt, Hertfordshire, UK

Ingredients: 4 oz. pudding rice 4 T soft brown sugar 2 pints soy milk	1 eating apple or small cooking apple, cored and sliced thinly

Directions:
1. Place half the rice in a 1 pint dish (casserole base or pie dish).
2. Spread half the sugar on top. Place the sliced apple in a layer on top of the sugar.
3. Spread the rest of the sugar on the apple.
4. Spread the rest of the rice on top.
5. Pour 12 fl. oz. milk over the layers and bake at 300° F/150° C for an hour.
6. Remove from the oven and push a spoon down through the layers to the bottom in half a dozen places.
7. Pour half the remaining milk over so it dribbles down through the layers and bake for another 30 minutes.
8. Repeat the last 2 steps.

The rice should be soft and fluffy, the top crusty and golden, and the sugar and apple
should spread sweet toffee flavours through the whole dish.

Oreo Balls

Contributed by Cindy Bryant
Muscatine, Iowa, USA

I made these for Davy.

Ingredients: 1 package of Oreo cookies 1 block cream cheese, softened	1 pack cooking chocolate (Hershey's semi-sweet chocolate chips are the best)

Directions:
1. Place Oreo cookies in a bag/blender and smash/blend until it is the consistency of dirt.
2. Mix the softened cream cheese into the smashed Oreos.
3. Roll the mixture into balls.
4. Melt chocolate in the microwave.
5. Cover balls in chocolate then leave to set in the fridge.

Davy's Heavenly Devonshire Tartlets

Contributed by Lucille Ryder
Westhampton Beach, New York, USA
(originally printed in a 60s teen magazine as a Davy Jones Recipe)

Ingredients:
8 oz. cream cheese
½ C sugar
¼ C butter
2 egg yolks
2 C heavy sweet cream

½ t salt
¼ t nutmeg
1 T orange juice
1 box pastry mix

Directions:
1. Mix up pastry mix and line muffin tin with the mix.
2. Mix the cheese with the butter, sugar, yolks, nutmeg, and orange juice.
3. Prick the pastry and fill with the cheese mixture.
4. Bake in hot oven (450° F) for 10 min., and then reduce heat to 325° F and bake an additional 15 min. longer or until firm and brown.
5. When done, turn upside down to cool on a sheet of paper.
6. Spread each tartlet with your favorite jelly or jam and top with the heavy sweet cream.

Cherry Sorbet

Contributed by Cindy Bryant
Muscatine, Iowa, USA

Try this cherry sorbet recipe with
some more chopped cherries on top.

Ingredients:
4 C pitted sour or sweet cherries, fresh or
   frozen (not thawed)

1 C water
2-4 T confectioners' sugar or superfine sugar

Directions:
1. Puree cherries, water, and sugar to taste in a blender until smooth.
2. Strain through a fine sieve, pressing on the solids to extract as much liquid as possible. Discard solids.
3. Process in an ice cream maker according to the manufacturer's directions until firm and slushy.
4. Transfer to an airtight container and freeze until ready to serve.

Freeze in an airtight container for up to 1 week.

8 servings, about ½ cup each

Fun Chocolate-Dipped Bites

Contributed by Florence Henderson
Star of The Brady Bunch

Ingredients:	
1-2 C melted semi-sweet chocolate	strawberries, washed and well dried
1-2 C melted white chocolate	dried apricots
pretzels	bananas, peeled, cut into 4 equal pieces with a
butter cookies	popsicle stick inserted into each, then frozen

Directions:
1. Cover cookie sheets or baking pans with wax paper. Set aside.
2. Stir each of the melted chocolates until smooth. Zap them in the microwave if they start to set up as you are using them.
3. Dip the pretzels halfway into the chocolates and lay them on the wax paper. Repeat with the butter cookies, berries, apricots, and frozen banana pieces. Dip each only halfway so guests can handle them without getting their fingers messy. You can double-dip if desired.
4. Place the "bites" in the refrigerator until ready to serve them.
5. Arrange the "bites" in decorative patterns on serving platters.

Photographs by Ken Wilkinson
© Courtesy of Hazel Wilkinson

Florence Henderson
with Davy Jones
on TNN's *Country Kitchen*
March, 1991

Parkin Cake

Contributed by Cindy Bryant
Muscatine, Iowa, USA

Parkin is essentially the Northern English form of gingerbread. Different Parkins are characterized by where they are made and Yorkshire Parkin, one of the most famous, is made using oats. Yorkshire Parkin is eaten on Bonfire Night, November 5th, celebrating the famous failure of Guy Fawkes to blow up the House of Parliament in 1605. Guy Fawkes was a Yorkshireman. This is a celebration David's family was very involved in as a community event when he was a child. The last treat I made for David was this Parkin cake when he performed at the Isle of Capri in Bettendorf, Iowa on Guy Fawkes Day, November 5, 2011, thanks to a suggestion from his sister, Hazel Wilkinson. This Parkin recipe is easy to make and creates a lovely, moist, sticky cake. Although you can eat the cake almost immediately, it gets sticker if you wrap and store it for several days. The other beauty of this cake is that it keeps really well in an airtight tin. It can be eaten as a cake or warm as a pudding with a dollop of custard and it makes an interesting alternative to sponge cake in a trifle, giving it a more autumny flavor than a light summer trifle.

Prep: Heat oven to 275° F

Ingredients:	
(Note: It is not recommended that you substitute in this recipe. It can be done but it won't taste the same.)	7 oz. flour
	4 t ground ginger
	2 t nutmeg
8 oz. soft butter	1 t mixed spice (NOT allspice—see recipe below)
4 oz. soft, dark brown sugar	2 large eggs, beaten
2 oz. treacle (black strap molasses)	1 T milk
5 oz. oatmeal	
7 oz. golden syrup (similar to Karo Syrup but does not have vanilla. It is not recommended to use Karo.)	

Directions:
1. Grease an 8x8 inch square cake pan.
2. In a large heavy based saucepan melt together the butter, sugar, treacle, and golden syrup over a gentle heat. Do not allow the mixture to boil; you simply need to melt these together.
3. In a large, spacious baking bowl, stir together all the dry ingredients. Gradually add the melted butter mixtures, stirring to coat all the dry ingredients, and mix thoroughly. Gradually beat in the eggs a few tablespoons at a time. Finally add the milk and stir well.
4. Pour the mixture into the prepared pan and cook for 1½ hours until firm and set and a dark golden brown.
5. Remove the Parkin from the oven and leave to cool in pan.
6. Once cool, store the Parkin in an airtight pan for a MINIMUM of 3 days if you can resist eating it. You can leave it up to a week before eating and the flavors really develop and the mixture softens even further and becomes moist and sticky. The Parkin will keep up to two weeks in an airtight container.

(I am guessing that in spite of the oatmeal this is not a heart-smart recipe...LOL!)

To make mixed spice combine:	
1 T cinnamon, ground	½ t ginger, ground
1 t coriander, ground	¼ t allspice, ground
1 t nutmeg, ground	¼ t cloves, ground

Fresh Berry Pie

Contributed by Karen Baker
Redmond, Washington, USA

You can make this with whatever kind of fresh berries you prefer.
My favorite is raspberry.

Ingredients:
9 inch pie shell (baked) or use a pre-made shell	⅔ C water + ⅓ C water
1 quart of cleaned berries	scant ⅓ C sugar or to taste
3 oz. of Tofutti Better Than Cream Cheese, softened	3 T cornstarch
1 C berries	

Directions:
1. Spread the "cream cheese" on the sides and bottom of the pie-crust after it has cooled.
2. In a saucepan, simmer the berries, ⅔ cup of water, and sugar together for approximately 3 minutes. Stir while cooking so it doesn't scorch.
3. In a cup or small bowl, mix cornstarch with ⅓ cup of water until there are no lumps.
4. Pour this mixture into the saucepan with the cooking berry mixture.
5. Cook for 1 minute or until sauce has thickened.
6. Cool the sauce.
7. While sauce is cooling, arrange the remaining three cups of berries in the pie shell.
8. Pour the cooled sauce over the berries in the pie shell and refrigerate until set, about 2 hours.

When you use sweet ripe berries, this is the yummiest pie you'll ever have.

I Really Love...This
(No-Bake Chocolate Cheesecake)

Contributed by Daryl Goldfarb
Seattle, Washington, USA

Ingredients:
1 pre-made pie-crust (I use Keebler's Graham Cracker Crust)	Pure vanilla extract or any liqueur to taste
1 box of soft tofu (unrefrigerated type)	Sliced berries, bananas, or other fruit, and/or non-dairy topping for garnish
1 lb. or 1 bag of semi-sweet chocolate chips (I like Ghirardelli)	

Directions:
1. Put all the chocolate chips in a microwave-safe bowl and melt them. This happens fast, so if you have a very powerful microwave, watch carefully! It normally takes only a minute or two. Stir halfway, as you don't want them to burn.
2. When chips are melted, drain and dry the tofu. Beat the tofu and the vanilla or liqueur into the chips at high-speed until smooth.
3. Pour mixture into the crust. Refrigerate until it sets and then add the toppings.

Yum!

What Am I Doin' Hangin' Cinnamon Rounds

Contributed by Peggy Hanson
Seattle, Washington, USA

Ingredients:
1 C hot water	1 C whole wheat flour
1 t salt	2 t dry yeast
2 T butter or margarine	4 T butter or margarine, softened
¼ C honey	1 C brown sugar
1 C white flour	1 T cinnamon
1 C oat flour – makes the rolls softer	

Directions:
1. In a bread maker, place the water, salt, butter or margarine, and honey. Follow this with the flours. Make a dent in the mounded flours* and place the yeast in it. Set the bread maker for "dough" setting and start.
2. When that is completed, roll out the dough on a large piece of wax paper. It should be rolled out to a 10" x 12" rectangle.
3. Spread the butter or margarine thickly onto the dough, then sprinkle on the brown sugar followed by the cinnamon.
4. Roll it up so that you have a 12" long roll of dough.
5. Cut with a bread knife into 12 slices and place touching each other on a greased cookie sheet; insulated is best so the bottoms won't get too done.
6. Preheat the oven by turning it to 200° F for 5 minutes, then turn it off.
7. Place the wax paper over the rolls and put them in the warm oven to rise for 20-30 minutes.
8. Take them out, take off the wax paper, and preheat the oven to 350° F.
9. Bake for 15 minutes. When they are done, allow a couple of minutes to cool, then turn them over with a spatula.

The combo of equal parts oat, white, and whole wheat flours works well for many breads, making the result light and wholesome.

Makes 12 Rounds

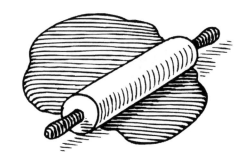

Lemon Curd/Cheese

Contributed by Hazel Wilkinson, Davy's sister
Manchester, UK

Ingredients:	
3 lemons (washed) 3 eggs 4 oz. butter	8 oz. loaf sugar (Loaf sugar is the old grocer's way of selling sugar, in a compressed block. No different from castor sugar.) jars and lids (for storing)

Directions:
1. Beat eggs with the grated zest and juice of the lemons.
2. Place in a strong pan (a heavy based pan such as a preserving pan or copper bottomed sauce pan, so you don't burn the bottom out!).
3. Heat the mixture gently, stirring it so it doesn't stick to the bottom or burn, until it's thick and smooth.
4. Heat the jars by immersing them in hot water (so they don't crack), pour the hot mixture in, cover with greased paper or jar lids, and leave to cool.
5. Serve on crispy bread.

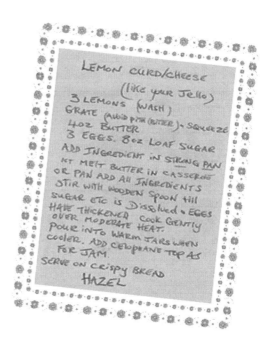

Photograph © Courtesy of Hazel Wilkinson

**Davy and Hazel
with one of Davy's horses
in Indiantown, Florida**

Christmas Pud

Contributed by Hazel Wilkinson, Davy's sister
Manchester, UK

Davy liked this recipe!

Traditionally you make Christmas pudding on Stir Up Sunday, which is the last Sunday before Advent. Everyone in the household gets a stir, and you make a wish while you stir, but you mustn't tell anyone the wish! People used to put silver tokens in the puddings. If you found a thimble it meant you would stay a spinster, a button meant a bachelor for life, and a sixpenny piece meant you'd be rich! That's the history, now the method!!!

Ingredients:	
8 oz. currants, raisins, and sultanas	¼ t nutmeg
6 oz. whole meal bread crumbs	4 fluid oz. sherry
1 oz. almonds	3 eggs
8 oz. brown sugar	lemon rind, grated
½ t mixed spice (not the same as allspice – see mixed spice recipe on page 208)	orange rind, grated
	4 oz. margarine

Directions:
1. Beat the margarine and sugar together until soft.
2. Beat the eggs and add to the sugar and margarine.
3. Stir in all the dry ingredients and add the sherry.
4. Grease the insides of a 2 pint pudding basin. Spoon the mixture in and level it.
5. Place a circle of greased paper on top, then cover with tin foil.
6. If you put a pleat in the middle of the foil it will expand when the pudding rises.
7. Tie the foil on with a string, making a string "handle" to lift the pudding out when cooked.
8. In a lidded saucepan, boil enough water to float the pudding basin. This stops it burning on the bottom of the pan.
9. Put the pudding in, turn down the heat, put the lid on, and let it simmer and steam for 6-8 hours.
10. As long as you keep topping up the hot water so it floats it really can't over cook.
11. Once done, lift it out and leave it to cool in the basin (so it doesn't break).
12. Wrap the cooled pudding in greaseproof paper and keep until needed, then re-steam for about half an hour.
13. In the weeks leading up to Christmas, you can dribble brandy over the pudding and let it soak in. It should traditionally be brought to the table flaming, covered in lighted brandy.

Photograph © Courtesy of Hazel Wilkinson

Hazel Wilkinson

Insanely Easy Fruit Cobbler

Contributed by Anita Williams Weinberg
Seattle, Washington, USA

Can be vegan - see notes in the directions.

Ingredients:
¼ C butter (or butter substitute)
1 ¼ C flour
1 C sugar
2 ½ t baking powder

1 C whipping cream (or cream substitute)
1 quart of your favorite fresh or frozen fruit

Directions:
1. Put butter (or butter substitute) into a 9x13 inch glass baking dish and put it into the oven while it preheats to 350° F.
2. Mix flour, sugar, baking powder, and whipping cream (or cream substitute).
3. Remove the hot baking dish from the oven and tilt it around to spread the butter across the bottom and up the sides.
4. Spread the batter into the baking dish and cover with fruit. This works really well with berries and peaches.
5. Bake 40-45 minutes.

Marshmallow Cream Fudge

Contributed by Ellen Donati
Burlingame, California, USA

Ingredients:
1 jar vegetarian marshmallow cream
1 ½ C sugar
⅔ C evaporated milk
¼ C butter
¼ t salt

1 (12 oz.) pkg. (2 C) semi-sweet chocolate
   morsels
1 t vanilla extract
½ C chopped nuts (optional)

Directions:
1. In a medium saucepan, combine marshmallow cream, sugar, evaporated milk, butter, and salt.
2. Bring to a full boil stirring constantly over moderate heat for 5 minutes. Remove from heat.
3. Add semi-sweet chocolate morsels; stir until morsels melt and mixture is smooth.
4. Stir in nuts and vanilla extract.
5. Pour into an aluminum foil lined 8 inch square pan.
6. Chill in refrigerator until firm (about 2 hours).

Nana Doris' Scottish Shortbread

Contributed by Karin Habert-Smith
Sudbury, Massachusetts, USA

Ingredients:	

¾ C (95 grams) all-purpose flour
¼ C (30 grams) rice flour (can use cornstarch/
    corn flour)
¼ C (50 grams) granulated white sugar or
    caster sugar
	½ C (113 grams) cold salted butter, preferably
	    frozen

Directions:
1. Preheat oven to 300° F (150° C) with the rack in the middle of the oven. Have ready an 8 inch (20 cm) tart pan with a removable bottom.
2. In a large bowl, whisk the flour with the rice flour (or corn flour/cornstarch) and the sugar.
3. Then take the very cold butter and grate it over the flour mixture.
4. With your fingertips, work the butter into the flour by lifting small handfuls and rubbing the butter and flour together until the mixture looks like breadcrumbs (you do not want a dough to form).
5. Evenly press the shortbread into the tart pan, smoothing the top as best as you can.
6. Prick the surface with the tines of a fork and then, with a sharp knife, score the top of the shortbread into 16 wedges.
7. Bake for about 40-50 minutes (watch carefully) or just until a light biscuit color.
8. Remove from oven and place on a wire rack to cool for about 5 minutes.
9. Remove from tart pan. Place the shortbread round on a cutting board and cut each shortbread round into 16 wedges (along the lines scored).
10. Cool completely on a wire rack. Makes 16 shortbread wedges.

Shortbread cookies will keep in an airtight container for about a week or they can be frozen.

Pistachio Cake

Contributed by Rebekka Bishop
Toledo, Iowa, USA

Ingredients:	
1 box Jiffy white cake mix 1 box pistachio pudding 3 eggs	2 t oil ¼ C water

Directions:
1. Combine all ingredients and beat until smooth.
2. Bake in a greased 9 inch round cake pan at 350° for 25 minutes or until tester in the center comes out clean.

Easy, easy, easy to make. Great for 2 people.

German Chocolate Vegan Cookies to Die For

Contributed by Shelley Calissendorff,
Pullman, Washington, USA

Ingredients:
1 ¾ C all purpose flour	½ C melted coconut oil or vegan margarine
¼ C unsweetened baking cocoa	⅔ C maple or agave syrup
2 t baking powder	1 t vanilla extract
1 t baking soda	1 t coconut extract
½ t salt	⅔ C of chopped or sliced almonds
½ C sugar	1 C unsweetened, shredded coconut

Directions:
1. Preheat oven to 350° F and line a baking sheet with parchment paper.
2. In a large bowl, whisk together flour, cocoa, baking powder, baking soda, salt, and sugar.
3. Mix in melted coconut oil, maple/agave syrup ,and vanilla and coconut extracts.
4. Add the almonds and shredded coconut and mix until no flour remains. The additions may not completely mix into the batter, but that's okay.
5. Shape into 15 rounded balls, flatten slightly, and place on prepared baking sheet(s).
6. Bake for 13 minutes at 350° F.
7. Cool on baking sheet for one minute and transfer to a wire rack to cool completely.

Makes 15 large-ish cookies

Estelle's Cherry Cheesecake

Contributed by Susan Rakis, Road Manager for The Buckinghams

This is my mom's greatest cheesecake recipe!

Ingredients:
½ C melted butter/margarine	16 oz. cream cheese
16 oz. crushed vanilla wafers	1 container Cool Whip whipped topping
2 C powdered sugar	45 oz. Red Ruby Cherry Pie Filling/Topping

Directions:
1. Mix melted butter/margarine and crushed vanilla wafers and line bottom of a pan with the mixture.
2. Bake at 350° F until the "crust" turns a bit brownish. Let cool.
3. While crust is cooling, mix powdered sugar, cream cheese, and Cool Whip together.
4. Layer this mixture over cooled crust and top with the Red Ruby Cherry Pie Filling/Topping.

Be sure to add LOVE while you are creating this extraordinary dessert.
Otherwise it really won't taste the same as my mom's!

Jody's Vegan Ice Cream Soda

Contributed by Jody Proetta
Putnam Valley, New York, USA

You will need a very large ice cream soda
glass for this very delicious dessert drink.

Ingredients:
2 scoops of vegan ice cream of flavor of your choice
A bottle of plain seltzer or vanilla flavored seltzer
At least 8 oz. of chocolate or vanilla soy milk or vanilla almond milk unsweetened or sweetened

vegan whipped cream (This is optional as this item is usually only found at a natural foods store or health food store unless your grocery store has a large vegetarian/vegan section.)

Directions:
1. Place your vegan ice cream into your ice cream soda glass. Use enough scoops to fill the glass halfway.
2. Pour your chocolate or vanilla soy or almond milk next to cover your ice cream 3 quarters of the way.
3. Now slowly pour your seltzer over the ingredients and it will fizz up nicely and form a foam of ice cream and your choice of milk.
4. You may have to stir a little bit and wait for the foam to calm down and add more seltzer to complete your soda.
5. If you have your vegan whipped cream you can add that on top.
6. I always add a sliced strawberry or other vegan garnish. Enjoy!!!

Rachel Bishop's No-Bake Cookies

Contributed by Rebekka Bishop
Toledo, Iowa, USA

Ingredients:
I C white sugar
1 C white corn syrup

1 (18-oz.) jar of peanut butter (creamy or crunchy)
large box of Rice Krispies type cereal

Directions:
1. Mix sugar and syrup in a large pan on stove. Cook until sugar melts and mixture is bubbly.
2. Add peanut butter and stir until melted.
3. Slowly add in 5-6 cups of cereal and mix well.
4. While still hot, drop by spoonful on waxed paper.

These are so easy to make and always a big hit at potlucks and picnics.

Avocado Chocolate Mousse

Contributed by Mandy Darmody
Melbourne, Victoria, Australia

Ingredients:
½ C dark cooking melts
2 ripe/soft avocados
½ C of agave nectar (can substitute 1 over-ripe
  banana or even ½ C brown sugar)

½ C of cocoa powder
1 vanilla bean
Note: All the ingredients above can be
  adjusted to taste.

Directions:
1. Melt the chocolate in a double boiler or in the microwave and set aside.
2. Cut the avocados in half and remove the pits. Remove the avocado flesh and slightly mash with a folk before adding it to a blender.
3. Cut the vanilla bean in half, lengthways, and remove the seeds with the back of a knife blade. Add the vanilla seeds to the blender.
4. Add the remaining ingredients as well as the melted chocolate to the blender and blend until no green avocado is visible.
5. Distribute mousse mixture into individual serving bowls and chill in the refrigerator for a couple of hours.
6. Serve on its own or with raspberry coulis.

Enjoy! (My non avocado liking husband LOVES this recipe).

Corn Pudding

Contributed by Rosinha Viegas
São Paulo, Brazil

Ingredients:
1 can sweetened condensed milk
2 cans of milk (use the same measure)
3 eggs

1 can regular corn (with water)
1 C sugar for the caramel

Directions:
1. Mix all ingredients in a blender.
2. Prepare the caramel (*) in a pudding form with a hole in the middle.
3. Pour the mixture into the pudding form.
4. Bake in water bath at 325° - 350° F for 20 minutes (or in the microwave for 12 min).
5. Allow to cool and refrigerate.

   (*) Melt 1 ½ cup sugar and ½ cup water over low heat without stirring until caramelized.

This recipe is also good with chocolate, grated coconut, or orange juice instead of corn.

Old Time Sugar-Cream Pie

Contributed by Mary Ann and Bobby Hart

*Bobby Hart is best known as half of the
songwriting team of Boyce and Hart, writing many
of The Monkees' hits and touring with Tommy Boyce,
Micky Dolenz, and Davy Jones as Dolenz, Jones, Boyce, and Hart.*

Ingredients:
1 C granulated sugar
¾ C brown sugar
½ t salt
½ C flour

1 C boiling water
1 C whipping cream (heavy)
⅛ t nutmeg
½ t vanilla

Directions:
1. Combine granulated sugar, brown sugar, salt, and flour.
2. Stir in boiling water, whipping cream, nutmeg, and vanilla.
3. Pour mixture into a 9 inch pastry lined shell.
4. Bake in a hot oven 450° F for 10 minutes.
5. Reduce oven to 350° F and bake for 40 minutes.

Photograph © Courtesy of Mary Ann and Bobby Hart

Homemade Ice Cream

*Contributed by Mary Ann and Bobby Hart
from an old family recipe*

Ingredients:
1 quart milk plus a little more
3 rounded T flour
3 eggs
2 C sugar (or honey)

pinch of salt
vanilla to taste
1 can Eagle Brand milk

Directions:
1. Heat milk.
2. Stir in rest of ingredients, except milk.
3. Add vanilla, extra milk, and Eagle Brand milk.
4. Pour into ice cream maker and follow manufacturer's instructions.

Pumpkin Pie Squares

Contributed by Linda Mathers
Drumbo, Ontario, Canada

Ingredients:	
1 ⅓ C flour	1 pkg. cream cheese, softened
½ C firmly packed brown sugar	3 eggs
¼ C sugar	1 can (15 oz.) pumpkin
1 ½ sticks cold butter or margarine	1 T pumpkin pie spice
1 C old fashioned oats (uncooked)	½ C sugar
½ C chopped pecans	

Directions:
1. Preheat oven to 350° F
2. Mix together flour, sugar, and brown sugar.
3. Add butter or margarine with pastry blender or two knives.
4. Stir in oats and pecans.
5. Reserve 1 cup of this mixture.
6. Press the rest into a greased 13x9 baking pan. Bake 15 minutes.
7. While crust is baking, beat in a mixing bowl: cream cheese, softened, eggs, pumpkin, pumpkin pie spice, and sugar.
8. When crust is done, pour mixture over crust.
9. Sprinkle remaining oat/pecan mixture on top.
10. Bake for 25 minutes.
11. Cool and cut into squares.

Sugar-Free Vegan
Chocolate Pudding

Contributed by Colleen Gruver
Lynnwood, Washington, USA

Ingredients:	
2 avocados	½ C water (or unsweetened almond or rice milk)
½ C unsweetened cocoa powder	stevia to taste (about 1-2 t powdered stevia)

Directions:
1. Place all of the ingredients into a food processor or a blender.
2. Blend until all avocado chunks are gone and the texture is creamy.

This is a super quick, super easy, and super healthy dessert!

White Chocolate Reeses Fudge

Contributed by Linda Mach
Kewaunee, Wisconsin, USA

Ingredients:
1 bag white chocolate Reeses peanut butter cups	½ t salt
	½ C butter
1 C sugar	2 ½ C white chocolate chips
½ C heavy cream	1 tub vegetarian marshmallow fluff

Directions:
1. Peel off all the white chocolate Reeses peanut butter cups wrappers and cut them in 4 pieces each.
2. Put parchment paper on the 9x9 inch pan. This keeps the fudge from sticking to the pan.
3. Put the white chocolate chips and marshmallow fluff in a big bowl. Set aside.
4. In a pan, melt the sugar, heavy cream, salt, and butter on medium heat until it starts to boil. Cook for 5 minutes.
5. Pour the hot stuff into the bowl of chocolate chips and mix with the blender until it's smooth and soft.
6. Mix (fold) in half the white chocolate Reeses peanut butter cups.
7. Pour into your pan.
8. Sprinkle the rest of the Reeses on the top.
9. Put in the fridge for 3-5 hours to let it set.

Rocky Road Candy

Contributed by Ellen Donati
Burlingame, California, USA

Ingredients:
1 (12 oz.) pkg. semi-sweet chocolate morsels	2 C chopped walnuts
1 (14 oz.) can sweetened condensed milk	1 (10 ½ oz.) pkg. vegetarian miniature marshmallows
2 T butter	

Directions:
1. In a heavy saucepan over low heat, melt morsels with sweetened condensed milk and butter.
2. Remove from heat. In a large bowl, combine nuts and marshmallows.
3. Fold in chocolate mixture.
4. Spread in a waxed paper-lined 13x9 inch pan.
5. Chill 2 hours or until firm.
6. Remove from pan and cut into squares.
7. Cover and store at room temperature.

Heaven In A Bowl
(Peanut Butter Brownie Trifle)

Contributed by Linda Mach
Kewaunee, Wisconsin, USA

Ingredients:
1 fudge brownie mix (13-inch x 9-inch pan size)	2 packages (5.1 oz. each) instant vanilla pudding mix
4 C cold 2% milk	4 t vanilla extract
2 packages (13 oz. each) miniature peanut butter cups	2 cartons (8 oz. each) frozen whipped topping, thawed
1 C creamy peanut butter	

Directions:
1. Prepare brownie batter according to package directions.
2. Bake in a greased 13x9 inch baking pan at 350° F for 20-25 minutes or until a toothpick inserted near the center comes out with moist crumbs. (Do not over bake.)
3. Cool on a wire rack and cut into ¾ inch pieces. Cut peanut butter cups in half; set aside ⅓ cup for garnish.
4. In a large bowl, whisk milk and pudding mixes for 2 minutes. (Mixture will be thick.)
5. Add peanut butter and vanilla. Mix well.
6. Fold in 1½ cartons whipped topping.
7. Place a third of the brownies in a 5-qt. glass bowl.
8. Top with a third of the remaining peanut butter cups.
9. Spoon a third of the pudding mixture over the top.
10. Repeat layers twice.
11. Cover with remaining whipped topping and garnish with reserved peanut butter cups.
12. Refrigerate until chilled.

Vegan No-Bake Cookies

Contributed by Brandy Burrow
Austin, Texas, USA

Ingredients:
1 stick (½ C) Earth Balance vegan buttery sticks	½ C natural peanut butter (creamy)
1 ¾ C unrefined sugar	1 t vanilla extract
½ C soymilk (or any plant based milk)	3 C oatmeal (quick oats)
¼ C unsweetened cocoa powder	

Directions:
1. Melt vegan butter over medium-high heat and add in sugar, soymilk, and cocoa powder.
2. Stir with whisk. Bring to a boil and stir constantly for 2 minutes.
3. Turn off heat and stir in vanilla extract and peanut butter.
4. Stir in the oatmeal with a wooden spoon.
5. Spoon a tablespoon size of the mixture onto wax paper. Let set for 40 minutes.

Enjoy! (makes about 2 dozen)

Zucchini Brownies

Contributed by Susan Wilson
Mount Olive, North Carolina, USA

Ingredients:

½ C applesauce
2 small or medium bananas, mashed
1 ½ C sugar
2 t vanilla extract
½ C cocoa powder

1 ½ t baking soda
½ t salt
2 C finely shredded zucchini
2 C all purpose flour
½ C walnut pieces

Directions:
1. Preheat oven to 350° F. Grease and flour a 9x13 inch baking pan.
2. In a large bowl, mix together the applesauce, mashed bananas, and sugar.
3. Add vanilla and cocoa and mix together.
4. Add baking soda, salt, and zucchini and mix together.
5. Add flour and walnuts and mix together.
6. Spread evenly into a prepared pan.
7. Bake for 25 minutes until brownies spring back when gently touched.

Vegan Blondies

Contributed by Kim Briggs
Atlanta, Georgia, USA

Ingredients:

3 ½ C flour
1 ½ t baking powder
½ t baking soda
½ t salt
1 ½ C sugar
1 C oil

2 t vanilla extract
1 C almond milk
1 ½ C semisweet vegan chocolate chips
    (I actually use Godiva dark chocolate and
    crumble it up.)

Directions:
1. Preheat oven to 350° F.
2. In a large bowl, stir together the flour, baking powder, baking soda, salt, and sugar.
3. Add the oil, vanilla, milk, and chocolate chips and mix together gently.
4. Pour mixture into a lightly oiled 9x13 inch pan and bake for 25-30 minutes.
5. Test with a toothpick for doneness.
6. Let cool 10 minutes before cutting into bars.

Carmella's Coffee Cake

Contributed by Linda Groundwater
Capalaba, Queensland. Australia

Ingredients:
1 C sugar
½ C margarine
1 C sour cream
2 eggs
2 C flour
1 t baking soda
1 t baking powder
2 T milk

chocolate chips, as much as you like! (I usually put about ¾ C)
½ C walnuts

separately, mix together:
¼ C brown sugar
1 t cinnamon
dash of nutmeg

Directions:
1. Cream the sugar and margarine.
2. Add sour cream, milk, and eggs.
3. Sift flour, baking powder, and baking soda, and then add to mixture and beat till smooth.
4. Grease and flour baking dish.
5. Put half the mixture in the dish. Sprinkle brown sugar mixture, chopped walnuts, and chocolate chips, then put remaining mixture, then brown sugar mixture, rest of chocolate chips and walnuts.
6. Bake at 350° F or 180˚ C for 40 minutes.

Sweet Potato Pie

Contributed by Patricia Walsh
Arlington, Massachusetts, USA

Ingredients:
3 C of mashed sweet potato (cooked)
1 C sugar
2 eggs beaten
½ C milk

½ C butter
1 C coconut
1 t vanilla

Directions:
1. Mix together and pour into 9x13 inch pan.
2. Top with topping below.
    1 C light brown sugar
    1 C self rising flour
    1 C walnuts or pecans
    ⅓ C melted butter
3. Mix first 3 topping ingredients together in a bowl and then add the ⅓ cup of melted butter.
4. Spread over the top of the potato mixture and bake at 350˚ F for 25 - 30 minutes.

Rum Balls

Contributed by Rose Ann Gillett
Beech Grove, Indiana, USA

Ingredients:
2 ½ C crushed vanilla wafers	1 lb. ground pecans
⅓ C Bacardi light rum	confectioners' sugar
½ C honey	

Directions:
1. Combine vanilla wafers, rum, honey, and pecans; mix thoroughly.
2. Shape into balls with melon baller.
3. Roll in confectioners sugar on wax paper.
Store in covered container 3-4 days before serving.

Chocolate Peanut Butter Bars

Contributed by Janet Prathaftakis
Bella Vista, Arizona, USA

Ingredients:
1 C peanut butter	1 T vanilla extract
6 T (¾ stick) butter/margarine softened	1 C all purpose flour
1 ¼ C sugar	¼ T salt
3 eggs	1 (11 ½ oz.) package (2 C) of milk chocolate
⅓ C applesauce (This is a healthy option replacing oil.)	morsels, divided

Directions:
1. Preheat oven 350° F.
2. In a large mixer bowl, beat peanut butter and butter until smooth.
3. Add sugar, eggs, vanilla extract, and applesauce. Beat until creamy.
4. Gradually beat in flour and salt.
5. Stir in 1 cup of the milk chocolate morsels.
6. Spread into ungreased 13x9 inch baking pan.
7. Bake 25-30 minutes until edges brown.
8. Immediately sprinkle remaining milk chocolate morsels over cookie layer. Let stand 5 minutes until morsels become shiny and soft. Spread morsels evenly on top. Cool.
9. Cut into 1 ½ inch bars. Makes approximately 48 bars.

Banana Dessert

Contributed by Darlene Haines
Crestline, Ohio, USA

Ingredients:
1 banana	pinch of salt
1 egg yolk	1 T butter
3 T water	¼ t vanilla
4 T sugar	chopped nuts
1 T vinegar	

Directions:
1. Beat egg yolk, water, and vinegar.
2. Add sugar and salt and boil until clear.
3. Remove from heat and add butter and vanilla.
4. Cool, pour over sliced banana, and sprinkle with chopped nuts.

Peach Cobbler

Contributed by Bonnie Musser
Milroy, Pennsylvania, USA

Ingredients:
½ C butter or substitute	4 C peaches (fresh is best, or drain canned and use the juice instead of sugar and milk)
1 C flour	1 T of lime juice
2 C sugar	cinnamon or nutmeg to taste
1 T baking powder	Note: fresh berries may be substituted for peaches
dash of salt	
1 C milk (soy, almond, or rice)	

Directions:
1. Melt butter in 13x9 pan.
2. Combine flour, 1 cup of sugar, baking powder, salt, and milk. Pour over butter.
3. Bring 1 cup of sugar, peaches, and lime juice to a boil and pour over batter.
4. Sprinkle with nutmeg and cinnamon.

Kit Kat Crusted Strawberry Cheesecake

Contributed by Linda Mach
Kewaunee, Wisconsin, USA

Ingredients:

The Crust:
2 C Honey Graham Crackers, crushed
16 Kit Kat Fun Size Bars, crushed and divided
¼ C butter, melted
¼ t baking soda

The Filling:
12 oz. cream cheese, softened (fat free works well)
⅓ C powdered sugar
1 egg
1 egg yolk
1 t vanilla extract
¼ t cinnamon
1 C frozen strawberries, thawed

The Topping:
1 C frozen strawberries, thawed
1 package vegetarian gelatin substitute*
1 C hot water
red food coloring
whipped cream for garnish

Editor's note: Preparation method may vary depending on which type of gelatin substitute you choose. Prepare according to manufacturer's directions.*

Directions:
1. Preheat your oven to 350° F.
2. Spray a pie form with cooking spray and set aside.
3. Start by crushing your crackers and Kit Kat bars in separate bowls.
4. In a large bowl, combine crushed crackers, melted butter, and baking soda. Stir until well combined.
5. Add half of the crushed Kit Kat Bars. Stir until combined.
6. Now press the crumbles into your pie form. Try to spread it out as evenly as possible.
7. Press remaining Kit Kat on top of the cracker crust.
8. Bake for 12 minutes.
9. Meanwhile, in a large bowl, combine all filling ingredients besides the strawberries and mix until smooth.
10. Pour filling into pre-baked crust.
11. Place strawberries on top all over the filling and bake for another 35 minutes.
12. Let cool completely (about 1 hour in the fridge).
13. Now combine gelatin substitute, hot water, and red food coloring (about 10 drops) and stir until gelatin substitute is dissolved.
14. Place strawberries on top of the cooled cake and pour gelatin substitute spoon wise over them, just until all strawberries are covered.
15. Place in fridge until set (about 30 minutes), then right before serving top with whipped cream.

*Unknown to many, gelatin is a protein that is derived from animal bone, cartilage, tendon, and skin. Gelatin is usually found in yogurt, marshmallows, cereals that are frosted, gelatin desserts, and Beano. Animal products are not always explicitly stated on some package labels, and therefore the consumer is unaware they are present in the foods. The good news is that there are vegetarian sources of gelatin readily available in your health food store so you are able to enjoy the delicious recipes here in this book that contain gelatin as one of the ingredients. Vegetarian gelatin is sold as plain or fruit flavored and is used the same way as conventional gelatin. You may be familiar with agar, one form of vegetarian gelatin. Just follow the directions of the manufacturer's label to adapt the ingredient to the recipe, and enjoy.

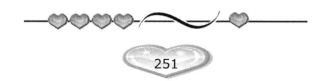

Soy Fruit Smoothie Ice Cream

Contributed by Jody Proetta
Putnam Valley, New York, USA

This makes a delightful vegan ice cream without the dairy fat. I use unsweetened soy or almond milk, but I do add stevia to it because it is dessert and I like a sweeter taste. Use the sweetener of your choice. To keep this recipe vegan, do not use refined sugar.

Ingredients:	
2 large frozen bananas sliced before frozen	8 oz. vanilla or chocolate, sweetened or
2 C of frozen mixed berries	unsweetened, soy or almond milk depending on your preference

Directions:
1. Place all of the above ingredients into a blender and puree to a thick but smooth consistency.
2. If you have to add a little more fruit to thicken up, add what flavor you'd like to dominate your ice cream.
3. You will then freeze the mixture into the containers for serving sizes of your choice. Make sure you choose containers that will not crack with freezing.

Lemon-Basil Snaps

Contributed by Marian Allen
Corydon, Indiana, USA

Ingredients:	
½ C fresh lemon basil leaves*	1 large egg
1 ¾ C sugar, divided	3 C all-purpose flour
½ pound butter or margarine, softened	sugar
⅛ C fresh lemon juice	

Directions:
1. Process basil, sugar, and butter in food processor until creamy. Add lemon juice and egg, beating until blended. Transfer to a bowl big enough to add flour. Work together with hands if necessary.
2. Shape dough into 1-inch balls and place 2 inches apart on lightly greased baking sheets. Flatten balls slightly with bottom of a glass dipped in sugar.
3. Bake at 350° F for 10-15 minutes or until lightly browned. Remove to wire racks to cool completely.

*Regular Italian ('Genovese') basil may be substituted for lemon basil. Makes 6 to 8 dozen, depending on what size the balls turn out to be.

Lemon Squares

Contributed by Lyn Tomkinson
Finksburg, Maryland, USA

This is my Aunt Jan's recipe.

Ingredients:
Crust:	Filling:
1 C flour	2 eggs
½ C butter	1 C granulated sugar
¼ C confectioner's sugar	½ t baking powder
	¼ t salt
	3 T lemon juice plus 1 t grated peel

Directions:
1. Blend flour, butter, and confectioner's sugar
2. Press into 8x8x2 inch pan. Bake at 350° F for 20 minutes.
3. While the above is baking, combine other ingredients.
4. Pour over baked crust and bake 20-25 minutes at 350° F.
5. Cool and cut into squares.

Peanut Butter Pie

Contributed by Lyn Tomkinson
Finksburg, Maryland, USA

This is Rick's recipe, my husband and a fantastic cook.
It's a mouth-watering family favorite!

Ingredients:
Crust:	Filling:
1-¼ C chocolate cookie crumbs	1 (8 oz.) package cream cheese, softened
¼ C white sugar	1 C creamy peanut butter
¼ C butter or margarine	1 C white sugar
	1 T unsalted butter, softened
	1 t vanilla extract
	1 C heavy whipping cream

Directions:
1. Combine cookie crumbs, sugar, and butter or margarine; press into a 9 inch pie plate.
2. Bake at 375° F for 10 minutes and cool.
3. In a mixing bowl beat cream cheese, peanut butter, rest of sugar, butter, and vanilla extract until smooth.
4. Whip the cream and fold into the peanut butter mixture.
5. Gently spoon filling into crust.
6. Garnish pie with chocolate or cookie crumbs if desired.
7. Refrigerate.

Black Bean Brownies

Contributed by Madelyn Warkentin
Fullerton, California, USA

This is vegan and gluten free.

Ingredients:
1 ½ C black beans (1 15-oz. can, drained and rinsed very well. 250g after draining. I made my
    own black beans instead of using a can. I salted them lightly after cooking them thoroughly.)
2 T cocoa powder (Dutch or regular—10g— add a little extra if desired.)
½ C quick oats (40g—I used whole grain oats instead of quick oats that I ground up first.)
¼ t salt
⅓ C pure maple syrup (75g)
2 NuNaturals stevia packs, or omit and increase maple syrup to ½ C. (I added increased maple
    syrup and skipped the stevia.)
¼ C coconut or vegetable oil (40g)
2 t pure vanilla extract
½ t baking powder
½ C to ⅔ C chocolate chips (115-140g. Not optional. Omit at your own risk.)
Optional: 2 drops of an edible citrus blend essential oil (such as doTERRA "citrus bliss "essential oil)
Optional: more chips, for presentation

Directions:
1. Preheat oven to 350° F. Combine all ingredients except chips in a good food processor and blend
    until completely smooth. Really blend well. (A blender can work if you absolutely must, but the
    texture—and even the taste—will be much better in a food processor.)
2. Stir in the chips, then pour into a greased 8×8 inch pan. Optional: sprinkle extra chocolate chips
    over the top.
3. Cook the black bean brownies 15-18 minutes, then let cool at least 10 minutes before trying to
    cut.

Makes 9 to 12 brownies

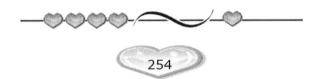

Image © Courtesy of Cindy Bryant

Rice Pudding

Contributed by Marian Allen
Corydon, Indiana, USA

Ingredients:
½ C water
½ C uncooked instant rice
3 eggs, slightly beaten
½ C sugar
2 t vanilla

¼ t salt
2½ C milk, scalded
½ C raisins
cinnamon

Directions:
1. Heat oven to 350° F. Heat water to boiling. Remove from heat; stir in rice. Cover and let stand about 5 minutes.
2. Blend eggs, sugar, vanilla, and salt. Gradually stir in milk. Mix in rice and raisins. Pour into ungreased 1½-quart casserole. Sprinkle rice mixture with cinnamon. Place casserole in square pan, 9x9x2 inches. Pour very hot water (1¼ inches deep) into pan.
3. Bake about 70 minutes or until knife inserted halfway between center and edge comes out clean. Remove casserole from water. Serve pudding warm or cool.

Pineapple Rice

Contributed by Marian Allen
Corydon, Indiana, USA

Ingredients:
3 C (750 ml) cooked white rice
3 C (750 ml) coarsely chopped fresh or canned
   pineapple, drained

6 T (90 ml) margarine
¾ C (180 ml) brown sugar
¾ C (180 ml) pineapple juice or water

Directions:
1. Place one third of the rice in a greased baking dish.
2. Top with one third of the pineapple, margarine, and brown sugar.
3. Repeat twice.
4. Add the pineapple juice and bake covered in a preheated 350° F (180° C) oven for 30 minutes.

Serves 4 to 6

Bourbon Balls

Contributed by Marian Allen
Corydon, Indiana, USA

Ingredients:
For centers:
6 C (one 2 lb bag) confectioner's sugar
1 stick margarine
⅓ C bourbon
1 C chopped walnuts
whole walnuts for topping--not a WHOLE
    walnut, obviously, just one unbroken piece
    of walnut meat

For coating:
8 squares semi-sweet chocolate
1 T paraffin wax (plain white wax, like you use
    to seal jelly)
2 T margarine, more if needed to make the
    coating liquid enough

Directions:
1. Cream margarine and sugar. Add bourbon. Fold in nuts. Work together until thoroughly blended. Cover with wax paper. Refrigerate 24 hours.
2. Make into 1-inch balls or smaller, place on wax paper on cookie sheet, and refrigerate again to make firm.
3. Melt in double boiler over hot water (Do not let chocolate boil). Dip one center at a time. Place on wax paper. Put walnut on top. Refrigerate. Note: This is never enough. I recommend making two batches of coating.

Makes around 100 at about 60 calories each.

Cracker Candy

Contributed by Marian Allen
Corydon, Indiana, USA

Ingredients:
saltine crackers
1 C brown sugar
1 C butter or margarine

chocolate chips
crushed walnuts

Directions:
1. Line cookie sheet with foil. Arrange 40 saltine crackers in pan.
2. Bring brown sugar and butter to a boil and cook 3 minutes, stirring constantly.
3. Pour over crackers and spread with a spoon.
4. Bake at 450° F for about 5 minutes. Watch closely to make sure it does not burn.
5. Remove from oven and sprinkle on one 12 oz. package of chocolate chips and walnuts. Let stand to melt. Spread and refrigerate. Break apart and serve.

Mom's Rum Balls

Contributed by Nancy Bowman
New Albany, Indiana, USA

Ingredients:
1 stick butter
2 ½ boxes powdered sugar
½ can Eagle Brand Milk

1 package chopped pecans
½ C rum or other liquor

Directions:
1. Mix all ingredients.
2. Form into balls.
3. Refrigerate until good and cold.
4. Dip in chocolate. (See recipe below.)

Photograph © Courtesy of Bonnie Borgh

Chocolate Dip

Contributed by Nancy Bowman
New Albany, Indiana, USA

Ingredients:
1 lb. bitter baking chocolate
½ cake of food grade paraffin wax (vegetarian "friendly" Parowax)

Directions:
1. Melt chocolate and paraffin wax in double boiler over low heat. DO NOT LET WATER BOIL.
2. Remove from heat and dip balls. Keep stirring chocolate if it gets thick.

The Next Best Thing
to Davy Jones

Contributed by Chanin Russell
Indianapolis, Indiana, USA

Prepare 24 hours ahead of time.

Ingredients:
1 C flour
1 stick of margarine
1 C chopped nuts
8 oz. cream cheese
1 C sugar
12 oz. tub of Cool Whip, divided

1 large package instant vanilla pudding
1 large package instant chocolate pudding
3 C milk
mini chocolate chips (optional—amount varies)

Directions:
1. Combine flour, butter, and nuts.
2. Press into ungreased 9x13 inch pan.
3. Bake at 350° F for 15-20 minutes. Let cool.
4. Combine cream cheese, sugar, and half of the Cool Whip.
5. Blend until smooth.
6. Spread over cooled crust.
7. Beat together the two puddings and milk until blended.
8. Pour into crust.
9. Spread rest of Cool Whip on top.
10. Sprinkle with mini chocolate chips if desired.
11. Refrigerate 24 hours. Serve.

Watergate Cake

Contributed by Karen Jorgenson
Stationed in Misawa, Japan

Ingredients:
Cake:
1 package yellow cake mix
1 package instant pistachio pudding

Topping:
1 package instant pistachio pudding
1 small container Cool Whip
1 C milk

Directions:
1. Preheat oven to 350° F. Grease and flour 13x9 inch cake pan. Make cake according to directions on box, adding dry pudding mix. Bake according to directions. Cool.
2. Mix pudding with 1 cup of milk, then gently fold in pudding mix.
3. Spread over cooled cake.

Chocolate Cake

Contributed by Sherry Doyal
Centre, Alabama, USA

Here is the recipe that I received from Davy back in 1998
for our VIP section in a cookbook for my church to raise funds.

Ingredients:
Cake:
1 box chocolate cake mix
2 boxes instant chocolate pudding

Icing:
1/2 C cocoa
2 C sugar
1 stick butter
1/2 C milk

Directions:
1. Cake: Mix cake mix by directions on box and pudding by directions on box. Mix cake mix and pudding together in a bowl. Pour into cake pan and cook at 400° F. Cook until cake tester comes out clean.
2. Icing: Mix all ingredients in saucepan over medium heat. Bring to a boil. Test icing by taking a small amount and dropping it into cold water. If it forms a soft ball, it is done. Remove saucepan from heat, pour icing over cake, and spread evenly or beat until cool and spread over cake.

Jolly Good!!!

Pumpkin Chocolate Chip Squares

Contributed by Maria L. Weiss
Somerset, Massachusetts, USA

Ingredients:
3 C flour
1 can pumpkin
2 C sugar
1 C vegetable oil
1 t salt

2 t baking powder
2 t baking soda
3 t cinnamon
3 eggs
16 oz. bag of chocolate chips

Directions:
1. Preheat oven to 350° F.
2. Mix all ingredients until smooth.
3. Pour into a greased 10x15 inch pan.
4. Bake for 30 minutes or until done.
5. Cool completely and cut into squares.

Grandma Zella's Persimmon Pudding

Contributed by Ginny Fleming
New Albany, Indiana, USA

Ingredients:
2 C persimmons
2 C sugar
3 eggs
4 T melted butter
1 t baking soda

1 t cinnamon
1 t mixture of nutmeg, allspice, and ground
    cloves (your choice of proportions)
1 quart milk
2 1/8 C flour

Directions:
1. Mix all ingredients.
2. Pour into greased brownie-sized pan.
3. Bake at 350° F. Use toothpick to test for doneness.
4. Let cool completely.
5. Drizzle with Persimmon Pudding Sauce (recipe below).

Persimmon Pudding Sauce

Contributed by Ginny Fleming
New Albany, Indiana, USA

Ingredients:
1 C sugar
2 T flour
2 T butter
enough milk (not condensed milk) or cream to
    make a paste

1 C boiling water
1 t vanilla

Directions:
1. Combine first four ingredients in a saucepan.
2. Add boiling water and boil 5 minutes, stirring constantly.
3. Add vanilla.
4. Drizzle sauce over cooled persimmon pudding (recipe above).
5. Makes about 10 "brownie-sized" pieces.

Photograph © Courtesy of Saul Photography

"I make beautiful girls!"
~ Davy Jones

Beverages

Photograph © Courtesy of Rhino Entertainment Company

The Basics Of Juicing

Why should you consider adding fresh fruit and vegetable juices to your daily diet?

Very few of us actually consume the recommended five or more daily servings of fruits and vegetables. Frankly, that's a lot of fiber to process! Juicing is an easy way to obtain the healthy benefits of large amounts of fruits and veggies without overloading on bulk.

Many of the fruits and vegetables that we eat each day are cooked, thus destroying their naturally occurring enzymes that aid the digestive process. Eating cooked foods without enzymes places an added strain on the digestive system, while raw fruit and vegetable juices are very easy to digest because of their high enzyme content.

There are two basic types of juicing machines. The less expensive and simpler to use type is called a centrifugal juicer. A centrifugal juicer shreds and spins fruits and vegetables, passing the juice through a fine sieve to separate it from the pulp.

The second type of juicer is called a masticating juicer. This type of juicer grinds fruits and vegetables and thus is called masticating because of its similarity to chewing. More preparation time is required for this type of juicer since produce must be cut up into smaller pieces to fit into the smaller opening. Even though a masticating juicer is more expensive and involves more prep-time, it has superior health benefits compared to a centrifugal juicer. More vitamins and enzymes are preserved as there is less oxidation than what occurs when using a centrifugal juicer. A masticating juicer also has the advantage of more efficiently extracting a greater amount of juice and leaving a drier pulp behind. Over the long term, this can be a real money saver as you will get more juice out of whatever produce you purchase for juicing.

Fruit and vegetable juice is most beneficial when consumed immediately after juicing. Time, exposure to air, light, and heat will all gradually reduce the nutritional content of your juice. If you're unable to drink all of your juice immediately after juicing, store it in the refrigerator in a sealed container, preferably glass, filled to the brim to prevent oxidation due to exposure to air. Try to drink this juice within a few hours, and no longer than 24 hours. Small jelly-sized Mason jars work very well for short term storage of single sized servings of juice.

There are many tasty combinations of fruits and veggies to use when juicing. Carrots and apples add a particularly sweet flavor to any juice combo. Some fruits and veggies, such as bananas and avocados, cannot be juiced due to their low moisture content. Experiment with different fruits and veggies to find the combinations that most appeal to you, and remember that juicing doesn't eliminate the need to consume some un-juiced fruits and veggies daily as well in order to add sufficient fiber to your diet.

~ Colleen Gruver

Berry Cooler

Contributed by Theresa Archey
Oklahoma City, Oklahoma, USA

Ingredients:	
4 C hulled, chopped strawberries	1 C sugar
¼ C lime juice	½ C peeled and coarsely chopped fresh ginger

Directions:
1. Purée strawberries and lime juice in blender until smooth. Strain through fine sieve and discard seeds.
2. Bring sugar, ginger, and 2 cups of water to a boil in small saucepan. Reduce heat to low and simmer, stirring until sugar has dissolved.
3. Remove from heat, let stand 10 minutes, then strain and discard solids. Cool.
4. Whisk strawberry-lime juice and sugar mixture together in pitcher. Serve over ice.

"That's when I started drinking!"

~ Davy Jones

Dream Date Shake

Contributed by Suzanne Gee
Las Vegas, Nevada, USA

Ingredients:	
⅓ C pitted dates, coarsely chopped	¼ t cinnamon
½ C non-fat milk	⅛ t almond extract
1 ½ C vanilla ice cream	

Directions:
1. Place all ingredients in a blender and blend until thick and well combined.
2. Serve immediately.

Serves 1

Jen's Raw Vegan Mocha Chocolate Shake

Contributed by Jennifer Alexander
Lynn, Massachusetts, USA

Ingredients:
½ C almonds
½ C walnuts
4 Medjool dates
1 frozen banana
2 T cacao powder
Optional 2 T Dandy Blend (instant herbal beverage)

½ vanilla bean – OR 1 t vanilla flavor/extract
2 T sweetener (such as raw coconut nectar or maple syrup)
1 pinch Himalayan salt
3 C ice cubes
2 C water

Directions:
Blend all together.

One of my favorite memories of David involves an evening my best friend Hannah and I spent with him after his show at the Times Square Arts Center in NYC in November 2008.
Accompanied by his band, we strolled around the city arm in arm while he did Arthur impressions and shared stories about his days as the Artful Dodger. To top it off, at the end of the evening, he made us all Chamomile tea! I remain forever grateful to David for the music, laughs, and most of all, lasting friendships I gained and continue to

Photograph © Courtesy of Jennifer Alexander

gain both directly and indirectly thanks to him. He also encouraged and supported my artistic endeavors which meant the world to my teenage self. Truly a class act, David Jones was more than the quintessential showman. He brought people together. I miss him and will cherish our happy times.

~ Jennifer

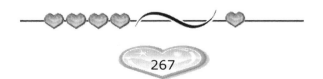

Riu Chiu Christmas Wassail

Contributed by Ginny Fleming
New Albany, Indiana, USA

Ingredients:	
½ gallon apple cider	2 cinnamon sticks
1 orange	1 t allspice in strainer
whole cloves	1 pint cranberry juice or orange juice
¾ C sugar	optional: your favorite rum

Directions:
1. Add apple cider and cranberry juice or orange juice to crockpot.
2. Add sugar.
3. Add allspice in tea strainer.
4. Float cinnamon sticks.
5. Float clove speared orange slices in apple cider. Leave orange just long enough for mixture to become hot. Remove before mixture becomes bitter.
6. Cover and cook for 1 hour.
7. Serve in festive mug with cinnamon stick.

Sing "Riu Chiu" or your favorite Christmas carol. Be merry and enjoy!

Easy Lemonade

Contributed by Andrea Gilbey
Cheshunt, Hertfordshire, UK

This is a recipe I made at school!

Ingredients:	
1 large lemon	1 pint water
2 oz. sugar	

Directions:
1. Wash the lemon and grate the zest from it.
2. Put the zest in a saucepan with 4 fl. oz. of water and add the sugar.
3. Bring to the boil, then reduce the heat, cover, and simmer for 5 minutes.
4. Squeeze the juice from the lemon and add to the saucepan with the rest of the water.
5. Strain into a jug. Stir and serve hot or cold.

Add a little ginger cordial for a warming winter drink.

Fine – So Fine Chocolate

Contributed by Ginny Fleming
New Albany, Indiana, USA

Ingredients:	
3 C milk	½ t ground cinnamon
⅓ C semisweet chocolate, grated	1 egg
1 T white sugar	

Directions:
1. Put milk into a microwave-safe container and cook on high in microwave for 2 minutes. Mix in chocolate, sugar, and cinnamon. In a small bowl, whisk an egg until smooth, then mix it into the chocolate mixture.
2. Return to microwave and cook on high for 3 to 4 minutes or until foamy. (Be careful not to let it boil.) Whisk until smooth and pour into 3 mugs. Makes 3 servings.

Optional: Add a large dollop to taste of Dekuyper's Buttershots (butterscotch schnapps liqueur).

It's fine... So fine. Yummm....

"We were having a little lemonade at the bar..."
~ Davy Jones

Boost Your Health Smoothie

Contributed by Reneé Baer
Bellmawr, New Jersey, USA

This smoothie is great to have if you feel a cold coming on.
The vitamin C will give your immune system a boost and help fight that cold!

Ingredients:	
1 C orange juice	1 C frozen strawberries

Directions:
Add ingredients to blender – blend and serve!

Apple Pie Milk Shake

Contributed by Jody Proetta
Putnam Valley, New York, USA

Ingredients:	
½ C apple juice	½ t of ground cinnamon
3 scoops of vanilla ice cream or frozen yogurt	

Directions:
1. Add apple juice and vanilla ice cream into blender. Blend on high until well-mixed.
2. When done, stir in your cinnamon to suit your taste. Enjoy your apple pie milk shake!!!

Breakfast Get Up and Go Smoothie

Contributed by Reneé Baer
Bellmawr, New Jersey, USA

A great smoothie to start your day!

Ingredients:	
1 C low fat or soy milk	1 C frozen strawberries or blueberries (or
1 C low fat vanilla yogurt	both!)

Directions:
Add ingredients to blender – blend and serve!

Coconut Cream Caribbean Smoothie

Contributed by Debbie Martin
Hazelton, Pennsylvania, USA

Ingredients:	
I carton pineapple yogurt	⅛ C coconut
½ C low fat milk	1 shot Captain Morgan Spiced Rum (optional)
1 medium frozen banana	creamy Reddi Whip

Directions:
1. Combine yogurt, milk, banana, coconut, and rum in a blender. Mix until smooth.
2. Pour in a tall glass, top with Reddi Whip, add a straw, and enjoy.

Roasted Barley Tea

Contributed by Marian Allen
Corydon, Indiana, USA

Ingredients:
¼ C (60 ml) whole-grain barley
8 C (2 L) water

sugar or honey to taste (optional)

Directions:
1. Toast the barley in a skillet over moderate heat, shaking the pan occasionally, until lightly browned and fragrant, about 10 minutes.
2. Combine with the water in a pot and bring to a boil over moderate heat. Reduce the heat and simmer covered for 15 minutes.
3. Strain and serve hot, chilled, or at room temperature with sugar or honey if desired.

Serves 6 to 8

Chai

Contributed by Marian Allen
Corydon, Indiana, USA

Ingredients:
3 sticks cinnamon
12 cardamom pods
½ whole nutmeg, grated
3 whole cloves

6 whole black peppercorns
2 tea bags (English Breakfast is excellent)
1 C (250 ml) milk or soy milk (or less to taste)
sugar to taste

Directions:
1. Place all ingredients except milk and sugar in a saucepan. Add 4 cups (1 L) of water. Cover and bring to a boil over moderate heat. Reduce heat and simmer 10 to 20 minutes.
2. Add milk until the color is a light brownish tan and heat through without boiling.
3. Strain and serve, adding sugar to taste.

Serves 4

Rootie-Tootie-Fruity Water

Contributed by Ginny Fleming
New Albany, Indiana, USA

This is especially good in the hot summertime.

Ingredients:	
your choice of fruit. Experiment, mix and match!	ice cubes water

Directions:
1. First, leaving skin on, thoroughly wash your favorite fruit, then slice into thin coin shapes.
2. In a gallon pitcher, layer fruit-coins and ice to the pitcher's top. Fill with water and refrigerate, allowing the fruit flavors to "meld" with the water.
3. Mix your fruit selections and create a colorful Sangria! Or instead of fruit, using sweet cucumbers makes a very refreshing drink.

Added bonus: Cucumber juice aids your body to shed retained water.

Soy Fruit Smoothie

Contributed by Jody Proetta
Putnam Valley, New York, USA

This smoothie will get you going in the morning.
I always keep my blender out on the counter everyday so when I get up in the morning the blender is there and waiting and I can make my smoothie without the fuss of digging the blender out of the cabinet.

Ingredients:	
8 oz. vanilla sweetened or unsweetened soy or almond milk depending on your preference 1 C frozen mixed berries	1 small frozen banana sliced before frozen, or ½ of a large frozen banana sliced before frozen

Directions:
Place all of the above ingredients into a blender and puree to a smooth consistency.

This will make two servings.

If you are calorie watching, you can use unsweetened vanilla soy or almond milk and add stevia, the zero calorie sweetener that is all natural, if you prefer a sweeter tasting smoothie, or the sweetener of your choice. To keep this recipe vegan, do not use refined sugar.

Super Energy Smoothie

Contributed by Reneé Baer
Bellmawr, New Jersey, USA

This smoothie is great to have first thing in the morning if you
are anticipating a busy or grueling day!

Ingredients:
1 C low fat or soy milk
1 banana

1 T peanut butter

Directions:
1. Add ingredients to blender – blend and serve!

Orange Jones Whip

Contributed by Beth Pinterich
Berwick, Pennsylvania, USA

Ingredients:
1 (6 oz.) can frozen orange juice
1 C milk
1 C water

¼ C sugar
1 t vanilla
10-12 ice cubes

Directions:
1. Combine orange juice, milk, water, sugar, and vanilla in a blender and mix well.
2. Add ice and blend until smooth.

Makes 4 servings
If you would like, you can add fresh fruit like peaches, bananas, berries, etc. before you add the ice.
Yummy!

Canaan's Delight

Contributed by T Lee Harris
New Albany, Indiana, USA

Ingredients:	
2 C milk, steamed or scalded	1 t cinnamon
2 T honey	pat of butter

Directions:
1. Put cinnamon and honey in the bottom of a mug.
2. Stir together slightly.
3. Pour hot milk over mixture.
4. Stir again.
5. Float butter on top of milk before serving.

2 servings

Cafe Borgia

Contributed by T Lee Harris
New Albany, Indiana, USA

Ingredients:	
1 C strong hot coffee or espresso	3 C milk
2 - 1oz. squares dark chocolate, grated	the grated peel from one orange
3 T granulated sugar	whipped cream
pinch of salt	

Directions:
1. In saucepan over low heat, stir chocolate into the coffee.
2. Add sugar and salt.
3. Stir in milk and heat through, but do not boil.
4. Serve garnished with whipped cream and grated orange peel.

3 servings

Kids' Recipes

Davy's Crazy Matey
Ice Cream Sundae

Contributed by Jody Proetta
Putnam Valley, New York, USA

Davy loved ice cream whether it was milk shakes or ice cream sundaes. His favorite place to drink milk-shakes or to eat ice cream sundaes was the Times Square Café, but sometimes we would buy all of the ingredients and he would make us ice cream sundaes. It was a real treat to watch him make it. He would get very serious. He called it "the crazy matey ice cream sundae" which meant in his British way, "a crazy mess" but it was awfully good!!! The ingredients we used were not as imaginative as nowadays, but this is what was available to us in 1963, and you can always add your own, but if you want it the Davy Jones way, here it is: This recipe is for two people.

Ingredients:	
Davy always used a scoop of chocolate and a scoop of vanilla ice cream.	about 10 Nilla wafer cookies, crushed
	1 large banana sliced
2 Hershey bars broken up into very small pieces	chocolate syrup
a box of Cracker Jacks	whipped cream

Directions:
1. Line the bottom of the ice cream bowl with the crushed Nilla wafer cookies. Davy would put them in a paper bag and jump on the cookies to crush them, but, of course, we would do it a little differently nowadays.
2. Place your scoop of vanilla and chocolate ice cream on top.
3. Sprinkle the broken Hershey pieces over the ice cream and pour some Cracker Jacks over that.
4. Sprinkle some sliced banana.
5. Pour some chocolate syrup on top of the entire sundae.

Add some whipped cream, and you are all set to enjoy Davy's original
ice cream sundae. We would sit on his fire escape and watch the
interesting sights in the city while eating his special creation.
ENJOY!!

Davy with his niece
Beverley Barber's children
Thalia and Thomas, 2011

Photograph © Courtesy of Beverley Barber

Breakfast Granola Bars

Contributed by Jody Proetta
Putnam Valley, New York, USA

Ingredients:	
2 C granola	dash of vanilla for sweetening (but this is
2 eggs beaten	optional)

Directions:
1. Combine the granola and eggs in a greased 8-inch square pan.
2. Bake at 350° F for 15 minutes.
3. Cut into 8 bars.

When serving, spread with jam, honey, or peanut butter. Very good and healthy!!!! Enjoy.

Watermelon Popsicles

Contributed by Jody Proetta
Putnam Valley, New York, USA

Ingredients:	
1 C seedless watermelon chunks	1 C water
1 C orange juice	popsicle sticks and cups

Directions:
Blend these ingredients in a blender, pour into molds, insert sticks, and freeze.

Have fun eating!!! Healthy, no sugar to cause cavities, and fun to make.

Hey Hey, Where's the Ice Cream?
A Monkee-licious Vegan Dessert

Contributed by Sarah Aujero
Glendale, California, USA

Ingredients:
4 large ripe bananas

Directions:
1. Peel and cut bananas into small pieces and freeze.
2. Blend, scrape, and blend until creamy.

Enjoy plain or add fruit, nut butter, cinnamon, or chocolate on top or with the blend.

Spicy Cheese Dip

Contributed by Jody Proetta
Putnam Valley, New York, USA

This is great for watching movies with friends.

Ingredients:
1 container of soft cream cheese (12 oz.)
½ C of salsa—mild

Tabasco sauce
1 bag of flavored tortilla chips

Directions:
1. Take your container of soft cream cheese and pour it upside down on a serving platter. Try to place it so it stays intact by tapping sides of the container.
2. Now pour your salsa directly over the cream cheese and sprinkle some Tabasco sauce on top to suit your taste. Use more if you like it really spicy.
3. Serve the cheese dip with your favorite flavored tortilla chips.

Potato with Melted Cheese

Contributed by Jody Proetta
Putnam Valley, New York, USA

Ingredients:
1 large potato washed well and patted dry
1 T of butter or margarine
garlic salt for shaking
a handful of freshly chopped herbs: parsley,
    basil, dill

½ C shredded Cheddar cheese
¼ C grated Parmesan Cheese

Directions:
1. Take a microwave safe bowl and place butter or margarine, chopped herbs, and sprinkles of garlic salt suited to your taste and cook for 10 seconds on high until your butter or margarine is melted. Set aside.
2. Cut your potato into ¼" slices but do not cut all the way through to the bottom of the potato. The slices should still be intact on the potato.
3. Now place your potato into a microwave safe bowl and pour your butter/margarine and herb mixture on the top of the potato and in between the slices. Cook your potato on high for 5 minutes. You may add an extra minute or more if needed so the potato becomes soft.
4. Let the potato sit for 5 minutes when done.
5. Sprinkle the potato with the cheeses and microwave once again on high for 1 to 2 minutes or until the cheeses are melted.

Enjoy your potato!

Edible Play Dough

Contributed by Darlene Haines
Crestline, Ohio, USA

Ingredients:	
peanut butter	dried milk
honey	

Directions:
1. Take "glob" of peanut butter and pour in some honey.
2. Add dry milk to make a consistency to roll and mold.
3. Cut with cookie cutter and design your own creation.

Carrot Curls

Contributed by Sharon Kenney Curran
St. Louis, Missouri, USA

Ingredients:	
whole carrots	1 t sugar
lemon juice or orange juice	

Directions:
1. Start with whole carrots. Clean and wash.
2. Slice or peel very thin; peel the long way.
3. Marinate in lemon juice or orange juice and 1 teaspoon sugar. Serve chilled.

Aussie Sunshine
Ice Cream Delight

Contributed by Kelli Bulfin
Queensland, Australia

Ingredients:	
2 frozen bananas, chopped	1 C of coconut water
1 x 250 grams punnet of strawberries, frozen	1 T LSA (linseed/sunflower/almonds)
8 chunky pieces of frozen pineapple	

Directions:
1. Place all ingredients into food processor/ninja (whatever kind you have).
2. Blend till creamy and smooth, like soft serve ice cream.
3. If you need it smoother, just slowly add more coconut water.

Eat straight away and enjoy!

Photograph © Courtesy of Anita Williams Weinberg

Davy's daughters and grandchildren

When Davy's family gathered at his Beavertown, Pennsylvania
home in June of 2013, they set about repairing this broken-down carousel
that Davy had purchased, and were able to bring the old carousel back to life.

Caramel Crispix

Contributed by Linda Mach
Kewaunee, Wisconsin, USA

Ingredients:
2 small boxes of Crispix Cereal	½ C light corn syrup
2 C butter	½ t vanilla
2 C brown sugar	½ t baking soda

Directions:
1. Melt butter in a sauce pan.
2. Add brown sugar and bring to a boil.
3. Add corn syrup, vanilla, and baking soda.
4. Put the cereal in a large bowl then pour mixture over the cereal.

"Now U Sea Mee" Buns

Contributed by Ginny Fleming
New Albany, Indiana, USA

Marshmallows dipped in melted butter, then cinnamon and sugar, wrapped in crescent rolls and baked. They're called "Now U Sea Mee" buns because the marshmallows disappear — Whoa — They were here a minute ago!

Ingredients:
4 oz. butter (half of a stick)	2 T cinnamon
4 large vegetarian marshmallows – halved	1 C sugar
1 tube of crescent rolls (makes eight buns)	

Directions:
1. Preheat oven to 350° F.
2. Roll marshmallows in melted butter.
3. Roll buttered marshmallows in cinnamon and sugar mixture.
4. Wrap marshmallows in crescent rolls.
5. Cook at 350° F for 12 minutes.

Options:
- *One section of a Hershey bar for each bun with or without the marshmallow, cinnamon, and sugar.*
- *For "painted" buns: 2 egg yolks in bowl, food coloring of choice = edible "paint". "Paint" buns before baking.*
- *Pastels for spring? Orange for Halloween?*

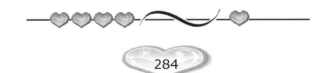

Chocolate Pops

Contributed by Jody Proetta
Putnam Valley, New York, USA

Ingredients:
1 (8 oz.) container of plain yogurt	2 T of brown sugar or honey
2 T cocoa or carob powder	popsicle sticks and cups

Directions:
1. Liquefy in a blender.
2. Pour into molds.
3. Insert popsicle sticks and freeze.

Have fun eating!!!!

Octopus Bubbles Drink

Contributed by Sharon Kenney Curran
St. Louis, Missouri, USA

Ingredients:
½ C pineapple juice	½ C club soda

Directions:
Mix together and drink. Oooh good!

Fruit Cheesy Bagels

Contributed by Sharon Kenney Curran
St. Louis, Missouri, USA

Ingredients:
¼ C cream cheese spread w/strawberries from 8 oz. container	1 banana, diced
¼ C diced apple	2 bagels, split and toasted

Directions:
1. Stir cream cheese in a small bowl until soft and creamy. Add apple and banana. Stir gently to mix.
2. Spoon and spread cream cheese mixture on toasted bagel halves.
3. Tip: Mix cream cheese and apple the night before. Stir in banana just before serving.

Photograph © Courtesy of Cindy Ferrier

**Davy's grandchildren: Phoenix, Harrison, and Lauren
in Beavertown, Pennsylvania, USA
June 15, 2013**

Ants On A Log
and Celery Hot Rods

Contributed by Jody Proetta
Putnam Valley, New York, USA

This is an old stand-by that I would let my son make himself. He loved them, and they are healthy and provide fiber, protein, vitamins, and iron.

Ingredients:	
celery sticks	raisins
cream cheese	tooth picks
peanut butter	circular carrot slices

Directions:
1. Stuff celery sticks with cream cheese or peanut butter and dot with raisins. These are "ants on a log."
2. Transform the ants on a log into celery hot rods by putting the tooth picks through the front and back ends and place your carrot slices on the ends of the toothpicks for wheels. The logs become hot rods for the ants.

My son loved these treats.

Snow Ice Cream

Contributed by Sharon Kenney Curran
St. Louis, Missouri, USA

Ingredients:
3 C freshly fallen clean snow
1 C canned milk (evaporated)
⅓ C sugar

1 t vanilla
dash salt, optional

Directions:
1. Combine milk, sugar, vanilla, and salt.
2. Pour quickly over the snow and stir just enough to mix.
3. Freeze until about as firm and as soft as sherbet.

Fruit Cones

Contributed by Jody Proetta
Putnam Valley, New York, USA

A very healthy and fun snack. Protein and fruit. Have fun!!!

Ingredients:
sliced strawberries
small cubes of various melons
mandarin orange sections
blueberries

grapes
fruit yogurt of any kind
whipped cream
flat bottomed ice cream cones

Directions:
1. Have your child place some fruit yogurt in the bottom third of the ice cream cones and fill the rest of the cone with the fruit.
2. Give a little squirt of whipped cream.

Pumpkin Seeds

Contributed by Sharon Kenney Curran
St. Louis, Missouri, USA

Ingredients:
seeds from Jack-O-Lantern

butter, oil, or margarine

Directions:
1. Wash seeds from Jack-O-Lantern.
2. Spread on buttered cookie sheet.
3. Toast at 350° F for 10 minutes or until golden.
4. Sprinkle with salt.

Eat. Crunchy!!

Granny's "Reesie-Bread"

Contributed by Vivian Bishop
Floyds Knobs, Indiana, USA

My ten kids remembered these simple-simple snacks I gave them when they were small. Now, my many grandchildren are building "Reesie" and "Hurry Up" memories with their own children.

Ingredients: 1 slice of bread peanut butter	chocolate icing

Directions:
1. Spread peanut butter on the bread slice.
2. Then spread chocolate icing over the peanut butter. Yum-Yum!

Granny's "Hurry Up Donuts"

Contributed by Vivian Bishop
Floyds Knobs, Indiana, USA

Ingredients: hamburger bun	chocolate fudge icing

Directions:
Spread chocolate fudge icing on buns, top and bottom. They look like big donuts!

Options: Ice the top for a "frosted" donut, or use a hotdog bun for a "footlong/bearclaw."

Ice Cream Cone Cakes

Contributed by Sharon Kenney Curran
St. Louis, Missouri, USA

Ingredients: flat bottomed ice cream cones 1 box cake mix (any flavor)	ingredients listed on cake mix package

Directions:
1. Mix cake mix according to package directions.
2. Fill cones half full. Place in jelly roll pan standing up.
3. Bake for approx. 60 minutes in a 350 degree oven.

You can top it with chocolate sauce, or dip into softened ice cream. Enjoy!

Home Made Play Doh
— NOT for Consumption —

Contributed by Sharon Kenney Curran
St. Louis, Missouri, USA

Ingredients:
2 C flour	2 T vegetable oil
2 C warm water	food coloring (liquid, powder, or unsweetened
1 C salt	drink mix)
1 T cream of tartar (optional for improved	scented oils
elasticity)	

Directions:
1. Mix all together, stir until completely mixed.
2. Add food coloring; mix throughout until color is even. I use plastic gloves for this part as the food coloring will stain your hands.

Finger Paints
— NOT for Consumption —

Contributed by Sharon Kenney Curran
St. Louis, Missouri, USA

Ingredients:
3 T sugar	food coloring
½ C cornstarch	pinch of detergent
2 C cold water	

Directions:
1. Mix sugar and cornstarch in pot. Add water. Cook over low, stirring constantly until well blended.
2. Divide into 4 or 5 portions (small margarine tubs work well).
3. Add food colorings, plus a pinch of detergent for easier cleanup. Cool and play.

Bubble Solution
— NOT for Consumption —

Contributed by Sharon Kenney Curran
St. Louis, Missouri, USA

Ingredients:
⅓ C soap or baby shampoo (Dawn is best)	2 t sugar
1 ¼ C water	1 drop food coloring

Directions:
Combine and put in an unbreakable bottle.

Treats For Our Animal Friends

Photograph © Courtesy of Michael G. Bush

Davy's Herd

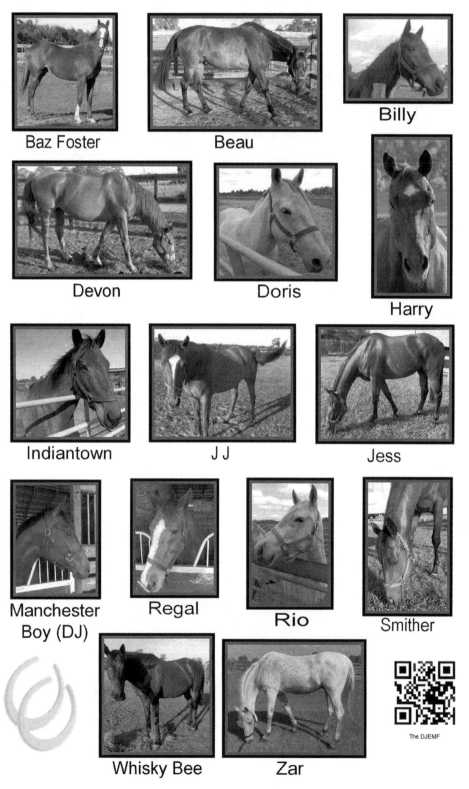

Baz Foster

Beau

Billy

Devon

Doris

Harry

Indiantown

J J

Jess

Manchester Boy (DJ)

Regal

Rio

Smither

Whisky Bee

Zar

The DJEMF

Photographs © Courtesy of DJEMF

Veggie Dog Biscuits I

Contributed by Susan Wilson
Mount Olive, North Carolina, USA

Ingredients:

3 t fresh parsley, minced (helps breath)	2 T bran
¼ C carrots, shredded	2 T baking powder
¼ C shredded Cheddar cheese	½ t flaxseed (optional)
2 T olive oil	½ C water
2 ¾ C flour	

Directions:
1. Mix parsley, carrots, cheese, and oil.
2. In a separate bowl, combine flour, bran, baking powder, and flaxseed.
3. Combine all ingredients, slowly adding water and mixing well. Dough should be moist but not wet.
4. Cut into desired shapes.
5. Bake at 350°F for 5-7 minutes. Baking time depends on size of biscuits.
6. Store in airtight container for up to 2 weeks or freeze.

Low-Fat Dog Biscuits

Contributed by Georgeann Maguire
Mechanicsburg, Pennsylvania, USA

Ingredients:

1 C uncooked oatmeal	3 C whole wheat flour
⅓ C unsweetened applesauce	1 ½ C cornmeal
1 ½ C hot water	

Directions:
1. Pre-heat oven to 325° F.
2. Put oatmeal and applesauce in a large bowl.
3. Pour hot water on top and stir; let stand for 5 minutes.
4. Stir in the cornmeal.
5. Add flour, 1 cup at a time. (The dough will become very stiff.)
6. Roll out to ½" thickness and cut with floured cookie cutter.
7. Place on cookie sheet and bake for 50 minutes.
8. Let biscuits cool until they are hard.

Peanut Butter-Applesauce Dog Biscuits

Contributed by Joey Jones
Santa Cruz, California, USA

Ingredients:
2 ½ C whole wheat flour
½ C quick oats
2 t ground cinnamon

½ C peanut butter (chunky or smooth)
½ C unsweetened applesauce
½ C water

Directions:
1. Pre-heat oven to 350°F.
2. Mix flour and cinnamon in a medium-sized bowl.
3. In another bowl, mix applesauce and peanut butter. (Works best at room temperature.)
4. Combine, adding water gradually to make dough. (Think the consistency of modeling clay.)
5. Roll out dough on floured surface to about ¼-inch thickness. Cut out shapes with cookie cutters or slice into bars.
6. Bake about 40 minutes, until lightly browned. Let cool completely.

Can also be cut into small pieces before baking to use as training treats.
Watch the baking time as small pieces will take much less time to bake.

Peanut Butter Dog Treats

Contributed by Susan Wilson
Mount Olive, North Carolina, USA

Ingredients:
½ C peanut butter (all natural or organic)
1 C water
2 T oil

1 ½ C wheat flour
1 ½ C white flour

Directions:
1. Combine peanut butter, water, and oil.
2. Add flours, 1 cup at a time, forming a dough.
3. Knead dough into a firm ball.
4. Roll to ¼-inch thickness.
5. Cut into desired shapes.
6. Bake at 350° F for 3-7 minutes. Time depends on size of biscuit.
7. Store in airtight container for up to 2 weeks or freeze.

Molasses Crunches
Horse Cookies

Contributed by Carole Miller
Lewistown, Pennsylvania, USA

When I had horses I'd bake these cookies for them quite often. One day I heard my husband telling someone that I bake cookies for the horses but not him, so the next time I baked Molasses Crunches I gave him one with a glass of milk.

I didn't meet Davy until July, 2008. I'm an Equine Massage Therapist. I live 20 miles from Davy's home in Beavertown, Pennsylvania. I was passing through Beavertown one day and decided to see if Davy was home so I could introduce myself to him and give him my business card. Two days later I went back to massage Jessie Jones, Whiskey Bee, and Regal Slew. What an honor! When I pass through Beavertown now I still get teary eyed knowing he is no longer there.

Ingredients:
1 C brown sugar	2 C flour
¾ C shortening	¼ t salt
1 egg	2 t baking powder
⅓ C molasses	4 T chicken scratch

Directions:
1. Cream shortening and sugar.
2. Add egg and molasses.
3. Beat well.
4. Chill thoroughly.
5. Roll into 1" balls.
6. Dip in chicken scratch.
7. Place scratch side up on greased cookie sheet.
8. Bake at 375° F for 12 - 15 minutes.

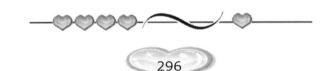

Birthday Cake for Rats

Contributed by Andrea Gilbey
Cheshunt, Hertfordshire, UK

This recipe will keep 4 rats happy for hours!

Ingredients:	
1 egg	¼ t crushed garlic
¼ carrot	1 T plain yoghurt
1 T plain flour	yoghurt drop rat treats (optional for icing/
a few raisins	frosting)
1 T porridge oats	

Directions:
1. Separate the egg.
2. Cut thin strips from the carrot for "candles" if required. (Obviously the right number for the appropriate age of your rat!)
3. Grate the rest of the carrot.
4. Mix the egg yolk, grated carrot, raisins, flour, yoghurt, oats, and garlic to a thick paste.
5. Whisk the egg white to peaks, as for making a meringue, and fold into the rest of the mixture.
6. Spoon into a greased muffin tin hole and bake at 180° C/350° F/Gas 4 for 15 minutes or until lightly browned on top and dry throughout when a skewer is inserted.
7. If you want to top your cake, melt a few rat treat yoghurt drops in a pan with half a teaspoon of water and "ice/frost" your cake.
8. Add carrot "candles" if desired.

Fido's Favorite Frosting

Contributed by Susan Wilson
Mount Olive, North Carolina, USA

Ingredients:	
8 oz. Neufchatel or cream cheese	2 T honey
2 T plain yogurt	2—3 T flour

Directions:
1. Combine cheese, yogurt, and honey until smooth.
2. Add flour to thicken to a good spreading consistency.
3. Spread on any dog biscuit or cookie.

Simple Simon's Birthday Bones

Contributed by Barbara Minnich
Georgetown, Indiana, USA

Ingredients:
2 C whole wheat flour
1 T baking powder

1 C natural peanut butter
1 C skim milk

Directions:
1. Preheat oven to 375° F.
2. In a bowl, combine flour and baking powder.
3. In another bowl, mix peanut butter and milk.
4. Using a stand mixer, add wet mixture to dry and mix well.
5. Turn out dough on a lightly floured surface and knead.
6. Roll out dough to ¼ inch thick and cut out shapes.
7. Place on a greased baking sheet and bake 20 minutes or until lightly brown. At this point, I turn off the oven and leave them alone overnight or for several hours.
8. Cool on a rack and then store in an airtight container. They freeze very well.

Cheese Treats for Dogs

Contributed by Georgeann Maguire
Mechanicsburg, Pennsylvania, USA

Ingredients:
4 C whole wheat flour
1 ¼ C shredded cheese
2 eggs, beaten

1 ¼ C milk
¾ C vegetable oil
1 T garlic powder

Directions:
1. Preheat oven to 400° F.
2. In a large bowl, combine flour and garlic powder.
3. Gradually stir in remaining ingredients.
4. Roll out the dough to desired thickness.
5. Cut out the treats with cookie cutter and place on cookie sheet.
6. Bake for 25 minutes. Cool completely before storing.

Caro's PAWS Good Dog Treats

Contributed by Mary Lee Woods
Des Moines, Iowa, USA
(Half of Sparkle Abbey, authors of the Pampered Pet Mysteries,
featuring Caro, Mel, and Dogbert, to name a few)

Ingredients:	
½ C creamy unsalted peanut butter	1 T honey
1 C oat flour	½ C finely grated carrot (Dogbert loves carrots
1 C brown rice flour (Caro uses organic.)	and so does Abbey.)
1 egg	water

Directions:
1. Preheat oven to 350° F.
2. In a big bowl, combine all ingredients with just enough water to make it the consistency of cookie dough.
3. Once you've got your treat dough all stirred up, put it between pieces of parchment paper and roll it out to about ¼ inch thickness, and then cut the dough with a cookie cutter. You can use whatever shape strikes your fancy. Caro often uses dog bone shapes of different sizes.
4. Next, put them on a regular cookie sheet.
5. Bake them between 15 –20 minutes or until they're Golden Retriever brown.
6. Let them cool and then put them in an airtight container. You can store your PAWS Good Dog treats for about a week (or you can freeze them for later use) but keep an eye on them. There are no preservatives, so watch out for spoilage.

This makes a couple dozen treats so there's plenty to go around.
Please share them with your dog.

Optional: You can also add a bit of grated cheese or other ingredients for flavor, but don't add too much or it will mess with the consistency of the dough and cause your treats to fall apart.

Talia Jones-Roston, Annabel Jones, Indiantown Jones, and Sarah Jones-McFadden
2012

Photograph © Courtesy of DJEMF

Dog Biscuits

Contributed by Pam Patrick
Pleasanton, Kansas, USA

I made these for Michael Nesmith's dog Dale.

Ingredients:	
½ C powdered milk	½ t onion or garlic salt
1 egg, beaten	1 t brown sugar
2 ½ C wheat flour	½ C water or bouillon
½ t salt	6 T shortening, butter

Directions:
1. Combine all ingredients.
2. Roll mixture to ½ inch thick.
3. Cut into desired shapes.
4. Bake on slightly greased cookie sheet at 325° F for 25-30 minutes.

Veggie Dog Biscuits II

Contributed by Georgeann Maguire
Mechanicsburg, Pennsylvania, USA

Ingredients:	
1 C white flour	1 t brown sugar
1 C wheat flour	1 egg
½ C wheat germ	6 T margarine/butter
½ C powdered milk	1 C mashed cooked vegetables
½ t salt	

Directions:
1. Preheat oven to 325° F.
2. In a large bowl, combine the dry ingredients.
3. Cut in the butter/margarine until it resembles cornmeal.
4. In a separate bowl, beat egg and brown sugar well.
5. Add the mashed vegetables to the egg mixture and stir.
6. When combined, add the vegetable and egg mixture to the flour mixture until stiff dough is formed.
7. Using your hands, blend completely, then knead.
8. Roll out the dough in a thick sheet.
9. Cut with bone-shaped cookie cutter (or your choice shape).
10. Bake just until lightly browned.

Kitty Krispies

Contributed by Andrea Gilbey
Cheshunt, Hertfordshire, UK

Ingredients:
¾ C wholemeal flour
½ C Rice Krispies (or similar cereal)
1 T sunflower oil
1 T clear honey

1 egg
1 T water, or enough to form a firm dough
pinch of catnip (optional)

Directions:
1. Mix all ingredients to form a firm dough.
2. Roll out to 1/4 inch thick and cut into cat-bite-sized pieces.
3. Place on a greased baking tray.
4. Bake for 10 minutes at 180° C/350° F/gas mark 4.
5. Allow to cool.

Store in airtight container for up to 2 weeks.

Obi's Favorite Cookies

Contributed by Beverly Maybo
Stamford, Connecticut, USA

Dog cookies ~ delicious ~ my granddog cannot get enough of these!

Ingredients:
1 egg
1 C oat flour
1 ¼ C brown rice flour
½ C unsalted peanut butter

1 T honey
⅔ C of water (Add gradually, you might not need all of it.)

Directions:
1. Combine all ingredients.
2. Roll out to ¼ inch thickness.
3. Cut into shapes, gather, and re-roll dough as needed.
4. Bake at 350° F for 20-25 minutes.

Cinder's Favorite Biscuits

Contributed by Barbara Minnich
Georgetown, Indiana, USA

Cinder is my first agility dog. I found her in a school parking lot and we both knew at first sight that we were meant for each other. She is a lab, beagle mix and has proven to be a fantastic agility dog. We have many titles, and many, many ribbons. She loves doing tricks and agility, and most of all we love being with each other. I could never repay her for all she has taught me, so the least I can do is make her favorite biscuits for treats at a trial. I hope your dog enjoys these as much as Cinder does.

Ingredients:	
Dough:	1 lb. peanut butter
2 ½ t instant yeast	3 eggs
3 C all purpose flour	3 C 1% milk
2 C whole wheat flour	
2 C cornmeal	Glaze:
1 ¾ C rolled oats	1 egg
¾ C soy flour	¼ C milk or water
1 C dry milk	

Directions:
1. For the dough, place dry ingredients into a large bowl and mix well.
2. Add the 3 eggs and peanut butter along with the 3 cups of milk.
3. Knead the mixture for 5 or 10 minutes until the dough holds together. You may add extra liquid or flour depending on the texture of the dough. It should be stiff, but not feel like "cement."
4. Return the dough to the mixing bowl, cover, and let it rest for 30 minutes.
5. Preheat your oven to 300° F and grease or line with parchment paper two or three baking sheets.
6. Working with about ⅓ of the dough at a time, roll it out to ¼ to ⅓ inches thick, then cut it into the size biscuits you want. The biscuits don't spread, so you can place them close together on the baking sheets.
7. Beat the remaining egg with ¼ cup of milk or water and brush it over the biscuits.
8. Bake the biscuits for 1 hour. Remove them from the oven and bake the second batch.
9. After all the biscuits are baked once, crowd them onto the amount of baking sheets that will fit into your oven. The biscuits may be overlapped.
10. Bake for 1 or more hours at 225° F until they are hard and dry.
11. Cool completely, then wrap well. Keep about 1 week's supply in a cool, dry place, and freeze the remaining for longer storage.

Marion's Recipe
for a Happy Horse

Contributed by Marion Seidel
Caretaker of Davy's horse Billy Jones
Port Saint Lucie, Florida, USA

Ingredients:
1 carrot, un-pared
1 apple, un-pared
1 or more Blowing Nose Kisses
2 parts patience
1 part love
1 big hug

Directions:
1. Feed horse first 2 ingredients.
2. Mix remaining ingredients and give to horse.
3. Happiness will result for both of you.

Marion is the author of:

Just Another Race Horse

Race Horse Training

*From Race Horse to Trail
Horse and Pet*

Billy
Jones

Marion

Seidel

Photograph © Courtesy of Marion Seidel

Memories

Photograph © Courtesy of Anita Pollinger-Jones Collection

Davy's *Oliver!* Days

These photos are from *Oliver!* at the Imperial Theatre on W. 45th Street & Broadway, New York City in 1963 as David played his role as the Artful Dodger. David Jones began his acting career at a young age in his native Manchester, England. Everyone took notice of the young David and his enormous talent as he performed in his church shows while his mum played the piano and his sisters ran the youth group. He then appeared in British soap operas including *Coronation Street* in his home country. He then spread his wings and began his American career with huge acclaim on Broadway in

Photograph © Courtesy of PHOTOFEST

New York City as the Artful Dodger in *Oliver!*, the musical adapted from the Charles Dickens book, *Oliver Twist*. His tremendous talent won him a Tony nomination, an award that many Broadway actors can only dream about. I bore witness to the Jones magic on stage in *Oliver!* here on Broadway many nights, and I can't remember a single show where David did not receive a standing ovation. His passion and his dedication to his audience was obvious to the packed theatre night after night

Photographs © Courtesy of PHOTOFEST

as he played his role like someone who had been performing on Broadway for many years. Many fell in love with the incredible talent and charm of this young man, leading to the formation of his first fan club of more than 500 members. Like the lights on Broadway that never go out, his too shall shine forever in the hearts of many. May you always hear our applause forever, David!

~ Jody Proetta

Photograph © Courtesy of PHOTOFEST

Put on the Rack

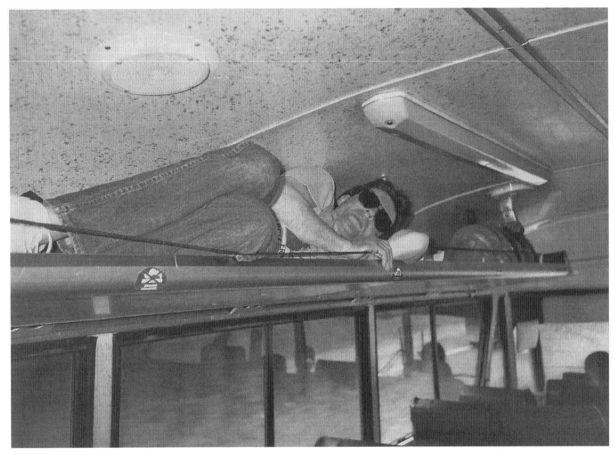

Photograph by Ken Wilkinson © Courtesy of Hazel Wilkinson

**"Taken somewhere between
Memphis and Shreveport - April 1992.
Put on the rack.
He shouldn't have told that rotten joke!"**
~ Ken Wilkinson

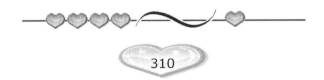

310

David's brother-in-law, Ken Wilkinson, was a lovely man with a great sense of humor. He would thumb through stacks of photos Bonnie Borgh and I had taken and announce they were "boring." Boring? Why was that? With a smirk he would say because there were no photos of him. So in an effort to make this cookbook less boring and to honor the memory of our friend Ken, I am sharing a diet plan that I have had on my refrigerator for years — one Ken recommended.

~ Cindy Bryant

Dieting Under Stress
Ten Rules on How to Combine a Successful Diet
with Life as a Normal Human Being

1. If you eat something and no one see you, then the food has no calories.
2. When you eat with someone else, the calories do not count if they eat more than you do.
3. If you drink a diet cola with a chocolate bar, the diet cola cancels the calories in the chocolate.
4. Broken biscuits contain no calories—the process of breaking causes calorie leakage.
5. Food used for medicinal purposes never counts, e.g. hot chocolate for relaxation; brandy for fortification; toast and cheesecake as antidepressants.
6. It is recommended that you fatten up everyone around you so that you appear slimmer.
7. Food licked off cutlery or out of a bowl has no calories if you are following a recipe, e.g. butter icing on a cake; remains of a scone mixture; cream for the top of a trifle.
8. TV and cinema food contains no calories as they are part of the whole entertainment package.
9. Foods of the same color have the same number of calories, e.g. spinach and mint ice cream, mushrooms and white chocolate, water and a large gin and tonic.
10. Athletes eat huge amounts of pasta before races like the marathon. It is a myth that you have to run 26 miles to work it off. One brisk trot around the settee is quite sufficient to wipe out one bowl of spaghetti. Twice around the living room will use up so much energy that a chocolate bar is required to supplement your sugar level and rebuild your strength.
Good luck!

Okay, Ken; you're in the book so it is no longer boring! Miss you, my friend!
~ Cindy

Photograph © Courtesy of Cindy Bryant

Ken Wilkinson, Davy's brother-in-law

In 1967, my mother Tina Dick and my sister Marilyn from Brooklyn visited me, my son Bobby Jr., and my then wife Joan in California. David and I had become good friends (both short). In any case, I suggested that my mom make her famous linguini ... David called them "noodles". So my mom made all the food at my apartment in Sherman Oaks and we went to David's amazing house in the Hollywood Hills. David was married to his first wife Linda, as I was married to my first wife Joan.

There were lots of Monkees Tour staff and friends at the house, and we had a great time. My sister, 11 years old at the time, loved David. My son Bobby Jr. loved his pool and his German Shepherd Susie.

~ Bobby Dick
of the Sundowners

Bobby Dick and The Sundowners toured with The Monkees during the 60s as their backup band and sometimes as their opening act.

Davy with Bobby Dick's mom, Tina Saratoga Performing Arts Center July 25, 1986

Photograph © Courtesy of Bobby Dick

I've known Davy since 1987. We did every Monkees tour from '87 till around 2006. In between The Monkees tours, Davy would tour solo and I was his drummer on those tours as well. We were very close and shared many, many unique and very funny experiences together. From riding horses together at his ranch in Beavertown, Pennsylvania to him staying over at my place because he wanted to help me build my rock wall on my property......all we'd do is laugh.

I miss him much and think about him often. Love you DJ - RIP.

~ Sandy Gennaro

Photographs © Courtesy of Sandy Gennaro

Photograph © Courtesy of Michael G. Bush

**Florence Henderson with Davy Jones
on TNN's *Country Kitchen*, March, 1991**

I fell in love with Davy Jones when I saw him many years ago as the Artful Dodger in *Oliver!.* He was absolutely brilliant!

Then, of course *The Monkees* gave him wide spread fame. We were all pretty excited when he came to guest star on *The Brady Bunch*.

I used to see him in Florida from time to time. We shared the same chiropractor.

Davy always remained the sweet person that he was when I first met him. He is missed by many and will always have a special place in my heart.

~ Florence Henderson

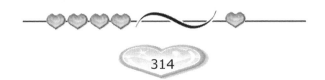

It was such a fun day when Davy and I recorded "Daydream Believer" for my new album! Davy came into the studio in Sausalito, California, Studio D. He came in like a whirlwind! Full of energy and jokes and fun! He made everyone feel comfortable right away.

When we started to go over the song, Davy was still singing "happy" instead of "funky" which was the original lyric that John wrote in the song. He said, "But I've been singing 'happy' for over forty years!" I said, "For forty years you've been singing the wrong lyrics!!!" It was a funny moment, and hard for him to adjust to "funky"! He said, "Of course; now the song makes sense!"

He also had never sung harmony on the song. He said, "I don't know harmony on this!" I said, "Well, you'd better learn some because I'm singing lead this time!" He laughed!

It was a great, fun day singing with such a pro. Such a natural singer. Easy is what it was. Everyone fell in love with Davy that day!

Davy was a great friend. He was a dear and sweet man. He would often call me just to see if I was alright and to check up on me and leave encouraging messages on my phone when I was not home.

Davy and *The Monkees* made a hit out of my husband's song "Daydream Believer"! That song is still paying the rent!!!

Thank you Davy... Monkees... My Johnny...

Davy died on my birthday. Leap year!
Of course! He would pick an unusual day
to leave this Earth and go into the Sea of
Grace...

I miss him.

~ Buffy Ford Stewart

**Buffy and Davy concluded the
John Stewart Memorial Tribute concert
with an emotional rendition of
"Daydream Believer" on May 3, 2008.**

Photograph © Courtesy of Sheri Prager

Photograph © Courtesy of Chris Pick

Chris Pick with Davy

When asked to share a memorable moment with David, I paused, questioning where to even begin. I never met a TV star more true to his character than David was to family, friends, and fans. How you remembered him on television was how he was in real life – always giving a good laugh, always giving a great smile, always giving! He was never truly acting, even on the show. He was always himself. And he once told me that he always knew how much he was loved by his fans, which is why he always gave back to them in many ways.

Occasionally my wife Michelle and I were asked to help run merchandise for him at concerts. He often gave two hour concerts, and once we remember him standing at his merchandise table for over two hours after the concert talking with fans, shaking hands, posing for pictures, leaving messages on fans' cell phones, etc. He was tired, but he took the time to give back to those who had given him so much. We had to keep all money exchanges out of his sight. He never liked to see that. If he had it his way, he would have given away all his merchandise, and he often did – even his personal things! I remember once someone commented on how much they loved a sweater he was wearing. He pulled it off (thank goodness he had a T-shirt on underneath), handed it to them, and said, "Here you go…It's yours!" He once even did the same with a Monkees watch he was given by Rhino Records.

I can remember back in '97, the three Monkees ended their 30th Anniversary concert at a big fair in Pennsylvania. A friend of mine and David's from Japan came in to see the show. I arranged for her to talk to David on a radio station that morning and then took her to the concert. Ward Sylvester gave us all backstage passes to meet all the Monkees. I spent some time chatting with friends who were there, including a couple members of the band. I briefly said hello and posed for pics with Micky and Peter, then we met up with David. They were all exhausted! Micky and Peter left early, but David stayed behind to greet more fans. Without saying goodbye, we walked out – only to be caught by David on the way out. He came over and asked if we were leaving. He then said goodbye to his friend and fan from Japan, gave her a hug, then we all said goodbye and we left, watching him walk back to meet more fans. It's memories like this that I treasure when I remember him or watch re-runs of *The Monkees* show. He truly was a loving and giving man!

~ Chris Pick

Photograph © Courtesy of Chris Pick

Chris and Davy

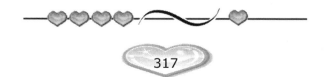

Photograph © Courtesy of Kevin Fulton

Davy was an inspiration to everyone around the world and I'm glad I got a chance to know him. He told me many times his family was more important than his career. I have lots of video and still pictures of our time together. He was easy to work with and I'm better off for knowing him. I love this picture because many people tell me how the picture shows he really thought of me as a friend, not just another TV guy.

~ Kevin Fulton

While doing *Boy Meets World* for seven years in the 90s, our cast was fortunate to have the pleasure of working with a plethora of iconic guest stars. Davy Jones made a permanent mark on *Boy Meets World* with his hilarious portrayal of the character, "Reg! Reginald Fairfield!" Not only did his character leave a lasting impression on fans of *BMW*, but Davy himself left a lasting impression on my heart. He was kind, funny, and always had a smile on his face. I can't help but have a smile on my face every time I think of him.

~ Danielle Fishel

Photograph © Courtesy of Danielle Fishel

A Chance Meeting, or Was It Fate?
We'll Choose Fate!

We first met David in 1965. We were standing in front of May Company on the corner of Wilshire and Fairfax in Los Angeles, California. Along came this good looking guy who had a transistor radio, and he started talking to us. We immediately noticed he had a beautiful English accent which attracted us to him right away! A Beatles song came on the radio station he was listening to, and we said, "I love that song," to which he quickly changed the radio to a different station. The next station started playing a Beatles song, and we said we loved the song, and he repeated what he had done earlier and changed to yet another station. This happened a couple more times and we finally caught on that if we said we didn't like the song, he would leave the station on the song we didn't like, so we did that from then on with the songs we really did like and got to hear our favorite songs all the way through. LOL!

He asked us how old we thought he was, and we told him about 14 years old. He got a little indignant and said, "I'm 19 years old!" He then asked our names, and Jill said, "What's yours?" He said, "David Jones." Then he repeated his question to us -- "What are your names?" and Jill replied "Jill Smith" and he said, "Yeah, sure, right!" So she took out her school ID and showed him that her name was in fact Jill Smith, and then he took out his driver's license and showed us that his name was David Jones and he was 19 years old. Then he told us he had just filmed a TV show coming out in about a year, and he asked if we liked The Beatles. We said of course we liked the Beatles. He asked who was our favorite. I said Paul McCartney and Jill said Ringo Starr, to which David replied that he had met them in person, and Ringo has a big nose, and if he stood under Ringo he could see right up his nose! He also told us he was going to be a household name and bigger than the Beatles within a year!

After that, he asked us if we knew of any good place nearby to get something to eat. We told him across the street was a Thrifty Drug Store which had a coffee shop in there and the waitress was a very pleasant lady, so he said, "Come on. Let's go." We said "OK." When he asked us what we wanted to eat, we told him just one order of French fries and one chocolate Coke. For those of you who don't know what a chocolate Coke is, it's a Coke with chocolate syrup. When our fries and beverage arrived, we put some ketchup on the side of the fries and proceeded to pick up our fries with our fingers and eat them. David said, "Ladies don't eat their fries with their fingers; they eat them by cutting them up with a fork and knife," and he picked up his fork and knife to show us. "Like this!" he said. We laughed. "You must be joking?" we said. He looked at the waitress and they both started laughing!

This was our very first of many Magic Memories to come with a man who blessed us by knowing him and touched us forever. We both miss him very much, and we thank God each and every day that fate brought us together and that he was a part of our lives!!!

~ Peggy Lublin and Jill Smith

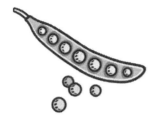

Snow Peas

I'd known Davy for a number of years, so there are any number of amusing stories that come to mind from time to time. This story involves one time we spent a day together just driving around doing errands or visiting places like the Buggy Museum in nearby Mifflinburg, Pennsylvania. (Davy always pronounced it "Boogie". "Do you want to go to The Boogie Museum?" he'd asked excitedly one time when we were in Mifflinburg. "Let's go to The Boogie Museum!!!")

We'd returned to the house in Beavertown after driving around all day doing errands and such, and Davy announced, "It's dinnertime - I'm stahving!" then turned to me and asked, "What would you like for dinner??? What's your favorite vegetable???" "Well, snow peas, I suppose," I said, as I do love snow peas, or Chinese pea pods. "Awright, then," Davy confirmed as he busied about the kitchen. "Snow peas it is!"

I don't know if you've ever had dinner at Davy's house, but he's the host and chef. He does all cooking and food preparation himself, and he doesn't want anyone's help; it's his show. So he's buzzing about the kitchen, like the busy little beaver from Beavertown that he was, jabbering away all the time about this and that, until, at last, dinner is set before us, including a large bowl of regular garden-variety peas which went untouched.

So, we're sitting at the table, enjoying dinner and chatting away, when suddenly, Davy stops mid-sentence, looks at the bowl of peas, then turns to me and says, "You haven't touched your peas, and you'd asked for them especially!" "But, Davy," I explained, "I'd asked for SNOW peas!" To which Davy replied, "Well, I got them from the freezer - it was the closest thing to snow I could find!!!"

He'd worked for that punch line; all during that evening, he was leading up to it! Davy was like that. He'd work to set up a situation where you'd eventually say something that would lead to him delivering a killer punch line! The seersucker suit joke, all his jokes — you just knew there'd be a funny line delivered by Davy in any situation in which you'd spend time together with him. I'm so blessed to have known him and to have this story, along with so many others, written in my heart, forever.

~ Susan Ritter

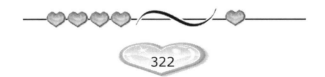

"Remember me the way you hoped I'd be."

David Thomas Jones

1945-2012

Made in the USA
Middletown, DE
20 December 2015